A Mind Frozen in Time

A PTSD Recovery Guide

Jeremy P. Crosby, Psy.D.

Contents

Acknowledgements

In life and professional work, nobody achieves solely on their own efforts. I have many people to thank for their contribution to my professional development and to my understanding of PTSD and therapy.

I would like to thank all those individuals who have contributed to my education, clinical training, and ultimately to the creation of this book.

I am most grateful to:

Lyle Sparkman, M.Ed., Ed.S.
David J. Lutz, Ph.D.
June Sprock, Ph.D.
Michael J. Murphy, Ph.D. ABPP
Carlene G. DeRoo, Ph.D.
William DeRoo, Ph.D. ABPP
Gary Dunn, Ph.D.

I especially thank Cynthia Dunn, Ph.D., for providing specialized training in the diagnosis and treatment of PTSD. I am grateful to Barbara Harrison, ARNP, CS, for logistic and clinical support in the implementation of this treatment approach.

I'd like to thank my family for all of their love, help, and support. It is worth more than words can say.

Jeremy P. Crosby

Start Here
(A Brief Introduction)

This book is for all survivors of traumatic experience and their families. While it was developed through working with individuals who have suffered traumas related to their military service, the themes and principles apply to most types of traumatic experience and their effects. (Note: The terms patient, client, and "person or individual with PTSD" are used interchangeably, as this material was originally used in a medical setting.)

This book is designed to function as a PTSD guide to recovery. It is designed to help individuals develop a basic understanding of PTSD, introduce coping skills to aid in symptom management, and provide information about some of the more difficult issues that need to be addressed in PTSD therapy. It can also be used by therapists to facilitate the educational component of therapy, to suggest a focus for group therapy sessions, and to provide brief reading assignments in individual therapy to help patients address a particular issue.

To the person with PTSD:
If you have experienced one or more traumas and now have PTSD, this book was written for you. The bad news is that you have an emotional condition that causes intense mental and emotional pain and makes it hard to manage life. The good news is that there are answers for what you are dealing with, and it is possible to get better.

Having PTSD does not mean that you are weak, that you lack courage, or that you are a lesser person than people without PTSD. You have suffered a mental/emotional injury, and it requires treatment just like a physical injury. To get better, you have a lot of hard work ahead of you – just remember it is possible to get better.

You are not alone in how you feel. Thousands of other people have also suffered traumas and have worked through the recovery process. You will probably have some symptoms of PTSD the rest of your life, but it is possible to live a healthy, fulfilling life in spite of your symptoms.

I wish for you the best on your journey of recovery. May God bless you with peace, love, self-acceptance, and true meaning in your life.

Jeremy P. Crosby

Background

Traumas are inherently confusing experiences. The person was not prepared for what happened, and they walked away from these experiences in a state of fear, feeling overwhelmed, and asking themselves "What just happened?" or "Did that really happen?" For individuals who go on to develop Post-Traumatic Stress Disorder, or PTSD, the person's efforts to cope after the trauma often result in numerous problems and can lead to a complete disruption of their life. At this point, we ask the question, "What do you do, when you don't know what else to do?" This is usually where many individuals find themselves at the beginning of treatment – confused, demoralized, and desperate. Many have said, "I guess this (therapy) is my last chance before I go kill myself." The good news is that thousands of people have found hope, answers, and reasons to live again. Recovery is possible and realistic.

A starting point for recovery from traumatic experience begins with basic education about trauma and its effects. Without a basic knowledge of what PTSD is and how it affects a person's life, a person will most likely remain confused and benefit only minimally from therapy, if at all. However, once we gain a basic knowledge of what we are dealing with, we can then begin to understand it and manage it. I've worked with many people who have looked back on their therapy experience and placed great value on the educational component of PTSD treatment. They have commented that it continues benefiting them in the long term. They have also stressed the importance of basic PTSD education to support the long-term healthy use of coping skills.

This book is organized according to a particular approach to treating PTSD that emphasizes understanding, education, and use of coping skills. This forms a foundation for building additional elements of treatment and overall recovery. Many traditional therapeutic approaches are woven throughout the material. A long-term management perspective is used here, and this is consistent with much of the current research literature on PTSD and its treatment.

While it is reasonable to begin at the beginning of the book and work through the chapters in the order they are presented, it is also appropriate to use chapters selectively when they are relevant to the issues being addressed in therapy. While almost every person will need to cover Sections I, II, and III at the beginning of treatment, the remaining chapters could reasonably be covered in almost any order depending upon the person's particular needs or stage of healing.

Please note that the information in this book is a basic groundwork for understanding PTSD and is intended as a supportive tool to help maximize the effectiveness of quality therapeutic work. Many individuals who read it on their own should find immediate benefit. Some people will most likely need to consult a therapist who specializes in the treatment of PTSD or other trauma-related conditions for further explanation, to have questions answered, or to work through some of the more intense elements of recovery. Family members might also benefit by increasing their understanding of their loved one's new challenge.

Why Outline Form?

Most individuals with PTSD experience significant concentration and memory difficulties. This greatly limits what can be accomplished in traditional talk therapy. If a person's understanding of their problem, options for coping, and degree of suffering are no different after years of therapy, we must ask whether the patient is receiving any benefit. This concern led to the outline format used in this book.

I've worked with many people who have found it helpful when the most important information was boiled down to the bare essentials and presented as bullet point statements or in outline form. In using this approach, many people have expressed how they recall the key information, understand more, and have experienced more success in implementing new healthy coping skills developed through therapy.

By utilizing this approach, I have seen many individuals stay focused in session, retain more of the necessary information, and more frequently apply the coping strategies that are suggested. Therefore, the information I have found most important for trauma recovery is presented in the following chapters mostly as concise statements.

The outline format is also intended to make it easier to look up key points or find specific information when the book is used as a reference or in group discussions. As such, this text can be used as a training guide for student therapists and also as a guide for more experienced therapists who are expanding their professional work to include therapy geared for patients with trauma-related issues.

Chapter Organization

Most of the chapters are typically a few pages in length. They are set up with an explanation about the topic or issue at the beginning and strategies for coping with that issue near the end of the chapter. While most of the chapters follow this format, a few chapters are purely descriptive and are intended to help individuals gain knowledge and/or insight. Some chapters include questions to be considered (or used as writing assignments) as part of the therapeutic work.

A Note about Writing Style

The type of language most individuals use in therapy often departs from the conventional rules of grammar, sentence construction, and overall "proper" writing. While in the therapy room, people tend to speak of their personal experiences using very personalized, incomplete, and informal expressions. This does not reflect a lack of education or intentional poor form in regards to the use of language. It is an artifact of the therapeutic context and the specific nature of the work. Due to this dynamic, the material presented in this book breaks many of the rules of grammar, sentence structure, and convention that would be expected in an academic journal article or other formal work. The intention of the material is to meet the person where they live on a daily basis and engage their thinking using the type of language that is typical of interactions in a therapy setting. Quotation marks (i.e., " ") are used to highlight or emphasize specific concepts and to identify ideas that have been expressed and gleaned from therapy sessions. All ideas or quotes from therapy patients in this book are used with permission, but no identifying information is provided in order to protect patient confidentiality. Direct quotations from other authors are identified immediately as such in the text. Finally, many sections use an "→" as a shorthand notation, meaning "leads to", "thus", or "therefore."

Section I of the book summarizes selected sources of information currently available on the topic of PTSD. The remaining sections consist mostly of my own integrative treatment approach which relies heavily on psychoeducation, development of new options for coping (i.e., based on new understanding, new thoughts, and new behaviors) and finally, the facilitation of personal empowerment and personal freedom.

How to Use This Book

This book is not designed to be a traditional book written in a traditional format, wherein chapters contain page after page of text in paragraph form. Instead, the information is presented in an outline format. This is intended to clarify the information, make it more convenient to locate the desired information, and also facilitate its use as a learning and therapeutic tool.

It is suggested that the chapters in this book be used to help people who are coping with PTSD do the following:

1. Gain knowledge of PTSD symptoms
2. Become aware of issues relevant to PTSD
3. Understand PTSD and how it affects a person's life
4. Identify strategies for coping and symptom management
5. Implement new behaviors and practical solutions for living a healthy life in spite of symptoms

As a Therapist:

1. Provide copies of relevant chapters to clients as a way to facilitate the therapeutic process.
2. Use specific chapters in individual therapy as educational homework assignments.
3. Use selective chapters to help clients focus on specific issues as part of their therapy.
4. Use chapters as an outline for discussion and educational purposes in group therapy settings.
5. Use the book as a basic primer for therapists or supervisees in training.
6. As a professional, please use the chapters contained in this book in other ways that are therapeutically helpful and appropriate (of course, abiding by the professional and ethical principles of your discipline).

Note: Photocopying of individual chapters is allowed if it is used as part of therapy by a licensed mental health professional or is intended to provide knowledge or help to a person with PTSD or their family member.

As a Person with PTSD:

1. Read the entire book as a way to learn about and understand PTSD-related issues.
2. Use chapters to identify key issues you are dealing with, and bring them up during your individual therapy sessions.
3. Share chapters (or the whole book) with family members or close friends to help them better understand PTSD and how it affects your life (please use good judgment in this).

4. Use the book as a reference and coping skills guide during especially difficult times or when unable to contact your therapist.
   (**Important Note**: If you are suicidal or thinking of harming someone else, please call 911 or your therapist's after-hours emergency number, or an emergency hotline such as 1-800-273-TALK (8255)).

As a Student Therapist in Training:
1. Use this book as a reference for understanding key PTSD-related issues.
2. Use key chapters as a tool to facilitate the integration of theory and practice in conjunction with your supervision and overall training.

As a Family Member (when your loved one has PTSD):
1. Read selected chapters (or the entire book) to increase your knowledge of PTSD and how you might be supportive of your loved one in their recovery.
2. Consider attending specialized PTSD therapy (individual, couples, or family therapy) to actively participate in the recovery process. Consider this an investment in your relationship and your family.

One final note – not every piece of information in every chapter will apply to you. Please take a practical approach. If the information seems to fit you and your experience, then use it. If some parts don't seem to apply, then move on and focus on the parts that do provide you benefit.

Philosophy of "Getting Better"

Every patient I've worked with has a unique personality, personal style, and specific needs. Therefore, not every approach or technique will work for every person. Find those things that work for you. If there is something you do not find helpful, then skip over it and move on. Try other things until you find the things that do help. In using this material, please be an active reader. Highlight or underline key information that applies to you and your experience. This increases the chances that you will learn and apply the information in getting better.

Goals of PTSD Recovery:
1. Reduce immediate suffering and emotional pain
2. See the world and interpret personal experiences more accurately
3. Get answers to symptoms and experiences that have been confusing
4. Reduce confusion that has perpetuated symptoms and added to ineffective coping
5. Reduce impulsive and reactive behavior
6. Reduce behaviors prompted by anger and their associated negative consequences
7. Increase coping skills (i.e., real life skills that empower a person to live in a more healthy and effective way)
8. Through increased skills, develop personal resilience to manage future challenges effectively
9. Build mental skills for problem solving and managing real-life challenges
10. Become able to use thinking skills to intentionally respond to and appropriately manage daily situations (i.e., called "responding, not reacting")
11. Increase your ability to act in ways that are effective (i.e., called "personal agency")
12. Build and support healthy self-esteem (i.e., feel valuable; feel that the things you do really matter)
13. See more positive, healthy options
14. Manage symptoms effectively
15. Achieve personal peace about past events through acceptance and forgiveness of yourself and others
16. Develop traits and a lifestyle that help you to become the person you truly want to be

Beyond the immediate individual goals for the person with PTSD, I envision a time when society changes its views of the trauma survivor. Instead of stigmatizing and labeling the person as "sick" or "mentally ill," I hope to see healthy reintegration of individuals back into their families and society as a whole. I hope for a time when many of the "symptoms" such as hypervigilance, high attention to detail, intense safety awareness, and intuitive awareness of corruption, can be valued and even sought out by employers. I anticipate an awareness that trauma survivors are strong, conscientious, loyal, and care about the greater good. I intend that we reach a place where trauma survivors are understood, cared for, and respected.

Section I: The Beginning

Patients with PTSD have said . . .

"In war, you die a death that you live with for the rest of your life."

"The vision of horror was now permanently stamped in my mind."

"When you get back to the world, your traumas become your everyday struggles."

"What do you do, when you don't know what else to do?"

"Before therapy, I didn't understand why I was acting the way I was acting."

Chapter 1 – PTSD? How'd I Catch That?

I.   **Description**

    A.   In order to start benefiting from therapy, a trauma survivor needs some very basic information about trauma, PTSD, and how their life has been affected.[1]

    B.   Without a solid understanding, most people remain confused and struggle with their symptoms.

    C.   Post-Traumatic Stress Disorder (PTSD) is an anxiety disorder that results from what is called a traumatic experience.[1,2,3]

        1.   <u>Definition of Trauma</u> – an extreme stressor involving direct personal experience or observation of an event that involves actual or threatened death or serious injury, or threat to one's physical integrity.[3]

        2.   The person's response to this event must involve intense fear, helplessness, or horror.

        3.   PTSD was first included in the official diagnostic manual of mental disorders in 1980.[1,2]

    D.   In a mental trauma, the person is exposed to one or more events in which he or she believes they will be seriously injured or killed, or they are extremely horrified at what they have seen.

    E.   Traumatic experiences are extremely intense, totally overwhelming, or life-threatening.

    F.   Examples of potentially traumatic events include physical assault, natural disasters, accidents, rape, and combat experiences.

    G.   Observation of these types of events without actually experiencing them directly can also lead to PTSD if by seeing what happened the person is completely horrified and/or overwhelmed by it.[3]

    H.   Any person who has had this type of experience could possibly develop PTSD.

    I.   <u>Note</u>: Not every person who has one of these kinds of experiences develops PTSD.[1,3]

    J.   It is not exactly clear at this time why some people develop PTSD in response to traumatic experiences and some don't.

    K.   PTSD continues to be researched to improve our understanding of the disorder and identify effective treatments.[4]

II.   **What Are the Symptoms of PTSD?**[1,2,3,4]

    A.   <u>Re-experiencing the Traumatic Events</u>

        1.   Upsetting thoughts of the trauma that force their way into your mind when you do not want to think about the trauma (called intrusive thoughts).

        2.   Terrible dreams about the traumatic events (nightmares).

3. Feeling as if you are back in the middle of the traumatic experience, and the event is happening all over again (called a flashback).

4. Mental pain or distress when you think of the trauma or related issues.

5. Physical reactions when thinking or talking about the trauma, such as increased heart rate, sweating, shaking, etc.

B. Avoidance Symptoms

1. Trying to forget about what happened in the trauma(s), but you can't forget, no matter how hard you try.

2. Avoiding people, places, or situations that remind you of the trauma(s).

3. Feeling as if part of the trauma(s) is blocked from your memory.

4. Loss of interest in activities you enjoyed before the trauma(s) ever happened.

5. Feeling rejected, threatened, or distant from most people most of the time.

6. Loss of the ability to have positive feelings; numbing or blunting of feelings.

7. Consistently pessimistic about the future.

C. Staying Extremely Alert and On Guard Ever Since the Event (called hyper-arousal symptoms)

1. Problems falling asleep or staying asleep.

2. Being easily angered or upset.

3. Concentration problems (trouble keeping your mind on track; losing focus frequently).

4. Feeling unsafe and being on guard most of the time.

5. An exaggerated startle response (i.e., being "overly jumpy").

III. **Other Patterns that are Commonly Found in Trauma Survivors (called associated features of PTSD)[3]**

A. Survival guilt

B. Guilt about what you had to do to survive

C. Phobic avoidance of reminders of the trauma

D. Difficulty regulating your emotions (feels like an emotional rollercoaster)

E. Self-destructive and/or impulsive behaviors

F. Dissociation (blanking out; spacing out mentally)

G. Somatic (physical) complaints

H. Feelings of ineffectiveness

I. Shame

J. Despair

K. Hopelessness

L. Feeling permanently damaged (mentally and/or emotionally)

M.   Hostility
N.   Social withdrawal
O.   Feeling constantly threatened (or constantly in danger)
P.   Impaired relationships
Q.   Personality change after the trauma

IV.   **Clues that You Might Have PTSD**[1,2]

A.   Some questions to consider (answer as honestly as possible)

1.   Have you had one or more experiences that were <u>so extreme</u> that you felt totally overwhelmed, you thought you couldn't handle it, or you were completely horrified at what you saw?

YES   NO

2.   Do you have terrible recurring dreams about an overwhelming experience that you've had in the past?

YES   NO

3.   Do you sometimes feel that you are reliving a horrible experience in your mind all over again and feel overwhelmed or frightened when this happens?

YES   NO

4.   Do you try to forget about a terrible experience you've had and can't seem to stop thinking about it, no matter how hard you try?

YES   NO

5.   Do you feel the need to be on alert for danger most all of the time?

YES   NO

6.   Are there certain people, places, or things you avoid because they remind you too much of extremely terrible experiences from the past?

YES   NO

B.   If you answered "Yes" to 2 or more of the above questions, it would be a good idea to get a professional evaluation by a therapist who specializes in the treatment of PTSD.

C.   If you have these symptoms, it is wise to seek therapy with a therapist who <u>specializes</u> in the treatment of PTSD.[1,2]

D.   While traumas are confusing experiences, the good news is that you don't have to stay confused.

1.   There are answers for what you are going through.
2.   It is possible to get better.

Chapter 1 Exercise

1. Write out the definition of a trauma.

_____

_____

_____

_____

2. List the re-experiencing symptoms that you have experienced.

_____

_____

_____

_____

3. List the avoidance symptoms that you have experienced.

_____

_____

_____

_____

4. List the hyper-arousal symptoms that you have experienced.

_____

_____

_____

_____

5. Which of the associated features of PTSD have you noticed in yourself?

_____

_____

_____

_____

6. How many "YES" responses did you have in Section IV? _____

7. If you had 2 or more "YES" responses, how do you feel about that at this point?

_____

_____

_____

_____

8. Are you willing to learn more about PTSD and/or possibly consider treatment?
    YES   NO

Chapter 2 – What's It Like if You Have PTSD?

I. **If You Do Have PTSD, What Is It Like?**[1,2]

    A.   Many people describe feeling <u>unsafe</u> and <u>confused.</u>

    B.   Anger is very common; some have feelings of hurt and disbelief about what happened.

    C.   It is common to ask "Am I crazy?"

    D.   A very important point:

        1.   PTSD is <u>NOT</u> the same as being crazy.

        2.   Many of the symptoms may "feel crazy", confusing, or bewildering.[2]

        3.   Even though many individuals with PTSD question their own sanity, PTSD symptoms are the result of real events that really did happen.

II. **Patients' Descriptions of Themselves <u>Before</u> Trauma**

    A.   <u>Before the Trauma, I Was:</u>

        1.   Happy-go-lucky; trusting (naïve), sociable, enjoyed friends, easy-going

        2.   Carefree, confident, future-oriented, independent

    B.   <u>Interests Before the Trauma:</u>

        1.   Sports, dating, cars, motorcycles, hobbies, social activities

        2.   Mechanics, music, writing, hunting, fishing, spending time with friends

III. **Patients' Descriptions of Themselves <u>After</u> Trauma**

    A.   <u>After the Trauma, I Was:</u>

        1.   Disconnected from self and others, didn't trust, wandered around

        2.   Felt lost, didn't have positive feelings, had nothing in common with past friends

        3.   Emotionally detached, didn't fit in anymore, didn't care about the future

        4.   Lost enthusiasm, became a workaholic, personality became very serious

        5.   People didn't understand me, detached from the world, more and more fatigued

        6.   Lived in 2 worlds: (1) public appearance, and (2) private misery (behind the mask)

        7.   Became physically aggressive, lost ambitions, couldn't stick with anything

        8.   Nervous, depressed, felt unworthy, fragile, felt rejected by others

        9.   Always considered worst case scenarios, always had contingency plans

    B.   Interests After the Trauma:
- 1. Drinking, getting stoned, getting high, driving fast, taking extreme risks
- 2. Shooting pool, spending time alone, just passing time, simple survival

IV.   PTSD from the Patient's Viewpoint

    A.   Personal Definitions of PTSD (written by actual patients who have PTSD)
1. PTSD is living with someone you don't have control of (and it's you!).
2. PTSD feels like forever and destroys the quality of your life.
3. PTSD is "traumatic experience" that is always present inside of you.
4. PTSD is a mental collapse. Every time I try something, I can only get so far. I am mentally challenged.
5. PTSD is a mystery compounded by my inability to understand it.
6. PTSD = fear $\times$ frustration $\times$ regret.
7. PTSD is my mind in total fear and confusion that has shaken life as I once knew it.
8. PTSD is a constant return of your worst nightmare.
9. PTSD is an angry, tired, hopeless existence.
10. PTSD is a silent hell, and not knowing why.
11. PTSD is a mind-boggling mixture of over- and under-reaction, and you don't understand why.
12. PTSD is like leprosy on the inside of your mind. If you don't treat it, you will fall apart and rot away.
13. PTSD is misery, loneliness, fear, and pain all rolled into one.
14. PTSD is the complete and total destruction of one's life.
15. PTSD is fear, on top of fear, on top of fear – a dark cloud you seem to always walk under.
16. PTSD is a condition of the mind that causes you to react to a situation in ways other than what is considered "normal."
17. PTSD is a life-crippling disorder brought on by trauma.
18. PTSD is a "mental problem" that controls your emotions and thoughts.
19. PTSD is a mental disorder that creates physical and emotional havoc in a person's life.
20. PTSD is a mental gloom about life and the future that never goes away.

    B.   How PTSD Has Affected Your Life (from the patient's viewpoint)
1. PTSD has not allowed me to be the person I want to be.
2. I've had divorce and alcoholism. It endangered my life and others around me.

3.   I never feel in control, but I always try to be.

4.   Family problems; no use for friends; total isolation.

5.   Paranoid and feel "less than" other people.

6.   Failure in relationships, "blown" opportunities to be successful, no self-confidence.

7.   Fear, suspicion, and doubt all of the time.

8.   Total withdrawal, no trust, "mad as hell."

9.   Feel totally worthless, feel that "I'm a loser."

10.   It's hard to love anyone – I don't think I even know what love really is.

11.   Depressed, lonely, and exhausted; living in turmoil.

12.   Loss of love, freedom, job opportunities, friendships, and family.

13.   PTSD slowly crushed me emotionally, physically, and economically until I had nothing left to live for.

14.   I have been displaced in time ever since [the trauma].

15.   My belief system vanished. I thought of suicide, dropping out of society, and hurting people.

16.   For years I could not look at myself in the mirror without walking away in disgust.

17.   Upset all the time, can't be around anyone, and keep everything bottled up inside.

18.   I would fight at the "drop of a hat," and I just didn't care anymore.

19.   Ever since [the trauma], I've always been looking over my shoulder.

20.   I've done a lot of stupid things and have been hard to get along with.

21.   I'm always in fear and searching for relief.

22.   PTSD ruined my life according to "being normal." I've never enjoyed anything [since the trauma], and I hate being around people.

23.   Anger became the norm, and I had a lot of rage.

24.   It has kept me from progressing in life for 38 years [my entire adult life].

25.   It is like a "merry-go-round" that's not merry.

26.   PTSD has totally screwed up my mental and physical health.

27.   PTSD has made me feel insignificant, hopeless, out of focus, lacking clear goals, and caused me to sabotage nearly every opportunity and/or relationship I've ever entered into.

C.   Themes from the Patient's Viewpoint [1,2,7,9]

1.   Lack of control; a ruined life; extreme fear and anxiety.

2.   Low self-esteem (feeling worthless; feeling a lack of value as a person).

3.   Inescapable symptoms; functional impairment; confusion; loss.

4.   Prominent awareness of one's own misery and feeling "abnormal."

5.   Anger; rage; irritability; destructive behavior.

6.   Depressed – hopeless; feel like a failure.
7.   Lonely, isolated, lack of healthy connections with other people.
8.   Gets progressively worse; eats you up inside; pessimistic outlook.

D.   <u>Don't Despair – As Bad as PTSD Can Be, It Is Possible to Get Better</u>

Chapter 2 Exercise

1.   What was your personality like before the trauma?

_____
_____
_____
_____

2.   What changes did you notice in your thoughts, feelings, and actions after the trauma?

_____
_____
_____
_____

3.   How did your interests change after the trauma?

_____
_____
_____
_____

4.   After reading the "patients' definitions," write your own definition of PTSD.

_____
_____
_____
_____

5.   How has PTSD affected your life?

_____
_____
_____
_____

Chapter 3 – What You Need to Know Up Front

I.   First Things First
- A.   You are not crazy!
- B.   When you have a flashback, it feels like you are losing control of yourself.
    1.   Feel overwhelmed all over again.
    2.   Think you might be losing your mind.
- C.   Recurring nightmares can make you fearful of going to sleep.[7]
- D.   Be aware:
    1.   There are some mental conditions that some people may call "crazy" or "insane."
    2.   PTSD <u>is not</u> one of them.
    3.   Understand that PTSD is one of the healthier ways of dealing with mental trauma.[1]

II.   How Does PTSD Work?[1,2,9]
- A.   A person's normal coping abilities get overwhelmed in a trauma, and overwhelming feelings are created.
- B.   <u>A big key:</u> The person loses the ability to feel safe.
- C.   The overwhelming feelings are pushed back in your mind because they feel unbearable.
- D.   A state of confusion is created and persists.
- E.   From that point on, you just survive the best you can (while staying confused, before therapy).
- F.   Every time the overwhelming feelings come up, you fight them off as best you can.
    1.   Mentally suppress the memories.
    2.   Drink or use drugs; become a workaholic.
    3.   "Just keep on runnin'."
- G.   Keep on this way until you hit bottom, break down, or don't know where else to turn.
- H.   Some people conclude that suicide is the only way out of the emotional pain (but it's not!).
- I.   Other people get into good treatment, find recovery, and regain a healthy life.

III.   It Can Be Dealt With [1,9]
- A.   Before treatment, PTSD can seem impossible to overcome.
- B.   Memories and feelings are overwhelming and generate high levels of fear and anxiety.
- C.   The thought of gaining control over these symptoms may seem impossible.
- D.   However, it is possible to get better.
- E.   If you are reading this book, then you have at least a little hope.

F.   If you have gone for treatment, then you are there for a reason.

G.   Make sure to hang on to that hope which started you toward treatment.

H.   Others have gotten better – you can too.

I.   Just how serious are you about healing, recovering, and getting better?

IV.   The Recovery Process [10,11,12]

A.   We first need to break through the denial → admit there is a problem.

B.   Realize that dealing with PTSD is tough, but possible.

C.   However, recognize that continuing to live in denial is harder (in the long run).

D.   A principle in PTSD recovery: <u>"You will probably feel worse before you feel better."</u>

    1.   This is because painful thoughts, memories, and feelings that you have been keeping back in your mind are now surfacing.

    2.   They need to be dealt with – don't let this make you stop treatment.

    3.   Thousands of other people have experienced the same thing in treatment and have made it through to the point of recovering.

E.   At times there are setbacks, but the long-term pattern is one of progress and improvement.[13]

F.   To get better, it might require several years of committed work.[1]

    1.   Remember: You are investing in your own health.

    2.   Your recovery can also benefit those people close to you that you care about.

Chapter 3 Exercise

1.   List the symptoms you have experienced that have "felt crazy."

_____

_____

_____

_____

_____

_____

2.   How does it feel to know that PTSD is not the same as crazy?

_____

_____

_____

_____

_____

_____

3.   What did you do to "fight off the symptoms" before you knew about PTSD?

_____

_____

_____

_____

_____

_____

4.   What do you hope to achieve through PTSD treatment?

_____

_____

_____

_____

_____

_____

Chapter 4 – How Does PTSD Affect a Person's Life?
(Why is it a problem?)

I.   **Why Is PTSD a Problem?**[1,2,7,9]
A.   Many people with PTSD go for years thinking they have no problem.
B.   It is common to think that everyone else is stupid and really messed up, while seeing yourself as having no problems.
C.   Some common patterns are frequently seen.
    1.   Using old behaviors to deal with new problems or situations.
    2.   Attempts at coping don't match the demands of the current situation or environment.
    3.   These patterns leave people thinking that their approach is "right" and that the problems are only caused by other people's incompetence or bad circumstances.
D.   Symptoms can cause levels of distress and suffering that limit our ability to function.
E.   Eventually, a person gets to the point of struggling, fighting, and not knowing what to do or where else to turn.[7,12]

II.   **Ways PTSD Can Affect a Person's Life**
A.   <u>Thoughts</u> [1,2,7]
    1.   Poor attention and concentration; trouble staying focused.
    2.   Often feeling confused or bewildered.
    3.   Expecting the worst most of the time.
    4.   Skeptical of most things → usually don't trust people.
        a.   Always wondering "just what do they want?"
        b.   "What is their ulterior motive?"
    5.   Disgust at incompetence, lackadaisical attitudes, or what we perceive as stupidity.
B.   <u>Emotions</u> [1,2,9]
    1.   Fear of the traumas happening again.
    2.   Fear of losing control of yourself and doing something you regret.
    3.   Fear of overwhelming emotions; grief, rage, anger, or shock.
    4.   Depression, guilt, and shame are common feelings.
    5.   Emotional numbing (certain feelings get shut down or blocked out in an effort to protect yourself; many people don't know how they feel when they are asked).
C.   <u>Biological</u> [6]
    1.   Trouble falling asleep or staying asleep often adds to extreme fatigue.
    2.   Physical hyper-arousal; increased startle response (jump at every little thing).

        3.   Lack of physical self-care (poor hygiene, diet, sleep, neglected physical appearance).

        4.   Multiple medical problems are common.[1]

        5.   Become susceptible to stress-related illnesses; never take any "down time" for yourself.

        6.   Severe wear and tear on the body.

D.   Relationships [14]

        1.   Feel detached, threatened, or rejected most of the time.

        2.   Isolation; avoid people most of the time if possible.

        3.   Don't get too close to anyone.

        4.   Don't let anyone get close to you for fear of hurting them or losing them.

        5.   Frequent arguments; strained relationships; multiple marriages.

        6.   Feel like you don't fit in (anywhere); often wind up feeling rejected.

E.   Other Problems Frequently Seen [1,2]

        1.   Drug and alcohol abuse; workaholism.

        2.   Panic attacks; uncontrollable worry.

        3.   Frequent job changes or unemployment.

        4.   Physical complaints or illnesses.

        5.   Family problems; legal problems.

F.   How many of these have you experienced since the trauma(s)?

III.   Expectable Course of Untreated PTSD [1,5,9]

A.   Memories of the trauma are avoided if at all possible.

B.   Alcohol and other drugs are used in an effort to avoid the painful memories.

C.   Some trauma survivors become workaholics to avoid thinking of the memories.

D.   Isolation becomes a way of life in an effort to manage stress and anger.

E.   Daily stress is more difficult to deal with; small things feel overwhelming.

F.   Anger becomes a chronic way of dealing with people and the world.

G.   Feel the need to stay on guard all the time to avoid danger and prevent another trauma.

H.   Stay emotionally numb so you don't have to feel the painful emotions (or feel much of anything).

I.   Sleep becomes disrupted most of the time; become afraid to go to sleep; eventually experience ongoing fatigue.

J.   Overall, a person's life feels chaotic and fear becomes the driving force behind most of their behaviors (all the while, the person believes "I'm not afraid of anything").

IV.   **Before and After Treatment** [1,9]
    A.   <u>Before Treatment</u>
        1.   Barely surviving (looking for a way to die)
        2.   Always pessimistic
        3.   Future looked unclear and bleak
        4.   Denial of PTSD symptoms and the impact on my life; "I don't have a problem, but all those other people out there are really screwed up"
        5.   Hide PTSD; feel shame; tell no one
        6.   Battling alone; (just barely hanging on)
        7.   Uninformed; why me? (total confusion)
        8.   Wondered if I might be crazy
        9.   Poor physical health
        10.   Not thinking (just reacting to everything)
        11.   Inner turmoil (always in confusion and conflict)
    B.   <u>After Treatment</u>
        1.   Looking for a way to live again
        2.   Hopeful
        3.   Future becomes more clear
        4.   Admission of symptoms; dedication to getting better
        5.   Acknowledge PTSD and use positive coping skills regularly
        6.   Tell my story in a safe way to people who understand
        7.   Coping each day; using healthy support systems; starting to live again
        8.   Well informed about PTSD and its impact
        9.   Have answers and increased understanding
        10.   Know that PTSD came from real experiences and you are not "crazy"
        11.   Improved health (taking care of yourself now)
        12.   Thinking (not always reacting); living in a thoughtful, intelligent way

Chapter 4 Exercise

1.   How did you typically view other people before treatment?

_____

_____

_____

2.   List how each of the following have been affected:

Thoughts

_____

_____

Emotions

_____

_____

Biological

_____

_____

Relationships

_____

_____

3.   Describe the direction your life was headed before treatment.

_____

_____

_____

_____

_____

_____

Chapter 5 – Why Coping Skills?
(Introduction to the Basic Techniques)

I. **What are Coping Skills?** [15,16]
    A.   Thoughts, behaviors, and skills that help us deal with stress, daily hassles, symptoms, and painful emotions (feelings).
        1.   These are actual skills that need to be practiced to be effective.
        2.   Everybody needs normal coping skills to manage the regular demands of life.
        3.   They are a key to effective living, but are not the final answer to everything.
    B.   If we don't develop these skills, our ability to deal with stress and make progress in life remains limited.

II. **Reasons for Ineffective Coping** [1,2,15,16]
    A.   Don't know that I have a problem.
    B.   Know that I have a problem, but not sure what it is (living in confusion).
    C.   Was never taught how to deal with stress or challenging experiences.
    D.   Just don't have the skills I need.
    E.   Have and understand the skills, but just don't put them into practice.

III. **Approaches to Coping When You Don't Know What Else To Do**
    A.   <u>Withdraw from people</u> [14]
        1.   Don't talk about it.
        2.   Don't let anyone get close enough to help you.
        3.   Isolate from most everyone else (avoid people).
    B.   <u>Become Aggressive</u> [1,9]
        1.   Be aggressive or violent before anyone else can hurt you any more.
        2.   Operate on the idea that "The best defense is a good offense."
        3.   Be harsh, rude, and nasty → this keeps people away and prevents further trauma.
    C.   <u>Become Depressed</u> [8]
        1.   This is a natural reaction to having been traumatized or abused (victimized).
        2.   Depression partly functions to protect us from further hurt or disappointment.
        3.   Depression is not desirable, but the feelings are very predictable.
        4.   Sometimes, people prefer what is predictable (i.e., feeling bad) over the unpredictable possibility of being hurt again in the future.

D. Abuse Alcohol and Other Drugs [12,13]
1. This brings some short term relief from the immediate emotional pain, but does not solve the deep-seated problem.
2. Drink or use drugs even though you don't like them → just to get some relief.
3. Trauma or abuse often feels like it "haunts you" → just want some escape from it all.

E. Tension-Reduction Rituals [1,9,16] – behavior patterns that are repeated over and over again to release some of the tension or emotional pain.
1. Get into a fight once per week or once per month (every time the tension builds up).
2. Have an argument in order to be able to express anger or other emotions.
3. Go into a rage → act out inappropriately; hurt myself; hurt other people; destroy property.
4. Self-mutilation → cutting on (or otherwise harming) your own body to release emotional tension or pain; going to extremes to get some relief or feel better.

IV. **Basic Skills – Coping Skills Everyone Needs**
A. Deep Breathing [17,18]
1. Used to calm the body when feeling anxious, upset, overwhelmed, or close to panic.
2. Can be used most anywhere – most any time.
3. Requires daily practice to master.
4. DO THE FOLLOWING:
    a. Take a slow, deep breath.
    b. Hold for a count of "3."
    c. Breathe out slowly.
    d. Repeat several times (slowly).
5. Many therapists and patients consider deep breathing to be absolutely essential.

B. Take a TIME OUT! [17,18]
1. Take a break from the upsetting situation before becoming more angry, violent, or destructive.
2. Remove yourself from the place or situation.
3. Take some time to cool down, relax, and think it through.
4. Come back and deal with the situation when you are in a calmer and more productive frame of mind.

C.   <u>Mental Focus</u> [1,15,16] – the ability to fix your thoughts on one thing at a time and gain perspective.
1.   When feeling overwhelmed, our thoughts usually race.
2.   We usually think of things that are not likely to happen.
3.   We often focus on things that are unrelated to the real issue (get sidetracked).
4.   We can quickly lose perspective.
5.   Our thoughts become distorted, leading to faulty conclusions.
6.   Instead, we need to pick one thing and focus <u>only</u> on it.
   a.   Look at a point on the wall until you regain control of your thoughts.
   b.   Focus only on your breathing.
   c.   Have a preplanned word, which calms you down and helps you focus, that you repeat over and over to yourself.
   d.   Eat a piece of candy slowly and without biting it, focusing your attention on the feeling, taste, texture, etc.

V.   **Using Coping Skills to Your Advantage** [1,2,15,16]
A.   We need to practice using these skills every day.
B.   Begin by mastering the above very basic skills.
C.   Work on more complex skills as you make progress.
D.   While some of the symptoms may never completely go away, your ability to deal with symptoms and difficult situations gets better the more you practice.
E.   As you make progress, your ability to manage stress, daily hassles, frustrating situations, and painful feelings increases to the point that you are no longer out of control or overwhelmed by them anymore.
1.   Coping skills are like tools.
2.   They don't help you if you never pick them up or use them properly.

VI.   **Coping Skills – The Bottom Line**
A.   No matter what your diagnosis is, what medications you take, or what your doctor says, you still have to live your life!
B.   EVERYBODY needs coping skills!

Chapter 5 Exercise

1.   List the coping strategies you used <u>before</u> therapy and their consequences.

Coping Strategy	**Consequences**
_____	_____
_____	_____
_____	_____
_____	_____
_____	_____
_____	_____
_____	_____

2.   What happens to a person when they use unhealthy coping skills?

_____

_____

3.   What are the benefits of the deep breathing technique?

_____

_____

4.   Describe the steps involved in taking a "time out"

a. _____

b. _____

c. _____

d. _____

e. _____

5.   If used properly, what benefits do the deep breathing and time out techniques offer?

_____

_____

_____

_____

_____

_____

Chapter 6 – Deep Breathing

I. **Why Deep Breathing Is Important** [1,2,17,18]
   - A.   With PTSD, we tend to become too excited mentally and physically to cope effectively with many situations.
     1.   Get upset easily; over-react.
     2.   Hyperventilate.
     3.   Heart racing; body shaking.
     4.   Racing thoughts; feel shaky and uneasy.
   - B.   This over-arousal can lead to over-reacting, fits of rage, and creation of even more problems.[9]
   - C.   We need a technique for calming ourselves so we can control ourselves and better manage the situations we encounter each day.

II. **How Deep Breathing Works** [17,18]
   - A.   In deep breathing, you focus on using your diaphragm when you breathe, instead of using your chest or back muscles.
   - B.   The diaphragm is a muscle that looks like a large pancake that lies beneath your lungs, but above your stomach.
   - C.   When breathing properly, the diaphragm moves downward, which pulls the lungs down and forms a vacuum.
   - D.   Air is drawn into the lungs; oxygen goes into the blood stream while carbon dioxide comes out of the blood stream.
   - E.   Then, we exhale.
   - F.   When we breathe correctly, the stomach and abdomen bulge outward when breathing in.
   - G.   When breathing out, the stomach and abdomen should move back in – like when you suck in your stomach.
   - H.   When breathing in this way, after a few breaths the body naturally begins to relax.

III. **The New Way**
   - A.   The deep breathing technique can be used almost any time and anywhere.
   - B.   It causes the body to automatically begin to relax.
   - C.   As we calm down, we get to be more in control of ourselves and we can think more clearly.
   - D.   This increases our chances of handling stressful situations more effectively.
   - E.   Practice this form of breathing in a quiet and comfortable place, focusing only on your breathing.
   - F.   With repeated practice, you will learn to control your breathing and be able to calm yourself when in pain or experiencing stress.

IV.   **Steps to do "Deep" Breathing** [17,18]

A.   <u>Note</u>: While you are learning, place one hand on your chest and one hand on your stomach to get the "feel of it."

B.   <u>Specific steps</u>

1.   Inhale slowly for a few seconds until the lungs feel full.

    a.   While breathing in, let your stomach and abdomen stick out.

    b.   The hand on your stomach should move out as the stomach begins to bulge out slightly, while the hand on your chest stays still.

2.   Hold the air in for a count of 1 – one thousand, and then slowly breathe out.

    a.   When breathing out, let your stomach slowly come back in to its normal position.

3.   If you feel light headed after a few breaths, you may need to breathe more slowly.

4.   Start with 2 or 3 slow, deep breaths.

5.   With practice, you can breathe this way for many minutes at a time.

6.   You will feel more relaxed as you learn to breathe this way more often.

C.   When you notice that you are starting to feel anxious, tense, or angry, that is your cue to use the deep breathing relaxation technique to relax yourself.

D.   Practice this form of breathing in a quiet and comfortable place, focusing only on your breathing.

E.   With repeated practice, you will learn to control your breathing and be able to calm yourself when in pain, under stress, or feeling panic.

F.   After you learn this technique, you no longer need to put your hands on the stomach and chest.

G.   Some people find benefit from combining counting with the in-breaths and the out-breaths. Utilize this approach if it helps you to focus and benefit more.

H.   Deep breathing has now become your new "normal" way of breathing and calming yourself, and can be used most any time you need it.

Chapter 6 Exercise

1.   List some situations in which deep breathing might be beneficial.

_____
_____
_____
_____
_____
_____

2.   What cues let you know that it is time to use deep breathing?

_____
_____
_____

3.   What benefits have you noticed since starting the deep breathing technique?

_____
_____
_____

Chapter 7 – Taking a "Time Out!"

I. **What's All the Fuss About?** [1,2,15,16]
  A. Many individuals with PTSD can become upset so easily, that they become unable to manage the upsetting situation.
  B. At this point, nothing productive will happen until they can calm down and think more clearly.
  1. Become upset quickly and easily.
  2. The frustration and anger take over.
  3. Get stuck mentally; get tunnel vision.
  4. Focus on proving yourself and being "right."
  5. Become aggressive or violent in trying to accomplish your task.
  C. We need a technique to help us calm down and get back in control of ourselves so we can handle upsetting situations properly.

II. **A New Approach to Frustrating Situations**
  A. "Time Out!" means taking a break from an upsetting situation.
  B. It should be used when you are beginning to feel angry, tense, irritable, or out of control.
  C. "Time Out!" helps a person regain their composure, manage their anger, and calm down.
  D. The Purpose of Time Out! [1]
  1. To prevent yourself from doing something you might regret later.
  2. To more appropriately manage your anger.
  3. To exercise healthy self-control.
  4. To help you relax, cool down, and think clearly when a situation begins to escalate.
  5. To prevent a violent outburst of anger.
  6. To remove yourself from a situation so that you don't overreact.
  E. When we think more clearly, we are better able to maintain proper self-control.[2]

III. **How to Use "Time Out!"** [18]
  A. First – Get away from the person or situation.
  1. Tell the other person that you are feeling angry or tense and need some time to calm down.
  2. Completely leave the place or situation.
  B. Second – Calm yourself physically and mentally.
  1. Use deep breathing to calm the body (see the deep breathing exercise).
  2. Do a physical activity such as walking.

3. Use calming thoughts to replace angry thoughts.
   a. "I can handle this."   e. "I don't have to react."
   b. "I am calming down."   f. "I will stay in control."
   c. "I only have to breathe." g. "I will choose how to handle this."
   d. "I refuse to let them   h. "I have survived much worse."
      push my buttons."

C. <u>Third – Give yourself enough time to calm down and get control of yourself.</u>
   1. Take enough time to make sure that you are calm and thinking clearly.
   2. It's more important to stay in control of yourself than to prove yourself to others.

D. <u>Fourth – During the time out, don't drink alcohol or use other drugs.</u>
   1. Alcohol and other drugs will only cloud your mind in this situation.
   2. This will make the situation worse instead of better.
   3. Don't drive, operate machinery, or do any other potentially dangerous behaviors .

E. <u>Fifth – After you are calm, go back and deal with the situation in a responsible, controlled way.</u>
   1. Focus on fixing the problem (not on placing blame).
   2. If you are about to lose control of yourself, then take another Time Out!

Chapter 7 Exercise

1.   What does it mean to "take a Time Out"?

_____

_____

2.   What is the purpose of Time Out?

_____

_____

3.   Describe the steps involved in taking a "Time Out"

    a. _____

    b. _____

    c. _____

    d. _____

    e. _____

4.   List some recent experiences where using Time Out could have helped.

_____

_____

_____

_____

_____

_____

Chapter 8 – Triggers

I.   **Trauma-related Trigger [1,2,9] (anything that brings to mind the overwhelming feelings associated with the trauma[s])**

    A.   A hallmark of PTSD is re-experiencing of the traumatic event(s).

    B.   Often things we experience in daily life can "trigger" this.

    C.   At first, triggers catch a person by surprise and cause them to feel unsafe and overwhelmed.

    D.   However, with some learning and practice, we can anticipate most triggers and have healthy options for how to manage the situation.

II.   **Examples**

    A.   <u>Triggers</u>

          1.   Smells, sights, sounds, people, objects, situations, etc., that remind you of the trauma.

          2.   Events such as holidays, specific dates, anniversaries, etc. can be triggers.

          3.   Particular slang or jargon used in a certain situation or place; tone of voice.

          4.   Current stresses can also be triggers, such as difficulties at work or home, emotional strains, financial or medical problems, crime, witnessing or being involved in a current traumatic experience, etc.

    B.   <u>Common Reactions to Triggers</u> [1,9,15]

          1.   Anger.

          2.   Rage.

          3.   Increased isolation.

          4.   Self-blame.

          5.   Craving food, drugs, alcohol, or other things.

          6.   Increased flashbacks.

          7.   Self-mutilation.

          8.   Depression.

          9.   Self-hatred; suicidal/homicidal thoughts.

          10.   Worsening of physical pain.

          11.   Headaches; activation of a chronic medical condition (for example, high blood sugar if you are diabetic).

          12.   Destructive behaviors, or other reactions.

          13.   Feel attacked; paranoia.

          14.   Decreased self-esteem; feel worthless.

15. Many individuals have reacted to triggers and then did not under-stand their own behavior.
    a. Could not explain the reasons for their actions.
    b. Wound up feeling embarrassed or humiliated.
    c. Felt out of control; questioned your own sanity.
C. Triggers and Traumatic Memory [1,2,9]
    1. When a trigger is experienced, the traumatic memory (or part of it) is brought to your conscious awareness.
    2. The emotional pain is felt, and often a person "feels traumatized" all over again.
    3. Immediately, a person tries to seek a place of safety, or might react by trying to take control over a situation (even if it calls for taking extreme measures).
    4. To get better, we need to figure out how these triggering experiences relate to the original trauma(s)?
    5. What traumatic memories do they bring up?

    _____

    6. Why does this trigger make you feel unsafe or vulnerable?

    _____

    7. What are healthy options for managing it?

    _____

III. Identifying Triggers[1]: (to increase understanding and options for positive coping)
    A. List the things that remind you of the traumas or cause you to react in one of the ways listed above.
    B. Next, list the way you typically react (old reactions).
    C. Last, identify a new behavior you could do when you come in contact with these triggers, instead of the old reaction in order to improve coping.

Trigger	Old Reactions	New Coping Behaviors
1.		
2.		
3.		
4.		
5.		
6.		
7.		
8.		
9.		
10.		

IV.   **Application (new coping strategies)** [1,2]

    A.   It is important to anticipate the situations in which you might react as if the trauma were happening again.

    B.   Once I know my triggers, I have two options:

        1.   Avoid it.

        2.   Confront it and overcome it.

            a.   Take this slowly.

            b.   Maybe ask your therapist to help in confronting the trigger.

    C.   By knowing what to expect, this increases our feelings of control over symptoms.

    D.   We can now develop strategies to cope more effectively with the triggers and not get overwhelmed like in the past.

    E.   With increased understanding, I can manage my triggers and start rebuilding my life in the way that I want.

    F.   In time, we can learn or relearn that not all triggers will be harmful to us, thus promoting healing.

    G.   While my reactions to these triggers may never completely go away, I don't have to "be blind-sided" or "wiped-out emotionally" when I encounter them like in the past.

Chapter 8 Exercise

1.   Write the definition of a "Trigger"

_____

_____

2.   What are your "Triggers"?

_____   _____

_____   _____

_____   _____

_____   _____

_____   _____

_____   _____

_____   _____

3.   What have been your typical reactions to triggers?

_____

_____

_____

_____

4.   How would you like to handle these triggers in the future?

_____

_____

_____

_____

Chapter 9 – Anniversaries and Holidays

I. **Traumatic Anniversary Dates** [1,2,9] **(the specific date [or same time of year] that the original trauma(s) occurred)**
    A. The time of year is a reminder, and brings up memories of the trauma(s).
    B. <u>Note:</u> Some people prefer to call these "trauma dates" in order to preserve a positive connotation for the word "anniversary."

II. **Why Is Coping with PTSD More Difficult During Traumatic Anniversary Periods?**
    A. The time of year reminds us of the most terrible experiences of our lives.
    B. At first, we don't know why our symptoms are worse at these times each year.
        1. Feel anxious or depressed and don't know why.
        2. Time of year is a trigger for remembering all the bad memories.
        3. Symptoms often cycle depending on the time of year.
    C. During trauma dates, we are reminded of major losses.
        1. Through this we re-experience the pain of those losses.
        2. Have increased depression (sadness; memory of loss; grief).
        3. Isolate more during these times.
        4. Have more nightmares, flashbacks, and intrusive thoughts.
    D. The painful emotions that were created by the trauma are brought to the front of a person's mind.
        1. The time of year makes it difficult to avoid the feelings associated with the trauma(s).
        2. This increase in symptoms can often begin a few weeks before the trauma date, and can last for some time after (everyone is a little different on this).

III. **Coping Strategies**
    A. Be prepared → know when your anniversary periods are.
        1. Keep a personal calendar and mark the dates.
        2. Look back over the past several years and find the patterns.
        3. Refer to the calendar regularly so you will know what is coming up the next month.
    B. Plan ahead → don't get caught by surprise like in the past.
        1. Plan activities to keep yourself busy during those times.
        2. Pre-planned coping behaviors are important.
        3. It's best not to try to figure out how to cope in the middle of overwhelming feelings, because then it's too late.
        4. When we know what to expect and are prepared for it, our ability to cope improves.

C.   Use certain behaviors, tasks, or rituals that help you cope – make sure that you stay busy during this time.
Examples:
1.   Hobbies.
2.   Exercise.
3.   Light work at home.
4.   Prayer; meditation.
5.   Have someone to talk to.
6.   Work on a project.
7.   Reading.
8.   Distraction (music, movies, poetry, writing).

D.   Be active in your treatment.
1.   The natural inclination is to avoid everyone and everything during these times.
2.   Instead, come to the clinic as scheduled – don't avoid it.
3.   Schedule an extra session with your therapist.
4.   Continue to participate in group therapy.

E.   Make sure that you have social support when you need it.
1.   Spend some time with people you trust and feel comfortable with.
2.   Spend some time alone when you need it – but not all of the time.

F.   Write in a journal.
1.   Express your thoughts and feelings → get it out in a safe and controlled way instead of bottling it up.
2.   Sometimes getting it down on paper helps us manage it better.

G.   Take medications as prescribed.
1.   Don't skip doses or try to "tough it out" during these times.
2.   Try to remain as stable as possible.
3.   Some medication providers give "PRN medications" to be used as needed during times when symptoms are increased.

H.   Recognize that you will make it through these extra tough times.

IV.   Getting Better

A.   As you progress through therapy, the first few years are especially difficult during trauma dates.

B.   Over time, many individuals have expressed how the trauma dates become less intense.

C.   Some people report that each year gets a little better and somewhat easier to deal with.

D.   While it is difficult at first, many people get to the point that the time of year no longer overwhelms them or totally disrupts their life anymore.

Chapter 9 Exercise

1.   Write the definition of "Traumatic Anniversary Date":

_____

_____

2.   Why is coping more difficult during the traumatic anniversary date?

_____

_____

_____

_____

3.   List your Trauma Dates or worst times of year (to the best of your memory)

_____

_____

_____

_____

4.   What strategies do you plan to use during upcoming trauma dates?

_____

_____

_____

_____

5.   Who will you call if you start having a difficult time coping during an upcoming trauma date?

_____

_____

_____

_____

Chapter 10 – Understanding the Big Picture of PTSD

I.   **A Working Model of PTSD**

1. Trauma	3. New Worldview	6. Suffering
2. Overwhelmed →	4. Safety Focus	7. Struggling
	5. Anger →	8. Ineffective Coping

A.   How does PTSD affect a person's life?[1,2]

1.   <u>Trauma occurs</u> (overwhelming fear, completely helpless, totally horrified).

2.   <u>The normal, typical coping strategies are overwhelmed</u> (i.e., are ineffective).

      a.   Survival is the bottom line (do whatever it takes to survive).

      b.   If you survive, you walk away fearful and confused.

3.   <u>A new worldview is created</u> (see the world in a completely different way now).[1,9]

      a.   Fear → the person loses the ability to feel safe.

      b.   See danger everywhere all of the time (constant perception of threat).

      c.   Survival mindsets become the core of our viewpoints.

            1.   All-or-nothing (no middle ground).

            2.   Now-or-never.

            3.   Perfectionism ("little mistakes can get you hurt or killed").

            4.   Denial of personal difficulty (never reveal that you are vulnerable).

            5.   Worst case scenarios (try to maintain an ultimate level of preparedness).

            6.   Fatalism (persistent pessimistic outlook).

      d.   Previous assumptions and viewpoints are shattered, crushed, or invalidated.

      e.   Spiritual and existential beliefs called into question → loss of trust and belief.

4.   <u>An extreme focus on ensuring personal safety is developed and maintained.</u>

      a.   Always on the lookout for danger.

      b.   Do anything and everything to try staying safe and in control.

      c.   Become over-protective of family members.

      d.   Frequent catastrophizing; worry; developing contingency plans.

5.   <u>Anger and irritability become prominent.</u>
   a.   Low frustration tolerance; Extreme self-reliance (believe you don't need anybody for anything).
   b.   Live in reaction mode most of the time.
   c.   Complete intolerance for the incompetence of other people, institutions, etc.
   d.   Short temper; irritable most of the time; outbursts of anger.
   e.   Inability to be assertive (usually very passive or totally aggressive; all-or-nothing thinking).

6.   <u>Suffering</u> [1,2,7,9]
   a.   Depression.
   b.   Self-blame; victim thinking.
   c.   Nightmares; flashbacks; intrusive thoughts.
   d.   Sleep problems.
   e.   Concentration and memory difficulty.
   f.   Lack of self-care compounds the suffering.
   g.   Panic attacks.
   h.   Extreme guilt.
   i.   Paranoia.
   j.   Extreme fatigue.

7.   <u>Struggling with Issues</u>
   a.   Focus on safety almost constantly (pervasive fear, distrust).
   b.   Don't believe you can trust anyone at all.
   c.   Perceptions become skewed (see most people/things as a threat or danger).
   d.   Always feel the need to be in complete control of everything and everyone.
   e.   Anger outbursts cause additional problems (try to be in control and feel safe).
   f.   Anniversary reactions (trauma dates; specific times of the year are difficult).
   g.   Triggers cause you to feel helpless, out of control, or overwhelmed.
   h.   Emotional numbing (only allow anger, sadness, guilt, disgust; all other feelings are shut out).
   i.   Stress overload → every little thing is very stressful (everything is a big deal!).
   j.   Harbor grudges and resentments.
   k.   Grieving over losses does not happen appropriately (leads to depression).

    8.   Maladaptive (ineffective or destructive) coping behaviors
- a.   Anger; acting out (creates new problems).
- b.   Avoidance (of everybody and everything – unrealistic).
- c.   Isolation.
- d.   Hiding; escape; running away.
- e.   Facade ("wear the mask"; try to appear "as normal as possible"; don't let anyone know what's really going on).
- f.   Always defending yourself; always trying to "prove" yourself.
- g.   Self-medication.
- h.   Substance abuse.
- i.   Workaholism.
- j.   Destructive behaviors.

B.   How many of these things describe the way your life has been since the trauma(s)?

II.   Using the "Big Picture" to Get Better [1,2,9]

A.   With PTSD, we often stay focused on only 1 or 2 issues
1.   E.g., anger, isolation, perceived unfairness, nightmares, depression, etc.
2.   As long as we stay confused, uninformed, or have tunnel vision, we will not recover.

B.   To get better, we need to "see the big picture" and understand what happened in order to be able to restructure our lives.

C.   The big picture allows us to move beyond tunnel vision and focus on areas of recovery that have been neglected.

D.   What issues from the working model of PTSD did you not know about?

_____

_____

E.   Does seeing the big picture now cause your anxiety to increase or decrease?

F.   What does it feel like to finally "figure it out?"

G.   Now, every time you "feel stuck" you can stop, look at the big picture, and continue to apply those things learned in therapy for making better choices for how to cope effectively.

III.   The Big Picture of PTSD Recovery

A.   Re-establish safety → you need to feel in control of yourself and your environment[5]

B.   Figure it out → become educated about PTSD (being confused or uninformed keeps you stuck)[1]

C.   Manage your anger and cope effectively with stresses (big and small)[15,16]

D.   Learn and master healthy coping skills (the more, the better)

E.   Learn to live well in spite of symptoms, and become the person you really want to be

Chapter 10 Exercise

1.   Describe your "big picture" view of PTSD at this point?

_____

_____

_____

_____

2.   How has your mindset or worldview changed since the trauma?

_____

_____

_____

_____

3.   In what ways do you feel you are struggling?

_____

_____

_____

_____

4.   What destructive coping strategies have you used?

_____

_____

_____

_____

5.   Write the following statements on a card or small piece of paper and say them to yourself at least 2 times each day for the next week.
    1.   I'm here now.
    2.   They (it) can't hurt me now.
    3.   I'm safe now.
    4.   It's not happening now.
    5.   It was not my fault.
    6.   I'm in control.
    7.   I don't have to be afraid now.
    8.   I am a valuable person.
    9.   I am not alone in this.
    10.   I do not have to live in constant fear.
    11.   When I encounter a trigger, I will handle it; it <u>will not</u> control me.
    12.   I choose to take control of my own life.
    13.   I choose to confront the realities of my life.

14.   I will not be totally overwhelmed by my past anymore.
15.   I will not let fear and uncertainty rule my life.
16.   I don't have to be angry all of the time.
17.   Most people are probably not out to get me.
18.   I will manage my anger and control myself.
19.   I will get better.
20.   I'm going to make it.
21.   I'm not crazy.

Section II: A PTSD Recovery Plan

"In therapy, I've learned that you're not crazy and it's possible to get better."
-One PTSD group therapy member offering
encouragement to a new group member

"A person who begins a project without a plan is foolish."
-An Ancient Proverb

"When I came to the end of myself, I had to seek guidance from those who were
further along the journey than me."
-Veteran active in PTSD therapy

Chapter 11 – Warnings About PTSD Recovery
(Some Things You Need to Know Up Front)

I.   **Be Aware Up Front!**
- A.   <u>PTSD recovery is not easy business</u> (but it is possible to get better).
  - 1.   Starting into treatment often brings up memories and thoughts you have been trying to avoid.[1,2,15,16]
  - 2.   To confront those things that are necessary for getting better takes a high level of courage.
  - 3.   You will probably feel worse before you start to feel better, because we must work through many painful things to get to a place called "better."
- B.   <u>Why does it seem so difficult?</u>[19]
  - 1.   Some behavior patterns become habitual and are difficult to change.
  - 2.   Realize that the behaviors you adopted in response to surviving trauma(s) are survival skills.
  - 3.   The fact that you survived means that in some way or another they worked.
  - 4.   Therefore, you have been rewarded for your actions → why would you want to change now?
  - 5.   Even though we can see the difficulties associated with many of the post-trauma behavior patterns, it can be easy to revert back to them, because at a gut level we "know it works."
  - 6.   While we may be aware that we need to try something else, it can be frightening to let go of those things we have been using to cope.

II.   **Examples of Common Obstacles to Recovery[1,9] (see if any of these fit your behavior patterns)**
- A.   Trying to control everything instead of dealing with your own personal issues.
- B.   Blaming → it doesn't solve problems or fix anything.
- C.   Not really knowing what you want – just simply surviving.
  - 1.   Jumping from one thing, to the next, to the next.
  - 2.   Having no clear goal or objective → leads you nowhere.
  - 3.   Not being able to see past "just today."
- D.   Making repeated mistakes (not learning from the past or changing when things don't work).
- E.   Over reacting to minor incidents.
- F.   Poor decision-making; repeatedly exercising poor judgment.

G.   Not taking appropriate, healthy care of yourself.
H.   Being unwilling to learn (think you already know everything).
I.   Living in denial in spite of problems caused by the real issue.
        1.   Focusing on the wrong things (side issues).
        2.   Shifting the focus to other people, situations, etc.
        3.   Being unwilling to take a radically honest look at yourself.
J.   Being unwilling to change as life circumstances change.
K.   Harboring anger, grudges, resentment, hatred, and unforgiveness.
        1.   Staying agitated about things you can't change.
        2.   Maintaining a condemning and judgmental attitude toward others.
        3.   Having no patience or healthy tolerance for other people.
L.   Trying to live without any limits whatsoever.
M.   Failure to anticipate consequences → usually produces undesirable results.
N.   Rejecting help when you need it.
O.   Being rigid, stubborn, inflexible, and overly defensive.
P.   Complaining, but not putting forth effort to fix the problem.
Q.   Not really wanting the cure → just seeking temporary relief from pain and suffering.
        1.   Unwilling to do the real work of therapy.
        2.   Letting the fear keep you paralyzed and stuck.
R.   Expecting a pill to "fix" all your problems (unrealistic).

III.   **Guidelines for Overcoming the Obstacles**[19]
A.   To overcome obstacles to recovery, some things are required.
B.   Take the time to clearly identify those obstacles listed above that are holding you back.
        1.   Circle each one (above) that applies to your life.
        2.   Give an example of each from your own life.
C.   Have the courage to be really honest with yourself about what you are doing and what you really want.
D.   To make progress, we usually need to go around obstacles.
        1.   This requires a change in behavior.
              a.   Recognize the obstacle.
              b.   Choose a new path.
        2.   Usually, if we simply try to overpower the obstacle, we will become overwhelmed or get out of control.
E.   Work in therapy to clearly identify your own behaviors.
F.   Seek new behaviors that are more helpful in managing the situations you face.
G.   Cut yourself a break → there will be times that you fall back.
        1.   This is not a total failure if you keep coming back to treatment and working on it.
        2.   It can take time to develop new behaviors that last.

Chapter 12 – How to Get Better: Part I
(The Foundations of PTSD Recovery)

I.   **Diagnosis (a formal process conducted by a licensed mental health professional is needed)[1,2,3]**

    A.   We first need a formal diagnosis that is accurate.

    B.   If the diagnosis is not accurate, it is hard to get appropriate treatment.

    C.   To benefit from treatment, it is important to accept the diagnosis.

        1.   Acceptance does not mean that you want or like the diagnosis or the fact of the trauma(s).

        2.   It does mean that you come to terms with the fact that you have PTSD.

        3.   Full acceptance of the diagnosis can sometimes take many weeks, months, or years.

II.   **Steps in the Recovery Process[1,2]**

    A.   Acknowledge that the trauma occurred → a formal diagnosis of PTSD is made.

    B.   <u>Note</u>: Not every person who experiences a traumatic event has PTSD.

        1.   Traumas can cause other mental disorders as well.

        2.   If another disorder is diagnosed, a different treatment is needed.

    C.   The first order of business: → re-establish safety for the traumatized person.[1,5]

        1.   If a person is still in danger of being traumatized, recovery will not yet begin.

        2.   Basic safety forms a foundation to build upon.

    D.   Next, a person needs basic stabilization.

        1.   If their life is chaotic, it is almost impossible to benefit from therapy.

        2.   A safe, stable environment with structure and a regular routine are needed.

    E.   Now, the person needs some symptom relief to be able to engage in the therapy process.

        1.   Medications can be very helpful in getting initial symptom relief.[20]

        2.   Also, knowing that you are not the only person going through this provides some relief.

    F.   Become educated about PTSD and its effects.[1]

        1.   Figure it out! → we need a basic understanding of PTSD in order to get better.

        2.   In dealing with PTSD, if you stay confused, you won't get much better!

G.   Learn and practice coping skills.
  1.   Begin developing coping skills to manage symptoms, anger, stress, and daily life.
  2.   An explicit focus on developing these skills is essential.
  3.   Without developing new, more effective coping skills, a person is likely to become overwhelmed easily in the future.
  4.   We need to <u>stop using</u> unhealthy coping strategies (e.g., drinking, drugs, violence, etc.).
  5.   Replace PTSD ways of reacting with more productive thoughts and behaviors.
  6.   Develop your adult mind and learn mature strategies for living in a more effective way.
  7.   <u>Note</u>: Coping skills are not the final answer to everything in life.
      a.   They do not answer questions of right and wrong, spiritual issues, or philosophical questions.
      b.   They are intended to help a person be able to function in a healthy way, and then become able to address the more important questions of life.

III.   **Areas of Life to Focus on During Recovery**[1,9]
  A.   <u>Physical</u>
    1.   Begin taking care of yourself physically again.
    2.   Practice good hygiene; do the basics to take care of yourself.
    3.   Start eating balanced, healthful meals.
    4.   Use medication appropriately, but not as your exclusive approach to coping.
    5.   Begin exercising at least 3 to 5 times each week (possibly start with walking; consult with your physician about exercise).
  B.   <u>Mental</u> (psychological)
    1.   We need courage to "speak the unspeakable" to someone who understands (i.e., a good therapist).
    2.   The goal is not to forget what happened, but to remember and integrate it into your life in a healthy way (this is a difficult process, but can be done).
    3.   Rebuild your belief system and start to value yourself as a person.
    4.   Begin going easier on yourself (less self-blame, increased understanding).
    5.   Practice skills for managing your stress each day in a more healthy way (i.e., become less reactive).
    6.   Progress is seen when you can talk about the traumatic events without being overwhelmed.

C.   <u>Social</u>
1.   Rebuild and reestablish relationships.[14]
2.   Reconnect with other people; isolate yourself less and less.
3.   Get plugged back into healthy social groups.
4   Become able to have a friend and be a friend.

IV.   Recovery Pitfalls (if you focus on these things, you won't get much better!)
A.   Exclusive reliance on medication.
B.   Aiming to "get rid of" the traumatic memories (the fact is, we can't erase memories).
C.   Revenge fantasies (this doesn't fix the real problems).
D.   Belief that monetary compensation alone will bring healing (it won't fix your PTSD symptoms).
E.   Belief that PTSD is similar to a terminal illness (in fact, people do achieve high levels of recovery).
F.   Your primary identity becomes "I am a person with PTSD."
G.   Expecting to "get better without working at it" (a lot of hard work is required).

V.   Signs of Progress
A.   First, understand it is possible that healing may never be complete, but a good and healthy life is possible.
1.   Healthy long-term management is a more realistic goal.
2.   Know that symptoms may cycle depending on the time of the year.
3   Understand that progress builds slowly over time – you did not get into your current condition "overnight."
B.   Your understanding of PTSD increases more and more as you progress through therapy.
1.   This gives you a better grasp on what you are dealing with.
2.   In PTSD recovery, knowledge is power if we use it to help us get better.
C.   With enough practice, coping skills become a healthy habit in managing your symptoms.
D.   Increasing reconnection with others and less isolation develops (i.e., healthy relationships).
E.   Moving away from being a complete victim and moving toward living your life again in a healthy way.
F.   Overall, progress occurs when a trauma survivor moves away from feeling a sense of helplessness and confusion about the trauma.
G.   New feelings of control, understanding PTSD, and feeling empowered to live life again are developed and become the new patterns of your life.

Chapter 13 – How to Get Better: Part II
(What It Takes to Recover)

I.   **The Three Elements Necessary for Recovery**[1]
- A.   In PTSD recovery, three things must happen for a person to recover.
- B.   They are three separate therapeutic areas that work together.
- C.   Area #1: Becoming Informed
  - 1.   Before treatment, a person is usually confused and uninformed about PTSD.
  - 2.   Confusion keeps us stuck and motivates us to keep using the old survival skills, which today are often harmful.
  - 3.   Knowledge of PTSD symptoms and how your life has been affected becomes a powerful resource for building skills and getting into a position to do something constructive about your situation.
  - 4.   Remember: Knowledge is power in PTSD recovery.
- D.   Area #2: Developing Coping Skills[15,16]
  - 1.   New coping skills are needed because the skills a person had at the time of the trauma became overwhelmed and were insufficient.
  - 2.   Ever since the trauma, it is easy to become overwhelmed frequently (i.e., poor coping).
  - 3.   When built on the knowledge from Area #1 above, a person becomes able to recognize symptoms or stress, and then apply the appropriate skill or tool to better manage it.
  - 4.   If our coping skills are underdeveloped, our ability to manage those things we encounter each day remains limited.
  - 5.   We may need to add new coping skills to our emotional tool box, or become reacquainted with tools we have not used in some time to better cope with the stress.
- E.   Area #3: Resolving the Emotional Damage
  - 1.   The third area of recovery involves healing the damage that was done to the emotions.
  - 2.   A trauma is essentially an emotional/mental injury.
  - 3.   Because these feelings are so painful, the natural tendency is to avoid them, fight them, or do anything to NOT feel them.
  - 4.   Remembering the traumas and working through the painful emotions is usually the most difficult part of PTSD recovery.
  - 5.   However, when this is done, most people report experiencing high levels of relief and healing, even if their symptoms never go away completely.

6.   The 3rd area of healing usually needs to be done in a safe environment with a therapist who specializes in trauma therapy (e.g., usually individual therapy).

II.   Understand that Past Learning Now Works Against Us

A.   Some behaviors that were learned in an effort to survive the trauma can now make recovery difficult, if not almost impossible (called survival skills).

B.   When we persist in old behaviors, we use strategies that are no longer useful.

C.   Which of the following do you still use?
1.   Try to control everything and everyone.
2.   Put intense efforts into staying safe, even though the dangers you encounter are usually not life threatening.
3.   Refuse to accept the truth about your past traumatic experiences; staying in denial.
4.   Negative consequences of a behavior outweigh the benefits, but you do it anyway.
5.   Believing that every upsetting experience is a full-blown trauma.
6.   Relying exclusively on past learning (i.e., survival skills) with no new learning now.
7.   Having a closed mind; insisting that you are right and have always been right about everything.

D.   It can be difficult to accept that those strategies you have relied on for so long are no longer helpful.

E.   To get better, we need to accept that new skills and strategies are required, and then work to develop them.

III.   Therapy as a Relearning Process

A.   To get better, we must become educated about the condition we are dealing with.
1.   Staying confused or uninformed leads to a poor adjustment and staying stuck.
2.   Understanding the symptoms increases our options for healthy coping.

B.   Many of our "automatic behaviors" are the product of past training or habitual behavior.
1.   Childhood instruction (might have been good or bad).
2.   Military training.
3.   Ways of doing things we just figured out on our own (self-training).

C.   If we stay stuck in these automatic ways of managing symptoms, stress, and life in general, we will continue to struggle with symptoms and the demands of life.

D.   To recover, a process of retraining is absolutely necessary.

1.   We need new mental habits.

2.   New behaviors that are more productive and effective are necessary.

3.   We need new coping skills that match up with the demands of current situations.

E.   We need to ask some questions to determine our retraining needs.

1.   Which of my coping behaviors are causing problems now?

2.   Do I accurately determine what is really dangerous and what is not?

3.   Am I looking to learn new things, or to just confirm my old beliefs?

4.   Do I have an open mind?

5.   Is it possible that I could be wrong about some things?

6.   Is it okay to change my mind about things in light of new information?

7.   Am I treating everything as life-and-death when it's not?

F.   New Training Requirements

1.   We need thinking skills and new behaviors.

2.   We need to stop treating everything as life-threatening when it's not.

3.   Learn when to be on the alert and when to be relaxed → then act accordingly.

4.   Develop skills to control your anger.

5.   Learn how to manage your daily stress without overreacting.

6.   Find ways to exercise control at the appropriate level (not too little or too much).

7.   However, when we don't learn from new experiences, we are doomed to repeat unhealthy behavior patterns.

IV.   What Do You Need to Work On At This Time?

_____

_____

_____

Chapter 14 – How to Get Better: Part III
(The Toughest Part)

I.   **The Deep Emotional Work**

    A.   To recover, we often will feel worse (i.e., experience the painful emotions) before we can get better → this keeps many people from going very far in therapy.

    B.   We need to stop suppressing and denying the feelings.

        1.   In PTSD, we are most fearful of the overwhelming feelings and memories.

        2.   We avoid thinking of the facts of the trauma(s) in order to escape the feelings that seem unbearable.

        3.   We need to stop running and avoiding everything.

    C.   To recover, we must be willing to confront the source of our symptoms and process the feelings so that they will not have power over us anymore.

    D.   For this process to be effective, you must come clean about it.

        1.   Have to talk about the hurts.

        2.   Have to be completely honest about what happened.

        3.   Have to be totally honest about how it felt and how it feels now.

    E.   There are some fears:

        1.   Just how much emotional pain will I go through in this process?

        2.   How much pain am I capable of experiencing?

        3.   Will I become overwhelmed and never recover?

        4.   Will I lose my mind and never get it back?

    F.   How to get better:

        1.   Once you fully experience the feelings, you no longer have to be controlled by them.

        2.   Then, you no longer have to put all that mental energy into fighting the feelings.

        3.   Realize that the anticipation of those feelings can sometimes be worse than the pain of the feelings themselves.

        4.   We gain control by letting ourselves have the feelings and becoming not afraid of them any more.

        5.   We recover by getting to where the memories are no longer overwhelming.

    G.   "I was helpless and horrified in the past, but I refuse to be a victim of the traumatic experiences or the painful emotions anymore."

    H.   Are you ready to heal from the painful emotions and stop running from this part of yourself?

II.   The Second Story of PTSD – How to Write and Use Your Narrative[1,2] (a story about the trauma)

A.   Remember enough about the traumatic events to form a narrative (a brief story about what happened to you).

    1.   Begin with the background and the details you can remember.

        a.   What was your life like before the trauma(s).

        b.   What situations led up to the traumatic experience(s).

    2.   At first, this is very painful because you don't want to think or talk about those things.

    3.   Begin writing these things down, and come back to it as you recall more of what happened (to the best of your memory).

    4.   This can take several days or a few weeks (as you are able).

    5.   At some point, what you have written will resemble a story of what happened and how your life was affected.

B.   How to use your story

    1.   Share your story with a competent therapist who understands PTSD and knows how to treat you.

    2.   This personal story may not tell every detail, but it is no longer just a collection of fragmented memories, confusing feelings, or over-whelming symptoms.

    3.   The after-effects of traumatic experience are no longer a mass of confusion, but are now starting to make sense to you.

    4.   Some of the confusion about the actual events begins to lift.

C.   As you progress through treatment, you develop a better understanding of what happened.

    1.   You understand what PTSD is (and what it is not).

    2.   You are now able to make sense of your symptoms.

        a.   You know where the symptoms came from.

        b.   You start to understand their purpose or function.

    3.   You can now provide some explanation of PTSD to other important people in your life when it is appropriate (but be cautious who you tell – not everyone will understand or wants to understand).

D.   As your understanding of PTSD continues to increase, you learn and prac-tice stress and anger management techniques.

    1.   You learn and practice ways of handling trigger situations.

    2.   You don't blow up or overreact all of the time.

    3.   You develop more healthy control over your life.

E.   You begin making healthy connections with other people.

    1.   You establish a trusting relationship with at least one other person.

    2.   You are able to talk about some parts of the traumatic event (or at least that period of time in your life) without becoming over-whelmed.

III.   Keys to Successful PTSD Recovery

 A. <u>Traumatic memories need to be confronted only when your mind is ready</u>

   1. Pressure to do this too early can cause many to stop treatment.

   2. Two therapeutic situations work best for this.

    a. In individual therapy with a therapist who specializes in the treatment of PTSD.

    b. In a very small trauma group (4 patients or fewer) with a therapist who specializes in the treatment of PTSD.

    c. Traumatic memory work <u>should not</u> be attempted in general therapy groups or in coping skills/education groups.

    d. If individuals discuss details of their traumas in general therapy groups, this usually causes agitation and "triggers" other group members (not therapeutic!).

    e. <u>Warning!</u> If this process is triggering or too overwhelming, try the deep breathing exercise or taking a Time Out. If you cannot continue, then come back and try again another time when you feel ready.

 B. <u>Feelings need to be identified and experienced in a way that they become no longer overwhelming</u>

   1. Once you fully experience the feelings, you no longer have to be controlled by them.

   2. You no longer have to put all that mental energy into fighting the feelings.

   3. Realize that the anticipation and fear of those feelings can possibly be worse than the pain of the feelings themselves once they have been confronted.

 C. <u>We need to regain control over our thoughts and the ability to manage feelings</u>

   1. We gain control by letting ourselves have the feelings and becoming not afraid of them anymore.

   2. We recover by getting to where the memories are no longer overwhelming.

   3. "I was helpless and horrified in the past, but I refuse to be a victim of the traumas anymore."

   4. "I can now handle those things that frightened and overwhelmed me in the past."

 D. <u>We need coping skills</u>

   1. When traumatized, a person's coping abilities were overwhelmed.

   2. To get better, we need to build strong coping skills to deal with PTSD symptoms and daily stress.

   3. When we have strong, healthy skills we no longer have to automatically fall back on the old behaviors we had used to simply survive → we gain control and begin to live again.

 E. <u>The Bottom Line:</u> Am I ready and willing to do this in order to heal and recover?

Chapter 15 – Talking with Your Medication Provider

I.   **The Choice About Medications**[20]
    A.   Some individuals with PTSD take medications as part of their overall approach to treatment.
    B.   This is often necessary in order to help a person stabilize their symptoms.
    C.   If some stability is not achieved at the beginning of treatment, it can be extremely difficult to benefit from talk therapy.
    D.   Some individuals choose not to take medications – this is a personal choice.
    E.   However, if symptoms are so severe that your ability to think clearly, function each day, or accomplish necessary tasks is impaired, most professionals recommend trying medication.
    F.   Many patients are able to do therapeutic work once symptoms start to be controlled or managed with medication.

II.   **How Medications Can Help**
    A.   Medication can provide some symptom relief.
    B.   It can possibly reduce the intensity of some symptoms such as depression and anxiety.
    C.   It can slow down racing thoughts and make it easier to think clearly.
    D.   Used properly, medication can help you gain some control over symptoms that previously you were unable to do much about.
    E.   Medication can also provide enough symptom relief and stability to make it possible to engage in talk therapy and work on getting better.

III.   **Things that Medication Cannot Help**
    A.   Medication cannot "magically fix" all of the symptoms associated with PTSD.
    B.   It cannot take away your traumatic memories.
    C.   It does not eliminate survival guilt or make you able to forgive yourself and others.
    D.   It is unable to resolve inner conflicts or magically straighten out a person's thought patterns.
    E.   In considering medication, make sure that your expectations are appropriate.

IV.   **Target Symptoms**
    A.   Medications need to be chosen based on specific symptoms that are causing problems.
    B.   Different people will choose to focus on different symptoms in their recovery plan.

C.   Begin by looking at the chart below:
　　1.   Which of these symptoms do you experience?
　　2.   Which symptoms are the most painful to you?
　　3.   Which ones are causing you the most difficulty?
D.   It is common to choose 1 or 2 areas to begin focusing on.
　　1.   Any combination of symptoms is acceptable to focus on depending on your own needs.
　　2.   Remember, some medications can be used to treat more than one symptom at a time.

V.   **A Word of Caution**
A.   We need to prioritize which symptoms to work on first.
B.   You might need to try several medications before you find what works for you – there are many to choose from; try to be patient in this process.
C.   Even if medication helps with symptoms, the issues also need to be worked on in talk therapy.
D.   Your medication provider needs to know exactly what is going on with your symptoms to be able to provide the most appropriate treatment.
E.   Ask what the medications are for, exactly how to take them, and what is reasonable to expect.
F.   Exactly what time of day should I take the medication?
G.   Do I have to take it with food? With milk? On an empty stomach?
H.   Are there certain things I have to avoid?
I.   Use the chart below to identify your symptoms and help you talk with your medication provider.

PTSD Target Symptoms That Medication Could Possibly Help

Category	Specific Symptoms	Notes: How Often? How Intense? Other?
1. Depression	Sad; Down; Low Mood	
	Loss of Interest	
	Irritability; Low Energy	
	Suicidal Thoughts	
	No Motivation; Appetite	
2. Anxiety	Nervous; Edgy; Keyed-up	
	Restless; Irritable	
3. Panic Attacks	Pounding heart; Sweating	
	Trembling	
	Choking; Chest Pain	
	Numbness/tingling	
	Fear of Losing Control	
	Nausea; Chills; Dizzy	
	Think You Are Going Crazy	
	Short of Breath	
	Fear of Dying	
4. Sleep	Falling Asleep	
	Staying Asleep	
	Wake Up Tired; Not Rested	
	Sleep is Restless	
5. Anger	Outbursts of Anger	
	Get Frustrated Easily	
6. Mood Swings	Unpredictable Moods	
	Extreme Ups and Downs	
7. Impulse Control	Impulsive	
	Act Without Thinking	
8. Mental Processing	Concentration Problems	
	Racing Thoughts	
	Paranoia	
9. Re-experiencing Symptoms	Nightmares	
	Flashbacks	
	Intrusive Thoughts	

Section III: Basic PTSD Education

Patients with PTSD have said . . .

"How can you fix something you don't understand? -You can't !!!"

"I started to heal when I got answers to those questions I'd had all those years."

"It's a lot easier to accept when you have some knowledge of what's actually going on in your head."

"Without knowledge and understanding, you just stay stuck and don't get any better – just worse."

Chapter 16 – The PTSD Re-Experiencing Symptoms

I.   **PTSD Re-experiencing Symptoms**
  A.   Feeling as if you are reliving the traumatic event (or certain aspects of it) all over again.
  B.   This can happen in at least 5 different ways.[1,2,3]
    1.   <u>Intrusive Thoughts</u> – thoughts of the trauma "force their way into your mind" when you are not wanting to think about it.
    2.   <u>Nightmares</u> – terrible, horrifying dreams about the trauma, or dreams that symbolize the traumatic experience(s) and cause you to feel extremely afraid or panicked.
    3.   <u>Flashbacks</u> – feeling as if the trauma or some critical aspects of it were happening again; feeling like you are reliving part or all of the trauma.
    4.   <u>Psychological Distress</u> – severe negative reactions (mentally or emotionally) when you come into contact with things that remind you of the original trauma.
    5.   <u>Physiologic Reactivity</u> – physical reactions when confronted with thoughts about the trauma including sweating, rapid heart beat, hyperventilation, nausea, hot flashes, chills, diarrhea, feeling frozen, etc.
  C.   The re-experiencing symptoms often cause people to "feel crazy" even though they are not.
  D.   This feeling is common before a person is diagnosed and understands their symptoms.

II.   **Why Do We Re-experience the Trauma?**
  A.   <u>Brain Processing</u>[1,6]
    1.   It is believed that the original traumatic experiences are not processed in the brain the same way ordinary memories are processed and stored.
    2.   The brain "knows" this, and is replaying the memories in an effort to get them into a more manageable, processed form.
    3.   The brain is trying to "heal itself" but can't seem to do it (a very specialized form of therapy is needed here, called memory reprocessing).
  B.   <u>To "Master the Trauma"</u>[8]
    1.   Traumas are completely overwhelming experiences.
    2.   Many people have a desire to master those things that have been overwhelming, confusing, or problematic in the past.

      3.   When we "master the trauma" or "get a grip" on what actually happened, we can then exercise control and stop living at the mercy of the memories and other symptoms.

C.   To Resolve Inner Conflict and Stop Feeling Overwhelmed[1,8]

      1.   Traumatic experiences can cause feelings of inner turmoil and conflict that might last for many years.

      2.   By re-experiencing the traumas, our mind is trying to give us "another chance" to make sense of what happened, to manage the experience, and reduce inconsistencies in our thoughts and feelings.

      3.   When we resolve the inner conflicts caused by the trauma(s), our symptoms reduce and we begin living in a more controlled, peaceful way.

III.   Coping Strategies for Dealing with the Re-experiencing Symptoms

A.   Understanding

      1.   Realize that nightmares and flashbacks are common experiences for people coping with PTSD.

      2.   These symptoms tend to occur more frequently during times of stress, loss, traumatic anniversary periods, and triggering events.

      3.   Accept the fact that these symptoms may never go away completely, but they can be reduced or somewhat controlled.

      4.   Say, "This is a part of my experience. I don't have to be overwhelmed by it anymore."

B.   Grounding – the process of connecting with the "here and now."[15,16]

      1.   Use the 5 senses (sight, hearing, taste, smell, touch) to bring you back to the reality of what is going on right now.

      2.   Focus on the fact that you are safe now.
          a. "I am here now."   d. "I am safe now."
          b. "It's not happening now." e. "Now I am in control."
          c. "I don't have to be afraid." f. "I'll be OK."

      3.   Examples of grounding techniques:
          a. Look at a current photo or picture; focus on the current month, day, and time.
          b. Listen to a favorite comforting song.
          c. Taste peppermint, coffee, etc. (anything connected with feeling safe).
          d. Smell vanilla, mint, chocolate, perfume, etc. (something calming).
          e. Touch a rough or smooth surface, velvet, leather, paper, an ice cube, table top.

    4.   Grounding can be used to minimize or stop the negative feelings when we start to re-experience the traumas.

    5.   The goal is to put current input into your brain, and get back in control of your thoughts and behavior.

C.   <u>Calm-Down Rituals</u>

    1.   Plan ahead what you will do when a nightmare or intrusive thought comes along, and then do it just like you had planned.

    2.   Use deep breathing to get back in control of your physical reactions.

    3.   Drink very cold water, listen to a favorite song, go for a walk, read a favorite passage/poem, color with crayons, ride an exercise bike.

    4.   If you are dealing with a flashback, take a time out from what you were doing, regain control and mental focus, and then begin again when you feel ready.

    5.   You can use most any activity that helps you calm down and feel more in control.

D.   <u>Keep a Journal of What Happens in Your Nightmares</u>[1]

    1.   Write out your nightmare in as much detail as possible.

    2.   Keep a notebook or tape recorder beside your bed and write/record immediately when you wake up.

    3.   Use the journal in therapy to work through the nightmares.

    4.   For some people, nightmares can sometimes be changed or reduced using this approach.

E.   <u>Use Medication Appropriately</u>[20]

    1.   Some medications have been used in PTSD to "block nightmares" and reduce intrusive thoughts, including some of the antipsychotic, antihistamines, and also hypnotic drugs.

    2.   While medication can help, psychological issues related to the trauma(s) need to be addressed and worked through in therapy to get long-term relief.

Chapter 17 – Substance Abuse and Workaholism

I. **When the Solution Becomes Part of the Problem**[19]
- A. Many people use alcohol or other drugs in an effort to get some relief from the pain of their PTSD symptoms.[13]
    1. This is a common coping strategy before you know the diagnosis and develop healthy coping skills.
    2. This approach usually provides some short-term relief, but is not a healthy long-term solution.
- B. This pattern is different from the person who abuses substances for the sole purpose of getting high, drunk, or stoned (i.e., just for fun).
- C. When substance abuse is an effort to cope with symptoms, the intention is to get relief from the emotional pain (i.e., self-medication).

II. **The Catch**[11,12]
- A. If we are really honest about it, using alcohol and other drugs is very effective for providing some symptom relief (in the short term).
- B. However, this approach usually causes more problems in the long term.
- C. While short term relief is found, we wind up in a worse place in the end.
- D. This method of only getting short term relief may eventually result in loss of jobs, ruined relationships, becoming out of control, and feelings of disgust at yourself.
- E. While alcohol can cause a person to fall asleep (i.e., "pass out"), it actually disrupts the various phases of sleep, resulting in poor rest.

III. **Workaholism**
- A. Many people coping with PTSD also become workaholics.
- B. This is not because they love to work more than anything else.
- C. When we are overly busy, we don't have much time to think about the traumatic memories or focus on symptoms (i.e., this is actually a combination of distraction and avoidance).
- D. This serves the same purpose as substance abuse → trying to find an effective distraction and get some relief from the emotional pain of symptoms (especially the traumatic memories).
- E. While the view of society toward workaholism tends to be more forgiving than for substance abuse, the result on relationships, families, and overall health can be just as damaging.

IV.   **Getting Better**

A.   If you are abusing alcohol or other drugs, the mental state caused by the drug use will prevent you from getting better and from coping effectively with your symptoms.

1.   You cannot think clearly when using.

2.   You will use denial, rationalization, and other strategies to protect yourself.

3.   Your efforts to cope actually hurt you in the long run.

B.   If you are using excessive work to cope, eventually your body will wear down to the point that you will not be able to do it anymore.

1.   If you have not developed other more effective coping skills, you will feel like you are falling apart mentally and physically.

2.   You will be forced to stop running from your symptoms and start confronting it.

C.   Getting better requires you to confront the fact that you have used these strategies to deal with PTSD symptoms, and choose to develop more healthy coping strategies.

V.   **A New Way**

A.   <u>Diagnosis</u>

1.   Once there is a correct diagnosis, then appropriate treatment can begin.[1,3]

2.   To start getting better, begin by learning as much as you can about the condition you are dealing with.

3.   Identify the patterns of drug use or workaholism you have been using.

4.   Try to see clearly the effects on your life.

B.   <u>Therapy</u>

1.   Treatment is not something that is done <u>to</u> you.

2.   Treatment is something that you must <u>actively participate in</u> for it to be effective.

3.   Many individuals require substance abuse treatment along with therapy for PTSD.

4.   Use therapy as a tool to help you build more healthy coping strategies.

5.   Work toward long-term symptom management – take one day at a time.

6.   Use therapy to develop a new positive identity – "I am no longer a drug abuser."

7.   We need to eliminate substance abuse as a coping strategy and replace it with healthier options.

8.   <u>Remember</u>: When you started abusing the alcohol or drugs, your emotional maturity got stuck at that age.[13]

9.   To get better, we need to start maturing again and try to catch up to our "real" age.

C.   <u>Proper Medication</u>[20]

1.   Take all medications exactly as prescribed.

2.   Work with your medication provider → give accurate and complete descriptions of your symptoms, side effects, and observations.

3.   Don't rely <u>exclusively</u> on medication.

a.   Antidepressants are not "happy pills."

b.   Instead, they help to regulate both the amount and functioning of chemicals in the brain that are responsible for your mood and some thought processes.

c.   Use medication to help you become stable, think more clearly, and function at your best.

d.   Use medication to become a more healthy, rational, well-functioning person.

4.   How medication is different from "self-medication" with alcohol and other drugs.

a.   Use pre-planned, fixed doses of medication to manage symptoms.

b.   The medication helps re-establish appropriate self-control.

c.   It increases our stability (instead of drug abuse, which causes you to be out of control).

d.   Medication helps us manage the emotional pain so we can build the healthy skills needed to live well and function better.

e.   <u>Remember</u>: Abuse of prescription medication reduces your ability to cope and is just as destructive as abusing alcohol or street drugs.[13]

D.   <u>A Final Word</u>

1.   Individuals who get significantly better for the long-term give up the alcohol and drugs and are committed to recovery.

2.   Is this what you want?

Chapter 18 – Emotional Numbing
(Fear of Feelings)

I. **What Contributed to My Current Emotional Condition?** [1]
- A. As a child you may have been taught certain attitudes that still affect you today.
    1. "Don't be a sissy."
    2. "Big boys don't cry" (or show emotion).
    3. "Emotions make you weak."
    4. "Feeling or expressing emotion is unacceptable and makes you weak."
- B. In a traumatic situation, emotional numbing is a survival skill.
    1. Didn't have time to consider how I felt – just had to do my job.
    2. The body numbs extreme pain when severely injured for survival.
    3. Similarly, the mind numbs extreme emotional pain in order to survive.
    4. "I got to where I just didn't care"; "It don't mean nothin'."
    5. Shutting down or blocking emotions is a common feature of PTSD.[1,3,9]
    6. Survivors of many different types of trauma show this symptom.
- C. Sources of Emotional Shutdown [9,63]
    1. The original trauma.
        a. At the time just tried to survive.
        b. Became skilled at turning off the feelings due to multiple traumas.
    2. Secondary wounding or other traumatic events.
        a. Got re-injured emotionally by the reactions of other people when they learned of what happened.
        b. This usually involved feeling blamed and rejected.
    3. Re-experiencing symptoms.
        a. Get overwhelmed every time I feel that I'm reliving the trauma.
        b. Develop the habit of using anger to feel in control and ward off feelings of vulnerability.

II. **How Emotional Numbing Helps You in the Short Term**
- A. In trauma, you do whatever it takes to survive.
- B. Shutting down emotions helps you focus on what you need to do to survive, and not be distracted by feelings at that moment.
- C. Emotional numbing has <u>immediate</u> survival value in the most extreme of situations.

III. **How Emotional Numbing Hurts You in the Long Run**
    A.   Emotions can be a good source of information.
          1.   If we ignore them, we may be ignoring useful information that could help us in a particular situation.
          2.   Many individuals with PTSD find that they get angry very quickly and do not see the warning signs of their own anger.
    B.   Other people often do not understand why things that are so upsetting to them are "nothing" to you.
          1.   You handle "big things" but overreact to minor events.
          2.   This makes us feel more disconnected from other people
    C.   If the only feeling you can experience is an adrenaline rush, your life will be chaotic due to dangerous behaviors engaged in on a regular basis in order to "just feel something."
          1.   Trying to feel good, alive, or to get some excitement.
          2.   Guilt, anger, disgust, sadness, and contempt become the only feelings you know how to experience.
    D.   Your ability to relate to other people is compromised.
    E.   If we don't recognize and express feelings mentally and verbally, they are not magically eliminated.
          1.   They will often be expressed in our bodies in the form of illness.
          2.   Examples: physical pain, ulcers, arthritis, headaches, chest pain, and other illnesses.
    F.   Staying emotionally numb takes energy and effort – this contributes to feeling tired or exhausted much of the time.
          1.   What we are really doing is wearing a mask to hide from underlying emotions, as a method of self-protection – all the while, wearing ourselves out.

IV. **How Ongoing Emotional Numbing Causes Problems**[1,9,63]
    A.   The trauma survivor becomes convinced that the painful emotions will always be unbearable.
    B.   This perpetuates the emotional numbing as a self-protection strategy.
    C.   However, this survival strategy is not needed now that you are not in the traumatic situation anymore.
    D.   Numbing blocks out <u>negative and positive</u> feelings.
    E.   Many people say this feels like you are walking around, but feel dead inside.
    F.   By numbing your feelings most of the time, you eliminate the ability to feel good things in life as well.
    G.   You may be close to dangerous levels of anger and violence because you don't notice any feelings to warn you.
    H.   Many patients speak of "going from zero to 60 in nothing flat!"

V.   Getting Better

A.   First, we need to learn that feelings won't kill us.

B.   Decide that it's okay to begin feeling again.

C.   Start trying out some new feelings a little at a time → go slowly!

D.   Understand that one of the most powerful ways to stop being fearful of feelings is to let yourself have the feeling.

    1.   It then starts losing its power to make you afraid.

    2.   We learn that this situation, person, or place does not have to be feared.

    3.   With practice, we come to see that those fears are not justified and don't serve our best interest.

    4.   By approaching feelings little by little, we become familiar with them in a way that does not overwhelm us anymore.

E.   Realize that having feelings doesn't make us weak → it makes us more fully human and helps us to experience and enjoy life.

F.   When we start to laugh again and allow ourselves to feel, we are then on the path of recovery.

Chapter 19 – PTSD and Sleep

I.   **Why Sleep Is Difficult When You Have PTSD**[1,9]

    A.   Most individuals with PTSD try to stay alert for danger at all times.

    B.   When sleeping, you can't stay on full alert → this causes you to feel vulnerable or unprotected.

    C.   Trauma-related nightmares are very painful experiences.

        1.   Some people try to avoid nightmares by not sleeping.

        2.   This only works for so long, and then you crash.

    D.   Over time, a person dreads going to sleep and a high level of fatigue builds up.

II.   **The Impact of Nightmares (caused by PTSD)**[7]

    A.   Fear of falling asleep (try to stay awake) → the nightmares might return.

    B.   Suddenly awakening in the middle of the night in a terrified and agitated condition.

        1.   Wake up in a cold sweat.

        2.   Feel helpless, vulnerable, out of control.

    C.   Don't want to fall back asleep after awakening.

    D.   In nightmares, we re-experience the traumatic events → don't want to think about them or experience the way they make us feel.

III.   **The Impact of Sleep Deprivation**

    A.   Feel tired; fatigued most of the time → this can increase depression.

    B.   Become very irritable and short tempered; frustration tolerance is reduced.

    C.   Increased anxiety; become physically, mentally, and emotionally drained.

    D.   Difficulty managing feelings and emotions; possible mood swings.

    E.   Extreme sleep-deprivation → hallucinations, irrational thinking, poor judgment.

IV.   **Coping with a Nightmare**

    A.   Focus on the here-and-now when you wake up using coping statements.

    B.   Repeat the following statements to get back in control of your mind.

        1.   "I am here now."

        2.   "It's not happening now."

        3.   "I'm OK."

        4.   "I am safe now."

        5.   "I don't have to be afraid."

        6.   "It can't hurt me now."

C.   Develop and use a calm-down ritual
1.   Go to a safe place and do 15 minutes of deep breathing.
2.   Drink very cold water.
3.   Listen to a favorite song.
4.   Color with crayons.
5.   Read a favorite passage/poem/scripture/lesson/etc.
6.   Other activities that help calm you down and help you feel more in control.
7.   Plan ahead what you will do when a nightmare comes, and then do it just like you had planned.
D.   Keep a journal of what happens in the nightmare[1]
1.   This can be used in therapy.
2.   Some people are able to change what happens in the nightmare through therapy using this method.
E.   Use medication appropriately to help you sleep better.[20]
1.   There are many different medications to choose from.

V.   Ways to Facilitate Improved Sleep[1]

A.   <u>Avoid</u>
1.   Excessive noise.
2.   Caffeine (a stimulant).
3.   Cigarettes (a stimulant).
4.   Alcohol (disrupts the normal sleep cycle).
5.   Napping (disrupts the proper timing of sleep).
6.   Catching an extra wink in the morning.
7.   Upsetting or stressful activities before bedtime (triggers).
B.   <u>Maintain</u>
1.   A comfortable and safe sleeping environment.
2.   Make the room a comfortable temperature (60-70 degrees).
3.   Exercise in daytime or early evening.
4.   Satisfying (safe) sex.
5.   Light snacks (carbohydrates, milk) – avoid colas, chocolate, other stimulants.
6.   Daily physical exercise.
7.   Try to wake up at the same time every morning.
8.   Imagine a tranquil (comforting) place as you are falling asleep.
9.   Listen to music; use a relaxation tape; do meditation.
10.   If repeatedly awakening, then try to relax in another room.
11.   Read or do something boring right before sleep.
12.   Many individuals feel safe going to sleep if there is a family member up and awake during that time (i.e., "pulling guard duty").

C.   <u>Remember</u>: Our behaviors are often the most powerful things that either help or hinder sleep.
D.   Become willing to <u>work with</u> the process of getting better sleep instead of fighting against everything the whole way.
E.   Sometimes, a person's schedule needs to be modified to fit a non-traditional sleep pattern that may help in coping.

VI.   How to Become an Insomniac
A.   Keep an unrealistic goal for the number of hours of sleep you should get.
B.   Catastrophize about not meeting this goal, especially in the middle of the night.
C.   Spend all of the desperate hours fighting to get to sleep in bed.
D.   Make the bed a center for many other daily activities.
E.   Worry very often that you will never sleep "normally" ever again.
F.   Stay angry about the difficulty you have with sleep.
G.   Keep your mind overly burdened with cares, concerns, and worries.

Chapter 20 – Isolation

I.   **What Is Isolation?**[1,9]
    A.   Actively avoiding contact with other people.
    B.   Intentionally being alone for extended periods of time in an effort to manage symptoms.
    C.   Many individuals with PTSD use isolation as a "blanket strategy" for dealing with others and as an attempt to manage their symptoms.
    D.   However, it is difficult to continue using isolation as your main coping strategy for the rest of your life.
    E.   Isolation makes it very difficult to function in situations that require contact with other people.

II.   **Why Isolate?**
    A.   <u>There is a fear that drives isolation:</u>
        1.   Fear of being vulnerable (unsafe).
        2.   Fear of "what I might" do if I become angry (and go into combat mode).
        3.   Results include distrusting others, feeling like "I don't need anyone", fear of others' judgment, and fear of my possible reactions to other people.
    B.   Isolation can help you cope with the disruptions PTSD has caused in your life by avoiding stress.
    C.   "If I am not around other people, chances are lower that I will become agitated and lose control."
    D.   "If anyone knew the things I have done (e.g., killed in combat; done things absolutely necessary for survival, etc.), then they would never accept me."
    E.   Don't have the energy it takes to relate to other people or engage in social activities.
    F.   When depressed, I don't want to be around other people.
    G.   It is hard to put forth the effort that it takes to pretend to be good company.
    H.   Don't want to deal with other people's comments such as:
        1.   "It's in the past. Why don't you just forget about it?"
        2.   "Just get over it!"
    I.   Don't want to share feelings of shame or guilt with others.
    J.   Isolation helps you avoid triggers or possible anxiety-causing situations.
    K.   Fear that symptoms (like flashbacks or panic attacks) might embarrass yourself or your family.

III.   **Isolation Becomes a Vicious Cycle** [1]
- A.   Withdraw and isolate to reduce anxiety and anger.
- B.   This leads to the pain and confusion of loneliness and despair.
- C.   I now feel abandoned, rejected, and betrayed.
- D.   This leads to more anger, anxiety, and depression.

IV.   **Pros and Cons of Isolation**
- A.   <u>Short-Term Benefits of Isolation</u>
   1.   Reduces stress and anxiety immediately.
   2.   Decreases the chances of acting inappropriately with others.
   3.   Helps avoid potential conflicts and/or other problems with people.
- B.   <u>Long-Term Consequences of Isolation</u>
   1.   Feeling detached or estranged from others.
   2.   Increases feelings of rejection.
   3.   Difficulty experiencing a wide range of feelings; staying emotionally numb.
   4.   Extreme emotional responses such as rage, depression, and panic.
- C.   However, trauma survivors who receive healthy social support after the trauma have a lower risk for developing PTSD.
- D.   If you did not have this support early on, it is important to find a PTSD therapy group where others understand your experiences and symptoms, and are supportive.

V.   **Steps in Reducing Social Isolation**
- A.   Anger Management Skills[15,16,21]
   1.   Learn to feel anger as a feeling without having to act on it immediately.
   2.   Develop the skill of <u>Not Reacting</u>, but instead choose how to respond to handle situations appropriately.
   3.   Develop ways to express anger that do not hurt yourself, do not hurt others, and does not destroy valuable property.
- B.   Assertiveness Skills
   1.   Learn to get your needs met by stating your needs and asking for what you want.
   2.   Learn to stand up for yourself without having to become aggressive or violent.
- C.   Identify and Cope with Your Triggers. [1]
   1.   Make a record of your triggers and your typical responses to them.
   2.   Practice Deep Breathing exercises and relaxation techniques to manage the anxiety they cause.
   3.   Learn to replace your typical reactions with productive coping responses.
   4.   Use physical exercise and other coping skills on a regular basis.

D.   Treatment
    1.   Become actively involved in individual or group therapy for PTSD.
        a.   This allows you to discuss your experiences with others.
        b.   Begin reconnecting with others through peer support and positive interactions.
    2.   Learn to give and receive feedback honestly and graciously.
    3.   Begin to value yourself more and more as a person, as your understanding of PTSD and your coping skills increase.

Chapter 21 – Safety and Risk

I. **Trauma and Safety**
   A. When a person experiences a traumatic event that produces PTSD, their sense of safety is shaken or feels taken away.[1,5,9]
      1. Feel totally helpless.
      2. Become completely overwhelmed by the situation.
   B. As a result, the person loses the ability to feel safe in most situations.
   C. From that point forward, they see the world as a totally and completely unsafe place.
      1. See danger or potential danger "everywhere."
      2. Feel the need to be alert and on guard at all times.

II. **What Is Risk? (the possibility of loss or injury; something that creates or suggests a hazard)**
   A. Risk is a natural and expected part of daily life.
      1. Risk is involved while driving or riding in a vehicle.
      2. Weather poses risk.
      3. Most types of financial investment involve the risk of losing money.
      4. A certain amount of risk is associated with most any part of life (this is normal!).
   B. Managing our risk is one of the keys to personal success.
      1. In business, proper risk management is crucial to making a profit.
      2. For health, certain behaviors can increase or decrease our risk of certain diseases (for example, smoking increases the risk of lung cancer and other diseases).
      3. For our mental health, we need skills for managing risk at the proper level so we don't become overwhelmed with anxiety.

III. **What is Safety? (the condition of being protected from hurt, injury, or loss)**
   A. Most people seek situations that offer personal safety on a regular basis.
   B. This need to feel generally safe and secure is normal.
   C. Traumatic experience compromises a person's sense of personal safety (i.e., lose the ability to feel safe most of the time).
   D. One of the hallmarks of PTSD is a continual pattern of effort to seek and re-establish personal safety.
   E. Traumatic experiences radically change a person's view of "what is safe" vs. "what is not."
   F. When coping with PTSD, staying safe is one of the most important motivators of our behavior.
   G. As a result, many people get to where they see danger, even in relatively safe situations.

IV.   Why is Feeling Safe So Important in PTSD?
- A.   Trauma compromises a person's sense of safety
- B.   <u>Hypervigilance</u> – " I have to be on the alert all of the time to prevent another trauma."
    1.   Walk around always on guard.
    2.   Always seem to be looking for the danger in a situation.
- C.   When living this way, our thoughts, feelings, and actions are being driven by the past trauma and the desire to ensure our safety.
- D.   Many of the extreme behaviors observed in people coping with PTSD are motivated by the desire to avoid another trauma.
- E.   The trauma was so painful and overwhelming, it is the last thing you would ever want to repeat or experience again.
- F.   Staying safe can take over all other priorities in a person's life, resulting in a continually paralyzing fear.

V.   Consequences of Feeling Perpetually Unsafe
- A.   Don't trust anyone – they might hurt you.
- B.   Be cautious in everything you do (which may become an obstacle to completing tasks).
- C.   Be suspicious of people and their motives.
- D.   Always be prepared for any kind of trouble.
- E.   Believe that "My paranoia keeps me safe."
- F.   Approach everything with a smile on my face and fully on guard inside.
- G.   Expect that "Whatever it is, it will be bad."
- H.   Live with the attitude, "Most people are stupid and unsafe to be around."

VI.   A New Way
- A.   Evaluate people, places, and situations as each day progresses → act according to the real level of threat or danger.
    1.   It feels safer to just see everyone as a threat.
    2.   This requires too much effort and also ruins our relationships.
    3.   We need to learn to relax when we really are relatively safe, and be alert when in more dangerous situations.
- B.   Some situations really are more dangerous than others.
    1.   When coping with PTSD, there is a tendency to see all situations as highly dangerous.
    2.   To cope more effectively, begin recognizing that some situations are quite dangerous and others are generally safe.
    3.   Begin using the question "What Are The Chances?" to reduce fear and worry.
    4.   If the chances of what you fear happening are very low, extreme efforts to be on the alert are not very helpful or productive.

C.   Tell the difference between real danger vs. perceived danger.
    1.   Deal with real dangers appropriately.
        a.   Avoid truly dangerous situations if possible.
        b.   Make your actions consistent with the severity of threat.
        c.   It is better to avoid a bad situation than be forced to deal with it.
    2.   Stop over reacting to perceptions of threat where no real danger exists.
D.   Use a strategy based on intentional choices to reduce your risks and regain control over your fear and your life.

Chapter 22 – Concentration and Memory Problems

I. **The Problem**

    A.   Many people coping with PTSD experience some difficulties with attention, concentration, and memory on an ongoing basis.[1]

    B.   This is a common symptom and is not limited to any particular type of traumatic experience that results in PTSD.

    C.   This is manifested in many ways.

        1.   Losing your train of thought (going blank).

        2.   Forgetting what you want to say if you don't say it immediately.

        3.   Misplacing or losing frequently used objects (keys, glasses, tools, etc.).

        4.   Difficulty reading or listening for an extended period of time.

        5.   Problems remembering what you read or what people say.

        6.   Trouble making decisions; indecisiveness; can't seem to make up your mind.

II. **The Process (why we have concentration problems)**

    A.   In PTSD, the mind is still trying to process traumatic memories.[1,6]

        1.   Traumatic memories intrude on current thought patterns or in the middle of unrelated tasks.

        2.   This makes it difficult to focus on current concerns or necessary tasks.

    B.   Dissociation – "blanking out"

        1.   When certain thoughts or memories are too painful or unacceptable, the mind will sometimes "space out" or "take us somewhere else mentally" as a way to cope.

        2.   This is a strategy the mind uses to protect itself.

        3.   While it offers some short-term protection against unbearable memories, a person is usually unable to function while this is happening.

        4.   A certain amount of dissociation is normal.

            a.   For example, when driving you don't remember the past few blocks.

            b.   When watching a movie you lose touch with where you are because you are engrossed in the show.

        5.   However, dissociation can become a frequently used automatic coping strategy during trauma dates or periods of high stress.

        6.   While taking a "mental break" can be helpful if used occasionally, it is not recommended as a first-line coping strategy.

C.   Long-term substance abuse in an effort to cope with PTSD symptoms can result in neuropsychological impairment.[1,22]
    1.   Long-term use of alcohol and other sedatives is associated with attention and concentration difficulty.[11,12]
    2.   Short-term and long-term memory impairment are frequently found when substance abuse continues for a significant time.
    3.   Heavy substance abuse for many years can result in permanent damage to the brain and cause severe memory impairment.
D.   Normal memory functioning usually declines some as we get older.[22]
    1.   The decline may be more severe for those with PTSD.
    2.   Memory decline is usually even worse in cases of more severe PTSD.

III.   **Coping Strategies**
A.   Difficulties with concentration and memory do not have to completely limit our ability to function.
B.   By practicing some specific coping strategies, we can still function well in spite of these limitations.
C.   Pocket Notebook
    1.   Carry a small notebook in your pocket and keep it with you at all times.
    2.   Always carry a pen.
    3.   Develop the habit of writing things down as you think of them.
    4.   Write checklists in the notebook and use them.
    5.   If you write it down, there is a better chance you can find it later.
D.   Sticky Notes
    1.   Write notes to yourself using some type of "sticky note" paper.
    2.   Put these notes in strategic locations around your home or at work (refrigerator, bathroom mirror, light switches, door knobs, computer, etc.).
    3.   Act on these reminders at the appropriate times.
    4.   Throw the note away when the task is finished.
E.   Use Daily Rituals
    1.   Rituals are "over-learned" behaviors that require little to no thought.
    2.   Habits develop when we use rituals.
    3.   Example: Each morning, take medication first thing and put a check mark on the calendar immediately.
    4.   Put frequently used items (e.g., keys, glasses, etc.) in the same place every time.
    5.   Healthy rituals help us function without the need for much thought or effort.
F.   Pace Your Activities[23]

1.   Read only a little at a time (5 to 10 minute bursts) – only 3 pages each day is more than 1,000 pages in a year.
2.   Work for 10-20 minutes and take breaks.
3.   "Down time" is just as important as "up time" for maximizing your productivity.
4.   Working in short bursts is usually more productive than trying to stay with it for long stretches of time.
5.   Practice "pacing" your activities and see how productive you can be.

G.   Use Alarms and Other Technology
1.   Get a watch or some device that has 3 or more alarms on it.
2.   Set the alarms for important tasks that correspond to certain times of day.
3.   Use a microcassette recorder or digital recorder.
4.   Speak into the recorder and save messages for yourself when you think of important things.
5.   Play back messages later and act on them at that time or write them down in your notebook for future reference.
6.   Many palm-sized or pocket-sized computers are available now with most any feature you would want.
7.   Some computer programs have reminder settings.
8.   Use a clapper alarm to find keys or other important items.
9.   Leave yourself a message on the answering machine at work or home.
10.   Make notes on a big calendar or dry erase board.

Chapter 23 – Fatigue

I.   **Types of Fatigue (exhaustion)**[24]

    A.   <u>Physical fatigue</u> – a subjective state of overwhelming, sustained tiredness or exhaustion.

        1.   Feeling tired or weak in your body; loss of strength.

        2.   Having little or no energy.

        3.   A decreased capacity for activities that require physical effort.

    B.   <u>Mental fatigue</u> – a feeling of mental tiredness associated with increased difficulty paying attention, concentrating, thinking, and remembering.

        1.   Confusion can arise at this point.

        2.   Our decision-making abilities may become compromised.

        3.   We can become indecisive and second guess ourselves.

        4.   At this point, mental mistakes are common.

        5.   We get to where we do not solve daily problems as well as expected, which can increase feelings of failure or frustration.

    C.   <u>Emotional fatigue</u> – a feeling of being "emotionally drained", irritable, moody, and/or fearful, with exaggerated emotions and loss of confidence.

        1.   We may feel the need to avoid other people.

        2.   If we work with other people, we might feel that we have "nothing more to give" at that point.

        3.   This emotional state can become a "vicious cycle" that contributes to increased anxiety and depression.

II.   **Causes of Fatigue in PTSD**

    A.   <u>Lack of Sleep</u>

        1.   One purpose of sleep is the recuperation and reenergizing of the body and mind.

        2.   When sleep is insufficient for a significant length of time, the body and mind can experience the negative effects of prolonged fatigue.

        3.   Nightmares and other symptoms can disrupt sleep on an ongoing basis.

        4.   Sleep deprivation results in reduced physical strength, inefficient mental functioning, and overall poor long-term health.

        5.   With prolonged lack of sleep, our ability to cope with daily stress and symptoms is greatly reduced.

    B.   <u>Excessive Activity</u> (Workaholism)

        1.   Use of excessive work is a common strategy for distracting ourselves from painful thoughts, memories, or psychiatric symptoms.

        2.   The mind and body eventually become exhausted as we continue using this coping strategy on a chronic basis.

3.   Many people work anywhere from 12 to 20 hours per day in an effort to avoid painful memories (i.e., make sure there is no time to think of the trauma).

4.   Using work in this way can be rewarding (e.g., financial success, high work productivity, feelings of accomplishment, etc.), but there can also be extremely high costs.

C.   <u>Mental Work</u>

1.   Coping with the re-experiencing symptoms of PTSD requires significant mental effort (the mind works overtime most all of the time).

2.   Efforts to avoid traumatic memories and feelings requires the mind to put forth a large of amount of energy to keep those thoughts out of our awareness.

3.   The effort required to deal with the confusion of trauma and other types of symptoms can result in long-term exhaustion.

4.   This is a type of hard work that is on-going, but no one else sees it.

D.   <u>Putting Up Appearances</u>

1.   When coping with PTSD and other mental disorders, we can wind up feeling as if we are "Living in 2 worlds."

    a.   Public World – "everything is fine"; "I'm fine like everyone else"; "Normal."

    b.   Private World – struggling to cope with the thoughts and memories inside your own mind, which no one else knows about.

2.   Trying to fit into society while struggling with PTSD symptoms is like doing double the work most of the time.

3.   Trying to hide our symptoms requires a high degree of effort and energy.

4.   The result can be exhaustion and feeling overwhelmed.

E.   <u>Poor Nutrition</u>

1.   Due to the chronic hyperarousal of the sympathetic nervous system in individuals coping with PTSD, many report that they rarely feel hungry.

2.   As a result, many individuals with PTSD eat one meal each day, or less.

3.   In an effort to always stay alert in case of danger, many individuals also drink excessive amounts of coffee, other caffeinated drinks, and use other stimulants. They also have inadequate intake of vitamins and minerals, and frequently become dehydrated.

4.   The long-term results can include malnutrition, especially when combined with heavy alcohol use in an attempt to self-medicate symptoms.

5.   With inadequate nutrition, the body struggles to repair itself and have adequate energy.

     F.   Lack of Basic Self-care
- 1. Many individuals coping with PTSD and other mental disorders simply do not engage in routine self-care behaviors on a regular basis.
- 2. Like machines or other valuable property, if the body is not maintained on a regular basis, it will tend to degrade and eventually fall apart.
- 3. One sign of therapeutic improvement is when you start to take care of yourself again.

III.   **Application**

     A.   First identify the causes of your fatigue.

_____

_____

_____

     B.   Make a plan for changing your behavior to reduce the negative impact on your mind, body, and emotions.

     C.   Begin taking good care of yourself on a regular basis whether you feel that you deserve it or not.
- 1. If you feel unworthy, at least do it for the sake of your family.
- 2. You cannot care for others if you are broken down.
- 3. At least give yourself a fighting chance to recover physically.

     D.   Actively use therapy to cope more effectively and be able to get some rest.
- 1. Practice until you master at least one relaxation technique.
- 2. Consider medication and behavior changes so that you get at least 5 or more hours of sleep each night.

     E.   Use medications to reduce anxiety and help you rest.

Chapter 24 – PTSD and Life Development

I. **Traumatic Experiences Often Disrupt Normal Development**[13]
    A. In the field of developmental psychology, it is believed that we accomplish certain "developmental tasks" at different ages throughout our life.
    B. When trauma happens, the necessary tasks involved in "growing up" may not be completed, and we stay at that age emotionally.[25]
    C. A person who has been traumatized may get "stuck" at a certain age.
    D. Do you ever feel that you are still stuck at the age you were when the trauma(s) happened?
    E. Example: If a person was traumatized at age 18.
        1. Have the feelings of an 18 year-old.
        2. Tend to react to situations "like a teenager"; "Still think, feel, and act like a teenager."
        3. Struggle to know "who you really are" or "where you fit in."
        4. "An 18 year-old in a 55 year-old body."

II. **Difficulties when Trauma Occurs in Early Adulthood**
    A. The developmental task of early adulthood is the need to <u>form a healthy identity</u>.
    B. When we have a healthy identity, we develop skills for handling life's problems appropriately.
    C. Identity problems associated with "getting stuck." [25]
        1. Confusion about feelings and emotions, anxiety, depression.
        2. Don't really know who you are anymore.
        3. Not sure that you can become the person you had always wanted to be.
        4. Not sure how to cope without using drugs and alcohol to "ease the emotional pain."
        5. It becomes difficult to pursue goals or to function at work or school.
        6. Feelings of loneliness, despair, deprivation, rage, or self-hatred.
        7. It can lead to feeling out of control or feeling lost.
        8. Blame yourself; feel shame about "what I had to do just to survive."

III. **Traumatic Experiences Disrupt Several Primary Abilities**[9]
    A. The ability to feel and manage a wide range of feelings.
    B. The ability to soothe and comfort yourself.
    C. The ability to trust.
    D. The ability to connect with other people in a healthy way.

    E.   The ability to maintain a positive identity.

    F.   The ability to feel valuable and maintain healthy self-esteem.

    G.   <u>Expectable Results of "Getting Stuck"</u>[26]
1. Low frustration tolerance.
2. Difficulty being persistent in reaching goals (e.g., change jobs frequently).
3. Feel hostile if you have to depend on someone else for something.
4. Constantly "testing the limits."
5. Feelings are expressed as behaviors (e.g., run away, fight, do "something extreme").
6. Emotions come and go quickly (i.e., tend to react to situations quickly).
7. Extremely sensitive to rejection.
8. Able to only see the present moment or current day (i.e., no view of the future).
9. Denial of what is really going on (before treatment, or early on in treatment).
10. All-or-nothing thinking (e.g., "you are either for me or against me").

IV. Several Viewpoints Can Result from "Getting Stuck" at a Certain Age (e.g., age 18)

    A.   "I have nothing in common with past friends."

    B.   "I see things through the eyes of a frightened 18 year old."

    C.   "My beliefs from growing up are all gone."

    D.   "I question my beliefs because of how the traumas have affected me."

    E.   "I gave up on church and society."

    F.   "My old belief system was destroyed by the traumas and had to be totally rebuilt."

    G.   "I'm always in a wait-and-see mode."

    H.   "I refuse to ever be impressionable, gullible, or naïve ever again."

    I.   "I don't remember who I am or who I was."

V. The Age at which a Trauma Occurs Will Affect the Person's Ability to Cope

    A.   Traumas are more difficult to cope with the younger you are (e.g., a child).
1. Children have less maturity and fewer coping abilities to rely on.
2. Children and the elderly generally have more difficulty coping overall.

    B.   The human brain is finally mature (physically) around ages 21 to 25.[27,28]
1. Traumas that occur before this age tend to bring strong challenges in coping ability.

C. It is important to develop coping skills now before we get older when most of our strength and abilities decline.

D. <u>Remember</u>: Most people continue to live with the level of coping skills that were typical at the age you were traumatized.

VI. Getting Better

A. To get better, we must start growing and developing again, but in a healthy way.[13]

1. Have to start growing again emotionally.

2. Need to "catch up" to your real (chronological) age.

B. How old were you when you experienced traumatic events?

1. In what ways have you continued to "act that age" since the trauma?

2. How long have you gone "at that age"?

C. Remember that recovery from traumatic experience is also a developmental process.

1. It will take time for the signs of therapeutic progress and personal growth to show.

2. The key is to be persistent in therapy over a period of time (usually at least a few years).

D. Two Keys to Growing Again

1. We need to create a positive, healthy Post-Trauma Identity.

   a. Decide who you want to be.

   b. Start working toward becoming that kind of person.

   c. Accept that it is okay to be a positive person.

   d. <u>Remember</u>: No amount of suffering, beating up on yourself, or negativity will help other people, fix problems, or do you any good.

2. We need to develop emotional maturity that helps us deal with life in healthy ways.

   a. How should a person your chronological age act?

   b. How would a mature person handle the things that have caused you to over-react in the past?

   c. Where are you headed in your healing process?

Chapter 25 – PTSD and Medications

I.   **What Are the Appropriate Uses of Psychiatric Medications?**[13,29]
   A.   To stabilize a person when they are feeling completely overwhelmed.
   B.   To get control over symptoms so that a person can benefit from education about their condition.
   C.   To help the person be able to develop more effective coping skills in the long run.
   D.   A person may also need to use small amounts of medication once in a while for a short time to get through a particularly rough situation – this is called "PRN" use (i.e., as needed).

II.   **Long-Term Outcomes**
   A.   We need to be careful that long-term medication use does not reinforce a complete reliance on "pills to fix everything".[29]
   B.   A view that sees all control as being outside the person reinforces the problem and keeps the person stuck.
   C.   We need to promote personal responsibility and development of new coping skills so the person can take back control of their life and live in a healthier way.
   D.   Short-Term use of medication allows a person to stabilize and then be able to develop better coping skills so that the symptoms don't control their life anymore.
   E.   While some people need to be on medication for the long term, this should be done in addition to education and therapy for specific symptoms and the person's overall condition.
   F.   Note: Some research has shown that people who received therapy only, or therapy + medication, did as well or better in the long term compared with people who received only medications.[29,30,31,32]
      1.   This relates to using therapy for developing skills in order to more effectively deal with stresses and life situations rather than just relying on a pill to fix everything.
      2.   Medications cannot fix the underlying psychological conflicts and other problems that caused and are perpetuating our symptoms.

III.   **Be an Informed Patient**[29]
   A.   Patients who take an active part in their own treatment usually do the best in the end.
   B.   Know the names of the medications you are taking, the dose, and how often you are supposed to take it.

C.   Look up the medications in a medical reference book or on the Internet.

    1.   For example, use the PDR (Physician's Desk Reference), or other medication references.

    2.   http://www.rxlist.com   http://www.medicinenet.com

    3.   http://www.mentalhealth.com   http://www.dr-bob.org/tips/ptsd.html

D.   Look up what the medications are supposed to be given for.

    1.   Note: Some medications can be used for multiple conditions and also for treatments other than what we might expect. Ask your doctor about this.

E.   Look up what the possible side effects of the medication could be.

    1.   Focus mainly on the most common side-effects.

    2.   All medications have side-effects.

        a.   Some can be tolerated.

        b.   Others might be severe and require a medication change.

F.   Know exactly when and how to take your medication

    1.   What time of day?   With food?   Without food?   With milk?

    2.   What should I avoid?

        a.   Grapefruit juice?   Alcohol?

        b.   Aspirin?   Antacids?   Over-the-counter cold medications?

        c.   Other things to avoid? (ask your pharmacist)

IV.   Attitudes about Medication

A.   Develop the attitude: "I will use medication if I have to, but I would like to use as little as possible, and get to the point where I use none if I can cope effectively without it."

B.   Some people can get to the point where they use no medications or very little.

C.   Other people need long-term medication treatment.

D.   However, EVERYBODY needs coping skills to deal with symptoms and daily stress.

V.   Healthful Benefits of Therapy + Medication[29]

A.   What things should improve by appropriately using psychiatric medication?

B.   See if you have "more" of the following as a result of actively participating in therapy and by taking your medication exactly as prescribed.

    1.   Increased self-control.

    2.   Good daily functioning – Able to do the normal, necessary tasks each day.

    3.   Coping effectively with daily stresses.

        a.   Not overwhelmed most of the time.

        b.   Use of healthy coping skills on a regular basis.

4. Think clearly the majority of the time (using your mind for the best benefit).

5. Make good decisions; think things through; anticipate possible consequences.

6. Deal with real issues (reality) – stop living in denial.

7. Live responsibly.
   a. Not out of control.
   b. Regularly fulfill obligations and commitments.

8. Accept yourself as a valuable person.

9. Not impulsive.
   a. Think things through before acting.
   b. Plan things out when possible.
   c. "Look before you leap."

10. Relate well with other people.
    a. Less irritable; less argumentative.
    b. More agreeable; able to compromise when appropriate; able to cooperate.

11. Able to enjoy the good things in life at a healthy level (enjoyment with moderation).

12. Patience – delay of gratification in order to get better rewards later.
    a. Not always going for the immediate payoff in every situation.
    b. Less urgency; not rushed all of the time.
    c. More thoughtful and intentional in your actions.

13. Mental Awareness.
    a. Awake and alert at the desired level.
    b. Able to focus your mind and stay on task.
    c. Not in a mental fog or having your mind in "neutral" the majority of the time.

14. Persistence.
    a. Consistently work toward goals until they are attained.
    b. Keep with things until you accomplish the goal.
    c. Stick with things; don't give up easily; able to work through difficulties.

15. A healthy, balanced life.

C. When therapy and medication work properly, we become able to restructure our lives, reduce symptoms, and live in a more fulfilling way.

Section IV: Anger Management

Patients with PTSD have said . . .

"I want to hurt those people so bad, . . . , but really, . . . , I don't want to hurt anyone.
I've seen enough of the hatred, the anger, the violence.
Why do we have to treat each other so inhumanely?"
-A new patient describing the effects of combat trauma

"I got to where I was angry all day long, every day.
I was angry all the time and didn't even know it."

"My greatest fear is getting angry and losing control of myself,
because I know just how destructive I can be, and that's no good for anybody."

Chapter 26 – Intro to Anger

I. **What Is Going On with Anger in PTSD?**[1,2]
   A. It is often a product of emotional damage (i.e., trauma).
      1. Anger covers pain → a way of trying to protect yourself.
      2. It becomes a self-protective reaction.
      3. An attempt to overcome hurt or feeling helpless.
   B. Anger can also be a result of learning.
      1. Learn to react (as in military training).
      2. Use anger to regain control.
      3. An attempt to not feel helpless.
      4. For some, anger is equated with power.
      5. After surviving trauma, it can be a method of "feeling alive again."
   C. While anger serves several purposes in PTSD, the overall long-term effects are usually detrimental.

II. **How Do I Know when I Am Angry?**[1,33]
   A. Certain things happen in my body, my thinking, and my actions.
      1. <u>Physical</u>
         a. Pounding heart; rapid, shallow breathing.
         b. Tightness in stomach, arms, shoulders, jaw, lips, forehead.
         c. Clenched hands/fists.
         d. Hair stands up on neck.
         e. Voice gets louder.
      2. <u>Thoughts</u>
         a. Blaming others.
         b. Thinking of hurting others.
         c. Negative thoughts about myself.
         d. Feeling or thinking "I'm helpless here."
         e. Mind reading.
         f. Exaggerating the importance of being right or getting even.
      3. <u>Behavior</u>
         a. Becoming very quiet.
         b. Sarcasm or inappropriate laughter.
         c. Not keeping a promise (to get back at them).
         d. Swearing or yelling.
         e. Driving dangerously.
         f. Throwing or breaking things.
         g. Hitting someone or something.

III.   **The Anger Sequence**[1]
- A.   <u>Event</u> → <u>Thoughts</u> → <u>Feelings</u> → <u>Actions</u> → <u>Consequences</u>
- B.   The upsetting event can be almost anything that is upsetting.
  - 1.   It might be harmful or it could actually be harmless.
  - 2.   Example: Somebody says something nasty to me; got cut off in traffic this morning.
- C.   Thoughts
  - 1.   Is this a threat? How dare they?
  - 2.   What's wrong here?   Where's the danger?
- D.   Feelings
  - 1.   Anger; rage; upset .
  - 2.   Felt attacked or victimized.
- E.   Behavior (actions)
  - 1.   Our behaviors now will either be productive (to fix the problem) or destructive (making it worse).
  - 2.   "How will I handle this situation?
  - 3.   "What possible actions can I take? (Think → OPTIONS)

IV.   **Anger in PTSD – Starting Halfway Up the Scale**[1]
- A.   Consider the anger continuum below

Calm - Mild irritation – Frustrated – Agitated – Upset – Angry - "Ticked-off" – Furious – Explosive - Rage

- B.   Notice that the further you move to the right of the scale, the stronger the anger becomes.
- C.   People who do not have an anger problem usually start at the calm point and then anger builds gradually.
- D.   In PTSD, we tend to start most days at the "upset" or "angry" point (already half-way up the scale).
- E.   What is your anger starting point most days? _____

V.   **How Do I Feel when I Am Angry?**
- A.   To get a grasp on our anger, it helps to name the angry feelings.
- B.   See the words associated with anger below.
- C.   Circle the ones you have experienced.

annoyed	furious	irked	stubborn	disturbed
bitter	hateful	irritated	touchy	troubled
contemptuous	hostile	outraged	unappreciated	snappy
distrustful	humiliated	overwhelmed	uneasy	sore
enraged	hurt	provoked	exasperated	vexed
impatient	resentful	ticked	bugged	
displeased	grouchy	offended	miffed	
sulky	rankled	riled	snarly	

Other words might be more descriptive for you _____

VI.   Situations Where You Might Feel Anger
   A.   Supervisor at work. Authority figures. Children act irresponsibly. Road rage.
   B.   A friend lets you down. People don't listen to you.
   C.   Parents' behavior. You feel criticized. Someone disagrees with you.
   D.   You get disappointed. Someone disrespects you. Chronically fatigued.
   E.   Feel pressure to do something   Something just "won't work right."
   F.   Sense that something bad is about to happen. People don't live up to your expectations.

VII.   To Deal with My Anger Effectively, I Need to Know Something About It
   A.   Was it O.K. to express anger in my home as a child?   Yes   No
   B.   How did I express anger when I was young? _____
   _____
   C.   How often do I get angry now? _____
   D.   When I'm angry, do I hurt other people or myself?   Yes   No
   E.   When I'm angry, do I tend to destroy things?   Yes   No
   F.   Do I like being angry?   Yes   No
   G.   What kind of person has my anger caused me to be? _____

VIII.   A Long-Term Goal for Anger Management → to Feel Anger as a Feeling, but without Acting On It Immediately
   A.   Is this possible   -Today ?   -In a few weeks?   -In 6 months?

Chapter 27 – Anger: Responding vs. Reacting
I Choose to Respond and Not React.

I. **Anger Can Have Several Possible Outcomes**[33,34]
   A. Destructive Outcomes
      1. When anger is destructive, we get hurt or wind up hurting other people.
      2. Things get broken or destroyed.
      3. We do things that we regret later (hurtful actions, angry words, valuables get broken).
      4. Things are done that cannot be reversed or fixed.
   B. Activities that may feel natural, but usually DO NOT lead to a desirable outcome.
      1. Yelling, shouting, or cursing.
      2. Punching the person immediately.
      3. Trying to cut, stab, or shoot the person you are angry at.
      4. Setting fires or setting off explosives.
      5. Stalking.
      6. Threatening or intimidating.
      7. Telling someone off.
      8. Throwing or smashing things.
      9. Other destructive acts.
      10. What are some examples of destructive outcomes from your own life? _____
   C. Productive Outcomes
      1. We deal with the event and our anger in a way so that the destructive things don't happen.
      2. We take action that fixes the problem or helps the situation.
      3. We recognize our anger, then choose a way to properly manage our behavior.
   D. Note: If anger has been a problem for you, either you will control your anger or it will become the primary thing controlling your actions!

II. **What Is Responding vs. Reacting?**
   A. Reacting – "I don't think, I just act."
      1. When reacting, we are not in control → we have given our control to the other person.
      2. We feel fully justified in our actions based on how we feel.
      3. Reacting in anger usually produces undesirable consequences or outcomes.

B.   <u>Responding</u> – "I don't have to act immediately."
1.   Responding means staying in control of yourself and handling the situation appropriately.
2.   STOP.
3.   THINK (of your options).
4.   Now, CHOOSE how to handle this!"

C.   <u>Example</u>: Someone makes a nasty remark about me.
1.   I have some options.
2.   Punching them in the nose immediately is a reaction.
3.   Or, I can stop, think how to handle it, and choose what I will do <u>to best handle</u> the situation.
4.   Do you <u>have to</u> react to what other people do?   YES   NO

III.   New Coping

A.   We need to change how we think in order to handle anger-producing situations more productively.

B.   <u>Steps in productive coping</u>[1,33]
1.   In a stressful situation I will first STOP!
2.   Now think, "What are my options?"
3.   What information do I have? ("What are the facts?")
4.   I <u>do not</u> have to react!
5.   "I will <u>choose</u> to express my anger in <u>non-destructive</u> ways."
6.   "What is the best course of action here?"
7.   Now, take action on the most reasonable, rational way of handling this situation.
8.   What outcome do you really want?

C.   <u>New Behaviors to try</u>
1.   Act the Opposite of how you feel as a starting point.
2.   Smile instead of frown.
    a.   This throws some people off guard.
    b.   You might get a better response from others this way.
3.   Speak softly (on purpose) instead of loudly.
4.   Relax instead of tighten up.
5.   Step back or walk away instead of attack.
6.   Try to understand instead of judging others.

D.   With practice, you can gain more control by choosing to respond (instead of react).
1.   Remember the key steps:
2.   STOP.
3.   THINK.
4.   CHOOSE.
5.   Now, RESPOND (with good coping).

Chapter 28 – How Anger Works

I. **How Does Anger Work?**[1,33,34]

    A.   First, you experience some kind of pain or upsetting event.

    B.   This causes trigger thoughts, which are perceptions, interpretations, or beliefs that make you feel victimized or deliberately harmed.

    C.   These thoughts blame others for our own painful experiences.

    D.   Finally, if you keep focusing on these trigger thoughts, it fuels your anger to higher and higher levels.

    E.   <u>Remember</u>: Anger is a warning signal that something is not right, or that you are feeling control slipping away.

    F.   We need to step back, identify it, and understand it in order to cope.

II. **Frequent Causes of Anger**

    A.   By knowing the causes of our anger, we can begin anticipating those things and manage them better.

    B.   <u>Simple Frustration</u> – something prevents us from reaching our goal.

        1.   Feel blocked in reaching my goal.

        2.   Murphy's Law – everything that can go wrong will go wrong.

        3.   The harder you try, the worse it gets.

    C.   <u>Feeling Provoked</u> – believe that somebody did something aggressively toward you on purpose.

    D.   <u>Feeling Unsafe</u> (not in control = vulnerable).

        1.   Anger is an attempt to get back in control of the situation.

        2.   When used chronically, we come to believe that anger is the only way to be in control or keep ourselves safe.

    E.   <u>Anger at Injustice or Unfairness</u> – anger is a reaction to the wrongfulness of what someone did.

        1.   We make an attempt to "right the wrong."

        2.   This form of anger can be both healthy or unhealthy depending on how it is expressed.

III. **Trigger Thought Patterns**

    A.   It is important to recognize trigger thoughts.

        1.   Trigger thoughts keep us focused on distressing ideas and feelings.

        2.   When we entertain these thoughts, this fuels the feelings of anger.

    B.   If you focus on the following thoughts, you will be angry very often.[33]

        1.   People are stupid or incompetent.

        2.   Someone rejects or tries to shame you.

        3.   You are kept waiting.

4.   People don't listen to you.

5.   Others seem threatening or dangerous.

6.   Someone disrespects you.

7.   You see things that are unfair or unjust.

8.   People are lazy or "don't do their fair share."

9.   Others act in an irresponsible way.

10.   People don't do the right thing or don't do things "the right way."

IV.   **What Anger Does to Our Minds (angry thoughts)**[1,2,33]

A.   Get tunnel vision.

B.   Focus exclusively on what we feel is the problem or threat.

C.   Tend to misinterpret events as threatening when they are not.

D.   When angry, we may feel provoked, taken advantage of, belittled, or abused even when no real threat appears to be present (we see something that is not there).

E.   With chronic anger, we may "go looking" for something to be angry about.

F.   Our ability to come up with reasonable solutions drops drastically when in the heat of anger.

G.   Solutions we think of when angry usually involve aggression, harm, retribution, revenge, pay-back, or some type of hurtful action.

H.   When angry, we tend to have distorted thoughts and perceptions, and our problem solving abilities are greatly diminished.

V.   **Anger and Our Behavior**

A.   People with anger problems tend to react quickly without considering consequences.

1.   Anger gets us "off-track" and produces hurtful behavior.

2.   We may be trying to change the other person, but this usually results in frustration.

B.   When anger gets out of control, we may act aggressively.

1.   Hurt self or others.

2.   Destroy valuable property.

3.   Get into legal problems.

4.   Do something that cannot be reversed or fixed.

5.   Do something I regret later.

6.   Ruin a relationship.

7.   Become a nasty, hostile person.

C.   Instead of aggression, we need positive actions.

1.   Change the situation.

2.   Change your response to the upsetting event (which might mean accepting the situation).

3.   Remember: Accepting something doesn't mean that you agree with it.

VI.   **Getting Anger Under Control**

    A.   If our thoughts are out of control, our behavior might be also.

    B.   To manage our anger, we need to think productive, coping thoughts.

    C.   New Thoughts (for coping with anger).

        1.   When I get angry, what exactly do I want?   What am I trying to accomplish?

        2.   If frustrated, what is blocking me?

        3.   What is another way to accomplish what I need here? **(Think Options!)**

        4.   If someone is trying to provoke me, then I choose to win.

            a.   **(I refuse to let them push my buttons!)**

            b.   Make it hard for them to get you upset → like trying to nail Jello to a wall!

        5.   As long as I stay calm, cool, and collected, then I am in control.

        6.   Am I really safe here or not? → is the danger I feel really real?

        7.   Just how important is this in the big picture?

            a.   If this is a big deal, then take appropriate action.

            b.   If this is only a small detail, then let it go.

        8.   Maintaining self-control is more important than proving myself to someone else (who doesn't really care anyway).

        9.   If it is not my place to judge, then I need to let it go.

        10.   Am I so perfect that I am justified in criticizing others?

        11.   How would a strong, compassionate, forgiving person handle this?

    D.   <u>The Rules for Expressing Anger</u>

        1.   Behaviors are okay as long as they follow 3 rules:

            a.   It does not hurt me.

            b.   It does not hurt somebody else.

            c.   It does not destroy valuable property.

    E.   As we get better at handling upsetting situations, our thoughts begin to work for us instead of against us.

        1.   Practice → practice every day → practice every day whether you need to or not

Chapter 29 – Anger and Self-Talk
I Choose to Respond and Not React

I.   **Anger Is Often Related to our Thoughts and the Things We Say to Ourselves**[35,36]

    A.   Certain types of thoughts "set us up" to become upset or to have difficulties.

    B.   These thoughts are in the form of unrealistic beliefs or expectations.

    C.   Anger Producing Thought Patterns.

        1.   <u>Blaming</u> – believe that other people are doing bad things to you.

            a.   Believe they are intentionally trying to hurt you.

            b.   Focus on "not letting them get away with it."

            c.   This makes us feel a little better immediately, but creates a sense of helplessness.

        2.   <u>Magnifying the Situation</u> – taking a small, negative experience and exaggerating it.

            a.   This intensifies the anger and other negative feelings.

        3.   <u>Global Labeling</u> – putting a complete negative judgment on people when we dislike their behavior.

            a.   Example: loser, jerk, no-good, retard, idiot, schmuck.

            b.   This approach turns the person into a worthless object in your mind and just fuels your anger.

        4.   <u>Jumping to Conclusions About the Other Person's Motivation.</u>

            a.   The first tendency is imagining the other person is trying to hurt you on purpose.

            b.   You are assuming that you know the other person's "real motives."

            c.   Catch yourself and see what assumptions you are making.

            d.   Then, check it out with the person.

            e.   Keep an open mind → look for other explanations.

        5.   <u>Over-generalizing in a Negative Direction</u>

            a.   Words such as always, never, everybody, no one, every time, etc. are used.

            b.   This stretches the truth of the situation.

            c.   It is a set up to be angry or to get an angry response from someone else.

        6.   <u>Placing Strong Demands on People and Situations</u>

            a.   Placing demands on how other people should act.

            b.   Notice using words like should, ought to, have to, got to, has to be, etc.

       c.   These are often seen when we feel things "must be done the right way" or if we see unfairness in a situation.

       d.   The problem is that other people will rarely do <u>what you think</u> they should.

       e.   It is more productive to state what you want as a preference, and learn to let things go if you have no control over them.

II. Additional Thoughts that Contribute to Anger [33,35,36]

A.   It is absolutely necessary to have love and approval from others almost all of the time.

       1.   If I don't, then I'm rejected.

B.   I have to punish or harm anyone who does things to me that I don't like.

C.   It is horrible, terrible, and catastrophic when things don't go <u>exactly</u> the way I want.

       1.   I should have complete control at all times.

D.   Things in my past <u>have to</u> continue to control me the rest of my life.

E.   I am only valuable as a person if I perform well.

III. Correcting the Thought Distortions

A.   Self-talk can be used in dealing with anger.

       1.   Remember that talking to yourself is normal.

       2.   Mostly, it is done quietly in your thoughts.

B.   Ask yourself, "What am I REALLY angry about?" _____

C.   How important is this situation in the big picture of life?

       Low   *Medium*   *High*

D.   Is this a catastrophe, moderate challenge, or just a minor inconvenience?

E.   What is the appropriate way to handle this?_____

F.   Choose to say things to yourself (silently inside your mind) that will help in dealing with the situation.

IV. What Coping Thoughts Should I Say to Myself? (silently inside your head)

A.   I don't have to react immediately.

B.   What are my options?

C.   I can stay calm.

D.   I will stay in control of myself.

E.   I don't have to prove myself in this situation.

F.   My anger is a signal to take a Time-Out!

G.   Is this a REAL threat or just a PERCEIVED threat?

H.   If people criticize me, I will survive. I don't have to be perfect.

I.   Is this really MY problem or THEIR problem?

J.   What are other ways of seeing this situation (that maybe I haven't thought of yet)?

K.   I don't have to take this so seriously.

L.   Getting upset won't help.

M.   Easy does it → getting angry won't gain me anything.

N.   Relax and just let it go.

O.   I choose to stay rational.

P.   Angry reactions won't fix anything.

Q.   It's just a minor hassle → I can handle it.

V.   **What Should I Do? (possible options)**

A.   Delay. If I just wait before I respond, sometimes the situation will take care of itself.

B.   Walk away (remove yourself from the situation).

C.   Be assertive. Stand up for your rights without being aggressive or violent.

D.   Take a TIME-OUT! (During Time-Out!, don't drive, drink alcohol, or use drugs!)

E.   Come back and deal with it in a better frame of mind.

F.   Tell the other person "I feel upset (angry, tense) and need a moment to collect my thoughts."

G.   Use calming, positive self-talk (silently inside your head).

H.   Use the deep breathing relaxation technique.

VI.   **Choose a Non-destructive Activity to Express Anger**

A.   Go for a walk or a run.

B.   Skip rocks across a stream or lake.

C.   Lift weights or do some kind of exercise.

D.   Take a drink of cold water.

E.   Play a musical instrument or listen to music.

F.   Write a letter or in a journal.

G.   Work in the garden; work on a hobby.

H.   Go somewhere alone and talk about how you feel.

I.   Squeeze a hand gripper (for hand strength).

J.   Play basketball or some favorite game.

K.   Talk to your pet dog, cat, or dinosaur.

L.   Other activity that lets you express feelings in a way that is not destructive.

VII.   **Overall, to Cope Effectively with Anger, We Need to Develop and Practice →
Self-Control!**

(through practicing the above skills).

Chapter 30 – Anger and Our Decisions
I Choose to Respond and Not React.

I.   **How Do I Make My Decisions in Life?**
  A.   Impulsively.
  B.   In a thoughtful way.
  C.   Have trouble even making a decision.
  D.   Don't give it much thought – I just do what I do.
  E.   Always motivated by anger, jealousy, envy, rage, revenge, etc.
  F.   What is your typical pattern? _____

II.   **Some Things Are More Important than Other Things in Life**
  A.   To be successful, we need to determine what is a "big deal" and what is not in making life decisions.
  B.   <u>Catastrophe vs. Details:</u>
     1.   Catastrophe – a sudden, terrible calamity; <u>a huge disaster</u>.
     2.   Details – a small or secondary part of the larger situation.
     3.   <u>Note</u>: To the perfectionist, everything is of ultimate importance (unrealistic).
     4.   Example: If I come home and find my house has burned down, that's a catastrophe. If I stub my toe in the dark, it's inconvenient and painful for a short while, but it's not a huge disaster.
  C.   <u>Proportional Responding</u>
     1.   Good coping requires us to distinguish between "what's a big deal" and "what's not" and then act accordingly.
     2.   I need to <u>choose my response</u> to a particular situation instead of simply reacting.
     3.   I need to make my response consistent with the intensity of the situation.
     4.   Overreacting is usually unproductive and often detrimental.
  D.   Making decisions when angry usually exaggerates our reactions, over-estimates the severity of the situation, and leads to poorly chosen courses of action. [33]

III.   **Choices Have a Large Impact on How Our Lives Turn Out**
  A.   Decisions we make usually have positive or negative consequences.
  B.   Good decision making can contribute to our success in life.
     1.   Helps us achieve goals.
     2.   Helps us avoid mistakes (that can be costly).
  C.   Poor decisions often create or perpetuate problems.
  D.   A secret to success in most areas of life is consistently making the best choices possible.

IV.   **Predictors of Decision Making Problems (circle all of the following that you have done)**

    A.   Having unrealistic expectations.

    B.   Making "snap decisions" – i.e., being impulsive.

    C.   Taking unnecessary action when no action on your part is really needed.

    D.   Failing to address the real problem.

    E.   Not making a decision for fear of making an error or mistake.

        1.   If you choose not to decide, then you still have made a choice.

        2.   This can be just as harmful as making a bad decision.

    F.   Not taking responsibility for your choices or actions.

    G.   Making decisions that really are not yours to make (forcing yourself onto a situation).

    H.   Having poor timing.

    I.   Putting things off → they will build up and eventually feel overwhelming.

    J.   Ignoring consequences.

    K.   Trying to make the perfect decision every time (perfectionism).

    L.   Ignoring risks or probabilities.

    M.   Not learning from past experience (yours or the experiences of other people).

    N.   Tunnel vision – not exploring options or possibilities; don't see the big picture.

    O.   Not being willing to reevaluate when the chosen course of action is clearly wrong or is producing bad results.

V.   **Mental Skills for Wise Decision Making**

    A.   Decide ahead of time that when an upsetting situation occurs that "I will NOT REACT immediately, but instead I will choose my response."

    B.   Think in terms of options. Say to yourself, **"OK, what are my options?"**

    C.   Anticipate the consequences of actions before doing them.

    D.   Weigh the pros and cons.

    E.   Remember similar events from the past, and use that information to help you think about the current situation right now.

    F.   Plan for upcoming events and situations ahead of time (without obsessing).

    G.   Ask yourself "What am I really working toward here?"

    H.   DON'T OVERREACT! Decisions made with a cool head are usually better in the long run.

        1.   Walk away – take some time.

        2.   Cool down – gather your thoughts.

        3.   Come back and deal with it in a better frame of mind.

    I.   Ask for the input of other people when you are not sure (get help when you need it).

J.   Don't rely exclusively on feelings in your decision making.
   1.   Pay most of your attention to the facts that you have and to your rational thoughts.
K.   However, don't ignore a feeling if it is particularly strong and won't go away for many hours (or days).
L.   <u>Remember</u>: Decisions made with a cool head are usually better in the long run.

Chapter 31 – Anger: Fueling vs. Self-Control

I.   **Mental Input**[1,33]
      A.   A person's mental input has a large impact on how often they become angry.
          1.   It is difficult to be angry about things you don't know about.
          2.   Your daily mental input either <u>fuels</u> or <u>helps you control</u> your anger.
      B.   Sources of Mental Input.
          1.   Television, radio, newspaper, talking with other people, books, magazines, lectures, observations, daily experiences, etc.
          2.   We usually have some control over our mental input, but not completely.
          3.   What are you feeding your mind?
      C.   Results of Mental Input.
          1.   The kind of person you become rests largely on your thoughts, beliefs, and actions.
          2.   If you think angry thoughts most of the time, you will become an angry person.
          3.   What kind of mental input will help you to become the type of person you want to be? _____
_____

          4.   What things do you focus your thoughts on most often?_____
_____

II.   **Fueling Anger**[33]
      A.   Feeding your mind upsetting information on a regular basis.
          1.   Certain TV programs, news shows, documentaries.
          2.   Newspaper columns, editorials.
          3.   Certain people that you interact with "get you going" or "worked up."
      B.   The more you focus on these upsetting things (which are beyond your control), the stronger your anger becomes.
      C.   These upsetting things become a poison to your mind and your mental health.
      D.   Your ability to cope with anxiety, depression, and daily stress is compromised and your personal stress levels become out of control.

III.   **Why Fueling Anger Is So Destructive**
- A.   When coping with PTSD, being agitated keeps symptoms at a high intensity level.
- B.   When agitated, our thinking is not clear.
  - 1.   We are more prone to make poor decisions .
  - 2.   The chances of doing something harmful goes up.
  - 3.   Our ability to cope with minor events becomes compromised due to the state of mind caused by fueling our anger.
- C.   Fueling anger perpetuates many PTSD symptoms.
  - 1.   Intrusive thoughts, nightmares, flashbacks.
  - 2.   Emotions feeling either shut down or out of control.
  - 3.   Sleep problems become worse.
  - 4.   Concentration and memory difficulties become more intense.
  - 5.   Hypervigilance (always being on guard).

IV.   **Making a Plan for Coping**
- A.   List the source of "fuel" for your anger.
- B.   How much control do you have over each one?
  Low   Medium   High
- C.   How could you reduce or eliminate this source of anger fuel?
  - 1.   Turn off the TV.
  - 2.   Change the channel.
  - 3.   Avoid certain people.
  - 4.   Other _____
- D.   Make your plan for better coping and then stick to the plan.
- E.   Get feedback about the plan from your therapist or therapy group.

V.   **Anger Management (appropriate control)**[1,33]
- A.   First, decide that you don't want to be angry all of the time.
  - 1.   Some people do want to be angry all the time, and are always looking for something to be angry about.
  - 2.   Do you want to be angry, bitter, and miserable, or contented and at peace?
- B.   Eliminate sources of information that "fuel the fire" of your anger.
  - 1.   Turn off certain TV programs; avoid certain people, situations, or places.
  - 2.   Choose positive, inspirational, uplifting things to focus your mind on.
  - 3.   Replace the negative mental input or it will drag you down.

C.   When forced to deal with problematic sources of information, limit your exposure as much as possible.

    1.   Use coping skills developed thus far to stay calm and think clearly.

    2.   Read the serenity prayer and practice it every day.

D.   Focus on feeling safe and in control without having to be angry.

E.   Realize that there are ways to get your needs met without having to be forceful or angry in every situation.

F.   Work to improve your attitudes.

    1.   Resentment and bitterness are hidden fuel for the fire of your anger.

    2.   Grudges keep you angry and do not add anything positive to your mental health.

    3.   Is that what you want?   Yes No

    4.   Critical and blaming attitudes can feel satisfying for a brief moment, but they keep you angry, nasty, bitter, and miserable in the long run.

VI.   Long-Term Outcomes

A.   What kind of person do you want to be in the long-term?_____

B.   Are you willing to do what it takes to become that way?   Yes No

C.   Every little choice changes you inwardly, making you either more angry and nasty or more mature, contented, and at peace.

D.   In what direction are you moving?_____

E.   Remember: You are either feeding your anger or contributing to your own mental health.

Chapter 32 – Anger: Aggression vs. Assertiveness

I. **Why We Need Assertiveness in PTSD**
    A.   Assertiveness is standing up for yourself at the appropriate level without becoming too passive or too aggressive.
    B.   In civilian life, assertive behavior is considered normal and healthy in most situations.
    C.   It is usually considered respectful and productive.
    D.   Most of the time, assertiveness is appropriate and helps us to get our needs met or get a task accomplished.
    E.   It is a balanced approach that helps us to get along with others.

II. **Some Coping Styles with Problems**
    A.   Passive Coping – a style characterized by trying to avoid offending people at all costs.
        1.   Keeping quiet.
        2.   Devaluing you own opinion.
        3.   Denying your needs and feelings.
        4.   Avoiding situations that might be uncomfortable; procrastinate; "drag your feet."
        5.   We rarely get what we really want or need with this approach.
        6.   People don't see you for who you really are.
        7.   Frequently "get walked on" or taken advantage of when they are too passive.
        8.   This approach often leads to feelings of resentment and bitterness.
    B.   Aggressive Coping – a style characterized by pushing people around to get what you want.
        1.   Expressive to the point of ignoring, hurting, humiliating, or putting others down.
        2.   Aggression might be direct (e.g., hitting someone) or indirect (e.g., manipulation).
        3.   Loudly demanding that you get your way; being obnoxious.
        4.   Punishing people who don't give you what you want immediately.
        5.   Aggressive people often do get what they want in the short term. This reinforces negative behavior.
        6.   However, the people you intimidate will often find some way to retaliate against you and "get you back later."
        7.   The aggressive person is never sure whether people are cooperative out of fear or love.

III.   Assertive Coping (a coping style characterized by expressing opinions, desires, and needs in a direct, open, and honest way)[33]
  A.   This style is based on the belief that people have the right to express their legitimate needs.
  B.   You can express how you feel, stand up for yourself, and set appropriate limits.
  C.   This can be done without violating the rights of other people.
  D.   Assertiveness allows you to work toward an agreeable outcome without anger or passivity.
  E.   It helps you be productive without having to blame others.
  F.   We can set limits without offending or turning other people off.
  G.   To be assertive, direct, clear, non-attacking communication is required.

IV.   Key Elements to an Assertive Response
  A.   Focus on the facts of the situation.
  B.   Avoid placing blame (it doesn't solve or fix anything).
  C.   State your response to (or feelings about) the situation in a matter-of-fact way.
  D.   Example: "When you _____, I feel _____ (about it).
  E.   Make a fair request. Be specific. Focus on only one thing at a time. (basically, say what you want in a matter-of-fact, non-blaming way.)
  F.   It is usually more realistic to expect people to change specific behaviors in response to your request, rather than their attitudes, values, or feelings.

V.   Some Specific Assertive Behaviors
  A.   Initiating Contact with Others – e.g., starting a conversation with someone.
    1.   Say "Hello" or "Hi."
    2.   "Good Morning."
  B.   Expressing Positive Feelings – e.g., telling someone that you like something about them.
    1.   Give sincere compliments.
    2.   Express satisfaction in yourself or others.
  C.   Accepting Compliments – e.g., thank someone for a compliment rather than denying it.
    1.   Say "Thank you" or "I appreciate that."
    2.   Stop denying or rejecting compliments or kind words from others.
  D.   Asking Questions – ask for more information if something is unclear.
    1.   "I'm not sure I'm clear on that."
    2.   "What did you mean by _____?"
    3.   "Could you tell me _____?"
    4.   "I'm sorry – I don't understand. Could you say that another way?"

E.   <u>Asking for Things/Favors</u> – requests should be reasonable, honest, and direct.
1.   "Would you please _____?"
2.   "I need _____. Would you help me with that?"

F.   <u>Expressing Opinions</u> – Agree or disagree with someone's opinion without putting them down.
1.   It's usually O.K. for people to disagree about things if they can disagree in an agreeable way.
2.   Sometimes we need to say "I guess we disagree about that" and then drop it.

G.   <u>Expressing Displeasure about Something</u>
1.   "When you _____, I feel _____ (about it)."
2.   "This (food, item, etc.) is not what I ordered."
3.   "This _____ is not what I expected."
4.   "This is not what I was wanting. Could we try again?"

H.   <u>Resisting Pressure</u> – Stand up for yourself without making excuses or always apologizing.
1.   "That won't fit my schedule."
2.   "I'll pass."
3.   "No thank you."
4.   "I choose not to _____."
5.   "I'm not comfortable with that."
6.   <u>Note:</u> With this one, you usually don't need to offer excuses or explain yourself.

I.   <u>Say "NO" to Unreasonable Requests or Demands</u>
1.   "I won't be able to do _____."
2.   "That won't work for me."
3.   "I'm not able to do that right now."
4.   "Maybe someone else could help you with that."

J.   <u>Take Criticism in a Non-defensive Way</u> – Evaluate what is said, and make up your own mind about it.
1.   Maybe they have a good point and maybe they don't.
2.   My worth as a person does not rest on their opinion.
3.   If I can learn something from them, that's great; if not, just move on.
4.   If they are off base, their opinion does not have to mess up my day.
5.   Possible responses:
    a.   "I'm sorry you feel that way."
    b.   "Thanks for your input."
    c.   "Thank you for the feedback."
    d.   "Interesting!"
    e.   "Oh!"
    f.   "Bless you!"

Chapter 33 – Letting Go of Anger: Approaches to Life

I.   **The Importance of Our Approach to Life**
    A.   An approach is a way of going about things in order to get a desired result.
    B.   It is a specific method for doing something.
    C.   The approach we take often determines success or failure in most endeavors.
    D.   What is your approach to life?
    E.   How do you go about getting your needs met? Reaching your goals?

II.   **Some Problematic (but common) Approaches to Life (circle all that apply to you)**
    A.   <u>Attack Mode</u> (the aggressive approach).
        1.   Get compliance by intimidation.
        2.   Try to control everybody and everything.
        3.   Think you can get everything you want by force.
        4.   Believe that negative consequences are never your fault.
    B.   <u>"I Know it All"</u> (the foolish approach).
        1.   My experience has taught me everything I could ever need to know.
        2.   Everyone else is stupid (they've not been through what I've been through).
        3.   "You can't tell me anything."
        4.   I can only relate to people who have had the same experiences as me.
        5.   Why don't people listen to me and all of my great wisdom?(at the same time, not applying it to your own life)
    C.   <u>Pleasure is King</u> (the hedonistic approach).
        1.   Avoid pain at all costs.
        2.   If it feels good right at this moment, then do it.(regardless of long-term consequences)
        3.   Put no limits on enjoyable things.
        4.   Feel disgusted and let down when things are no longer fun or you feel burned out.
        5.   Focus only on making yourself happy and on nothing else.
    D.   <u>Win at all Costs</u>
        1.   Focus exclusively on having power, money, and/or fame.
        2.   Do whatever it takes regardless of consequences.
        3.   Don't care about who you step on or hurt in the process.
        4.   "It's all about me!"
        5.   The only measure of success is "moving up" and having more.

E. Reaction Mode
    1. Base everything you do on emotional reasoning (not logic or common sense).
    2. Be irrational and unreasonable very often.
    3. Live in an out of control way.
    4. Most of your actions are a "knee jerk response" (i.e., reactions).
    5. React to situations in ways that do not connect to the reality of the situation.
    6. Feel fully justified living in the extremes of chaos (unstable).

F. The Hermit
    1. Avoid everything that you can.
    2. Isolate yourself from everything and everybody.
    3. Stay too busy to ever interact with another person in a meaningful way.
    4. Live in a cycle of perpetual fear (but never admit that you are afraid of anything).
    5. Misinterpret others' behavior as attacking and intrusive.

G. Live in a Fantasy World
    1. Live out of touch with reality.
    2. Think: "It's not real if I don't think about it."
    3. Place your hopes on things that are extremely unlikely.
    4. Convince yourself of things that are not true, and then be upset when they don't work out.

III. **A Healthier Way → Mindfulness**[37,38,39]
    A. Some approaches to life are healthier than others.
    B. With practice, we can begin to live in a way that is more productive and fulfilling.
    C. Characteristics of better living through mindfulness.
        1. Be intentional in your actions.
            a. Not impulsive.
            b. Not lackadaisical.
            c. This way, you become more in control of your life.
        2. Try to learn and understand as much as you can.
            a. Be informed about things you are dealing with.
            b. Knowledge is power if you use it to cope better.
        3. Make good, intelligent choices.
            a. Take your time.
            b. Think things through.
        4. Try to cooperate with people if at all possible.
        5. Listen to wise people and learn.
            a. Nobody knows it all.
            b. Be willing to learn something new or consider a new perspective.

6. Enjoy good pleasures in moderation.
7. Find humor in real life situations; Develop your sense of humor.
8. Choose your battles.
   a. Some things are worth a fight, and some things are not.
   b. If it's not critical, then let it go!
9. Practice responding, not reacting.
   a. Remain in control of yourself.
   b. Choose how to handle a situation.
   c. Don't let the other person "push your buttons."
10. Strive to be calm and relaxed when possible.
11. Practice being thoughtful, not impulsive.
12. Be conscientious (i.e., do what you say you will do; fulfill obligations).
13. Practice healthy flexibility (roll with the punches).
14. Try to be as rational and intelligent as you can; use "common sense."
15. If in doubt, wait → get input from someone who is wise and/or experienced.
16. Focus on the "big picture" when feeling frustrated.
    a. Take your time.
    b. Re-think things.
    c. Try again later.

Chapter 34– Masked Anger

I. **Identify the Type of Anger Pattern You Have**[33,34]

 A. Anger can be expressed in many different ways.

 B. To gain control over our anger, it is crucial to recognize our own anger patterns.

 C. It is difficult to cope when you don't know what you're dealing with or how it is affecting you.

 D. If anger has been a problem in your life, you will either get it under control or it will dominate your life.

II. **Masked Anger**[34]

 A. How masked anger works:

  1. A person does not allow him/herself to have feelings of anger. (This is doomed to fail → the reality is that everyone gets angry sometimes.)

  2. Anger is seen as a terrible thing.

  3. The person believes it makes them a bad person.

  4. Therefore, anger is hidden, avoided, distorted, expressed indirectly or used to frustrate other people.

  5. People with masked anger don't recognize their own true feelings and are often in denial.

  6. With the masked anger pattern, you don't get what you want and wind up feeling frustrated much of the time.

 B. See if any of the following patterns describe your experiences of anger.

  1. <u>Anger Avoidance</u>[34]

   a. Anger is frightening.

   b. Try not to become angry if at all possible.

   c. Scared of losing control if I get angry.

   d. Think "It's bad to be angry; I'm a good person because I don't get angry."

   e. Avoiding all anger makes me feel safe and calm.

   f. Unable to be assertive (either totally passive or overly aggressive most of the time).

   g. Feel guilty if you get angry or assert yourself.

  2. <u>Sneaky Anger</u>[34]

   a. Try not to let anyone know you are angry.

   b. Feel in control by intentionally frustrating other people.

   c. Anger comes out in passive-aggressive ways.

   d. Quickly become bored → use anger to get some excitement going!

e.   Have frustrating, unsatisfying relationships most of the time.

f.   Wind up using anger as a tool, but try to hide it.

3. Paranoid Anger[34]

a.   Always feel threatened by others (when in fact nobody is after you).

b.   See aggression and danger everywhere you look.

c.   Spend most of your time jealously guarding what you think is yours.

d.   Anger is disguised as self-protection (which is a rationalization).

e.   Confusion between your own feelings and those of others can lead to poor judgment.

f.   Find yourself always on the defensive and seeing threats when none are really there.

III.   Healthy Anger[1,2,33,34]

A.   Anger is a normal feeling that needs to be managed and expressed appropriately like other Feelings.

B.   Indications of Healthy (normal) Anger

1.   Anger is viewed as a natural, normal part of life.

2.   Anger is a signal that there is a real problem that needs to be dealt with (i.e., a warning sign).

3.   Behaviors motivated by anger are chosen carefully.

4.   You don't automatically get angry just because you can.

5.   Anger is expressed in a controlled (planned) way so that you don't get out of control.

6.   Feelings of anger are expressed in a clear way so others can understand.

7.   The real goal is to solve problems, not just to express anger or feel powerful.

8.   Anger is temporary – let it go once the issue is resolved.

C.   Do I want to be angry all the time?

D.   How do I want to manage my anger?

E.   Am I willing to become more healthy with regard to my anger?

F.   What will I do to deal with my anger appropriately?

G.   Once the issues are resolved → let it go!

1.   This is easier said than done, but is possible with time and practice.

2.   We need to actively take a different perspective to tolerate those things we don't like.

H.   We must choose to not let anger hold us back, beat us down, or keep us trapped.

I.   When anger is managed well, it no longer controls our life.

Chapter 35– Explosive! Anger

I. **Identifying Explosive! Anger**[34]
   A.   The person with explosive anger is like a time-bomb!
   B.   People around this person often feel like they are "walking on egg shells."
   C.   The angry outburst comes on fast and often with little to no warning (this person is possibly very dangerous).
   D.   People who don't know the person very well are often surprised.
   E.   Others who do know the person frequently think, "When will be the next time they have an outburst?"
   F.   The results of explosive anger can be negative and severe if we don't identify it as a problem and learn to cope in more effective ways.

II. **How Explosive! Anger Works**
   A.   People with explosive anger know they are angry, and they want to make sure everyone else knows it too.
   B.   The anger is either triggered by something or used to get what they want.
   C.   The person with explosive anger vents their own anger, and then they are "over it."
   D.   They don't understand how other people can "stay upset" for so long.

III. **Explosive! Anger (see if any of the following describe you or your behavior)**
   A.   <u>Sudden (explosive) Anger</u>[34]
      1.   Fly into a rage at the smallest upsetting event.
      2.   Release all negative, intense feelings at once.
      3.   Major problem → you don't see warning signs of anger; just suddenly lose control.
      4.   This person can be extremely dangerous to themselves or others with little or no warning.
   B.   <u>Shame-Based Anger</u>[34]
      1.   The slightest criticism creates feelings of shame and then anger.
      2.   Most of the time you feel unlovable, worthless, and "not good enough".
      3.   Try to get rid of shameful feelings by blaming, criticizing, or ridiculing.
      4.   Anger helps you get revenge at those people who "made you feel bad."
      5.   Wind up attacking people you love.
      6.   Expressing anger creates even worse feelings about yourself in the long run, but you are not sure how else to get rid of the shame.

C.   Deliberate Anger[34]
    1.   Anger is a planned thing (done in a calculating way).
    2.   Enjoy controlling people through anger, violence, threatening, or overpowering.
    3.   You are really looking to exert power and control (and not just vent angry feelings).
    4.   Anger is used as a tool to get what you want.
    5.   This approach eventually breaks down and can backfire when people "finally get enough" and retaliate.
    6.   Eventually, you will come across someone who is bigger, meaner, and nastier than you, and it won't be pretty.

D.   Addictive Anger[34]
    1.   "The only time I feel excited is when I'm angry."
    2.   Rageaholic → look forward to the "rush" or excitement of being angry.
    3.   Anger makes you feel alive and full of energy.
    4.   Become dependent upon anger as the only way to feel good.
    5.   Feel bored the rest of the time.
    6.   The anger winds up being used like a drug to make you feel better.

IV.   Regaining Self-Control
A.   First, realize the potential danger involved in explosive anger.
B.   Start looking for warning signs or cues that you might be getting angry .
C.   Don't be taken by surprise like in the past.
D.   Avoid trigger situations if at all possible.
E.   Practice expressing anger in degrees of intensity (instead of all-or-nothing).
F.   If long-standing feelings of shame are an issue.
    1.   Work through this with a qualified therapist.
    2.   Accept that expressing anger appropriately is an OK thing to do.
    3.   Learn other more healthy ways to deal with feelings of shame.
G.   If deliberate anger is a pattern, look for more appropriate ways of getting what you want.
    1.   Learn assertiveness skills.
    2.   Look back and count the costs of your deliberate anger.
H.   For the anger addict, develop new and more healthy ways to have excitement in your life.
    1.   You will probably need to rework some relationships.
    2.   Need to re-examine the use of power and control in your life.
    3.   Make a list of things you can enjoy without having to be angry.
I.   Work very hard to maintain self-control and not "lose it."
    1.   Remember: Self-control is highly valuable.
    2.   "Losing it" shows a lack of control.

J.   Consider the consequences of explosive anger.
       1.   Results can be severe.
       2.   It may result in outcomes that cannot be reversed.

Chapter 36– Chronic Anger

I. **The Nature of the Problem**[1,33,34]
  A. For some people, anger has become a chronic problem (ongoing; long-lasting).
  B. The anger has gone on for years.
  C. You might have held a grudge for a few decades.
  D. Other people might describe you as an angry person.
  E. See if any of the following three patterns of chronic anger are similar to your own experiences.

II. **Chronic Anger Patterns**
  A. <u>Habitual Anger</u>[34]
    1. Wake up irritable and go through most days looking for something to be angry about.
    2. You have been angry for so long, it has become a daily habit.
    3. Look for the worst in everyone and everything.
    4. The anger has become a part of your personality.
    5. This pattern sets you up to have frequent arguments.
    6. Life feels lousy, dim, and/or dreary, but is very predictable.
  B. <u>Moral Anger</u>[34] (the unhealthy type)
    1. Always looking for someone who "breaks the rules" so you can point it out and condemn them.
    2. Always feel outraged at "all those bad people" out there.
    3. You feel that your anger is 100% justified because "they're breaking the rules and doing wrong."
    4. Feel superior to everyone else (or at least try to).
    5. Not willing to compromise on matters of preference.
    6. You have set yourself up as the ultimate authority and claimed the right to judge everyone else.
  C. <u>Hatred</u>[34]
    1. Comes from anger that has built up, festered, and hardened.
    2. Anger → resentment → "how can I punish them?"
    3. Always believe you are "just an innocent victim."
    4. Create a world of enemies (in your mind) and attack them vigorously (with words or actions).
    5. Ultimately feel bitter and frustrated.

III.   **Overcoming Chronic Anger**
    A.   Do I really want to be irritable and angry most all of the time?
    B.   Do I like being this way?
    C.   Do I know how to be any other way?
    D.   Am I willing to develop a more optimistic outlook?
    E.   What am I basing my moral anger on?
        1.   Is this really justified?
        2.   Am I perfect in all regards?
    F.   Am I just as guilty as the people I condemn, but unwilling to look honestly at myself?
    G.   Can I maintain my beliefs without having to "come down hard" on everyone else?
    H.   What's the worst that would happen if I compromise on issues that are not critical?
    I.   Is my hatred making me a better person?
    J.   By giving up my resentments, will I be any worse off?
    K.   Is my hatred making things better or worse?
    L.   Who suffers the most from my hatred? → is that what I really want?
    M.   What will I do to move toward having a <u>more healthy</u> anger?

IV.   **Coping Thoughts and Behaviors**[33,34]
    A.   <u>"Cool Thoughts"</u>
        1.   These are reminders to use relaxation skills.
        2.   These thoughts and actions help us to stay calm.
        3.   In time, we can develop new habits that do not provoke anger.
    B.   <u>Problem-Solving Thoughts</u>
        1.   These are thoughts that identify good solutions without using anger.
        2.   <u>Remember</u>: the anger is a warning signal to look for a good solution.
        3.   Usually there is a good solution to most problems if we look hard enough and think clearly about the situation.
    C.   <u>Escape Routes</u>
        1.   These thoughts remind us that it is better to avoid a problem if possible.
        2.   Just walk away.
        3.   Remove yourself from the situation before it escalates.
        4.   It is better to leave a situation than to lose control or do some kind of permanent damage.

D.   <u>Confident Thoughts</u>
   1.   Remind yourself that you do have the ability to cope.
   2.   No matter the situation, your coping skills are continuing to improve.
   3.   Tell yourself that you have (mental) tools available for dealing with tough situations.

E.   <u>Getting Along</u>
   1.   To get along better with others, express your needs in a non-attacking way.
   2.   If you disagree, do it in an agreeable way.
      a.   Let the other person have their own opinion.
      b.   You won't convince them of something by arguing.
   3.   Describe the problem without blaming or attacking the other person.
   4.   Try very hard to understand the other person's point of view.

F.   In time we can develop more healthy, long term habits and live well without resorting to anger.

Chapter 37– Destructive Behaviors

I. **Problematic Attempts at Coping**[33]

   A.   Many destructive behaviors are an attempt to find relief from emotional pain.

      1.   Over time, symptoms can wear you down.

      2.   It "gets old" living this way.

      3.   "Get sick and tired of being sick and tired."

      4.   Ongoing frustrations can lead to inappropriate behavior if we don't cope with our stress effectively and appropriately.

   B.   What do you do when you don't know what else to do?

   C.   <u>Self-Mutilation</u>[1] – harming yourself through cutting, burning, hitting, or otherwise trying to injure your physical body.

      1.   These behaviors express pain that cannot be verbalized.

      2.   It converts emotional pain into physical pain (which many people say is somewhat easier to bear).

      3.   It can sometimes relieve pain.

      4.   The pain is a way to feel alive when you feel "dead inside."

      5.   It provides a feeling of power and control over the pain.

      6.   It might be an attempt to complete the unfinished past – "finish the job."

      7.   It is used to bring yourself back to reality when "spacing out."

      8.   Some people are trying to punish themselves or reduce (survival) guilt.

      9.   Potential consequences: shame, guilt, physical scarring, loss of intimate relationships.

   D.   <u>Destruction of Property</u>[33]

      1.   Anger and rage can lead to destructive acts.

      2.   While anger is intended to help you feel more in control, destruction of property usually just causes more problems.

      3.   Destroying property can also cost you financially.

      4.   What has this type of behavior cost you?

      5.   Sometime you might do something that can't be reversed or fixed.

      6.   Potential consequences: legal problems, jail time, fines, financial cost to replace property.

   E.   <u>Self-Blame</u>[1,40] – in PTSD, this is usually an attempt to convince ourselves that we had more control in the traumatic situation than we really did.

      1.   This is a attempt to "fix the past" in our mind.

      2.   If you feel worthless or unworthy, punishing yourself won't fix the problem.

      3.   This type of destructive behavior is internal (called beating up on yourself).

4.   It can be just as harmful to our (mental) health as external actions.

5.   Even if you were helpless in a situation in the past, remember that you did survive it and now have a chance to make your life better.

6.   Potential consequences: feel perpetually bad about yourself, continued deepening depression.

F.   <u>Examples of Other Destructive Behaviors</u>

    1.   Out of control eating.

    2.   Frequent "accidents."

    3.   Gambling.

    4.   Addictive behavior; Alcohol or drug use.

    5.   Reckless sexual behavior; prostitution.

    6.   Compulsive shopping; spending money you don't have.

    7.   Dangerous behaviors involving driving.

    8.   Extreme excitement-seeking behavior.

    9.   Other: _____

G.   What consequences have you experienced directly from your own destructive behaviors?

II.   Healthy Alternatives[1,2,40]

A.   When frustrated or angry, we need to express our anger in appropriate ways.

    1.   Rules for expressing anger.

        a.   It does not hurt me.

        b.   It does not hurt other people.

        c.   It does not destroy valuable property.

    2.   Examples:

        a.   Do some physical exertion to get your anger out (Note: not toward other people).

        b.   Do some walking or exercise (without straining or hurting yourself).

        c.   Sit inside your car or truck with the windows up and yell very loudly (please don't drive while doing this one!).

        d.   Squeeze a gripper (for hand strength).

        e.   Put a pillow over your mouth and scream.

B.   Decide for yourself.

    1.   "No matter how angry I get, I will control myself."

    2.   "I will express my anger appropriately."

C.   If you feel suicidal, reach out to those who can help.

    1.   Be willing to accept help.

    2.   Eventually, everyone needs help with something.

D.   Find purpose and meaning in your life – have a good reason for living.

E.   Actively work on your spiritual and religious beliefs.[37]

F.   Use your support system.

1. Have the names and phone numbers of 3 people you can call and talk to when feeling suicidal or needing encouragement.
2. Come to group therapy as often as possible.
3. Call your therapist, clergy, or trusted friend.

G. Ask for some individual therapy to get you through a rough time or crisis.

H. Focus on your family members and the fact that they need you.

I. Consider your contributions to the therapy group; your community; your family; your work; your church, temple, synagogue, etc., or other group where you are active. [14]

J. Focus on being a survivor and eliminate victim thoughts and behavior.

K. Commit to being productive, not destructive.

L. What type of person do you really want to be?

Chapter 38– The Costs of Anger

I. **Background**
    A.   Expressions of anger are usually motivated at first by feeling hurt and frustrated, and then trying to get back in control.
    B.   Other things that can trigger or motivate anger include feelings of guilt, shame, loss, helplessness, anxiety, emptiness, hunger, and feeling unworthy.
    C.   While there are benefits to anger (payoffs), there are also costs.

II. **Anger Payoffs**[33]
    A.   Anger has some benefits or people would not engage in angry behavior so often.
    B.   The rewards of anger can be very satisfying in the short term.
    C.   See if you have experienced any of the following anger payoffs.
        1.   Anger can reduce stress immediately → feel instantly relaxed or relieved.
        2.   Anger gets you what you want.
            a.   It is reinforcing (rewarding).
            b.   This increases the chances that you will act this way again in a similar situation in the future.
        3.   Anger sometimes hides emotional pain → this provides short-term relief, but the feelings usually come back later.
        4.   Anger gets you attention, but eventually may turn people off to where they won't listen to you at all.
        5.   Anger can be used to get revenge or punish someone.
            a.   This can feel good immediately.
            b.   However, it usually creates resentments and enemies in the long run.
        6.   Anger can motivate us to take action when it is needed (which is a valid survival mechanism).
        7.   Anger can be used to motivate or change the behavior of others.

III. **Costs of Anger**[33]
    A.   <u>Physical Costs</u>
        1.   Perpetual anger can cause high blood pressure.
        2.   It increases the chances of cardiovascular disease, heart attacks, and other illnesses.
        3.   Anger and hostility can potentially damage your heart and arteries.
        4.   It can possibly lead to an early death.
    B.   <u>Relationship Costs</u>

1.   Being an angry person can push friends and family away.
2.   People avoid you.
3.   You might wind up feeling lonely, isolated, and rejected as a result.
4.   Family conflicts.
   a.   Divorce.
   b.   Distant or non-existent relationships with your children.
5.   Loss of intimate relationships.
6.   Anger can make you into the kind of person that is hard to be around.

C.   Other Costs
1.   Physical fights.
2.   Someone finally retaliates and he's bigger and meaner than you.
3.   Physical injury or somehow getting hurt.
4.   Legal problems.
5.   Financial costs (things got broken, tickets, fines, repairs, court costs, etc.).
6.   Loss of your freedom.
7.   Anger turned me into the kind of person I really don't want to be.
8.   Has it taken you down certain paths you would rather have avoided?

IV. Conclusion

A.   What has anger cost you in your life?

_____

_____   _____

_____   _____

_____   _____

_____   _____

B.   Was it worth it?
C.   Do the costs of your anger outweigh the benefits?
D.   Is it possible to get the things you want and need without having to use anger?

V. Productive Thoughts for Dealing with Anger

A.   I can handle this.
B.   Getting upset won't help here.
C.   I'm in control as long as I stay calm.
D.   I refuse to let them push my buttons.
E.   I will stay calm.
F.   Anger won't solve anything here.
G.   They can all look foolish – I'll stay calm.

H.   This is just a small hassle – not a catastrophe.

I.   If they want me to get angry, they can just be disappointed.

J.   I choose to relax and stay in control.

K.   I will figure out my problems → I don't have to be reactive.

L.   I choose more acceptable costs to my behavior.

Section V: Stress Management

Patients with PTSD have said . . .

**"In PTSD, what gets shaken is your sense of safety and security.
You walk around in fear all of the time and don't even know it."**

**"The fear . . . I just can't have it controlling me anymore . . .
it was destroying me."**

"I didn't realize that I was actually afraid all these years . . . but I was."

**"You overreact to every little thing, and tell yourself that it's a necessary
and appropriate reaction, but really it's not."**

Chapter 39 – What Is Stress?

I.   **Type of Stress**[41,42,43]

    A.   <u>Physical Stress</u> – any specific situation or event that threatens the health of the body or has an undesirable effect on its functioning.

    B.   <u>Psychological Stress</u> – anything that challenges or interferes with a person's ability to think, make decisions, or function in life.

    C.   Different things are stressful to different people (e.g., people, places, situations).

II.   **How Do I Know when I Am Under Stress?** [41]

    A.   <u>The Body Reacts</u>

        1.   Heart rate speeds up.

        2.   Sweating; hands shaking (or the whole body).

        3.   Feel nervous or tense; "butterflies in the stomach."

        4.   Dry mouth.

        5.   Have to urinate frequently or might have diarrhea.

    B.   <u>Performance Might be Impaired</u>

        1.   Difficulty thinking or making decisions; Poor judgment.

        2.   Difficulty controlling your hands or other body movements.

        3.   Not able to perform familiar tasks as well as usual.

    C.   <u>Having Frequent Illness</u>

        1.   Changes in appetite; Long-term tiredness or fatigue.

        2.   Having frequent colds or infections; Can't seem to get over an illness.

        3.   Persistent physical problems such as headaches, asthma, stomach problems, back pain, skin break outs, sexual problems.

III.   **It is important to identify the specific things that I personally find stressful.**

    A.   <u>Stressful things in my life are:</u>

_____   _____

_____   _____

_____   _____

_____   _____

IV.   **What Are the Long-Term Effects of Stress?**[41]
    A.   Worry, confusion.
    B.   Feeling out of control.
    C.   Feeling overwhelmed → eventually hopeless and feel like giving up.
    D.   Changes in mood or mental state.
        1.   Depressed.
        2.   Anxious.
        3.   Frustrated.
        4.   Hostile.
        5.   Feel Helpless.
        6.   Impatient.
        7.   Frequently irritable.
    E.   Trouble Sleeping.
        1.   Hard to fall asleep.
        2.   Can't seem to stay asleep.
        3.   Wake up too early in the morning.
        4.   Sleep is restless or wake up tired.
    F.   Using more alcohol or smoking more than usual.
    G.   Life starts feeling out of control and our ability to function each day declines.

V.   **Some Stress Management Strategies**[42,43] **(to improve coping and your benefit from therapy)**
    A.   Maximize your best time of day.
        1.   Be productive during your good time of day.
        2.   Rest during your "down time."
        3.   Use "up time" and "down time" to your advantage.
    B.   Be prepared for things as much as possible (without obsessing) → plan ahead.
    C.   Stop living in denial.
        1.   Get in touch with reality.
        2.   Become willing to accept the realities of what has happened.
        3.   What is a good solution to the things you are encountering?
    D.   Stop avoiding → deal with real problems in a mature and productive way.
    E.   Keep a notebook of ideas.
        1.   Write down your ideas about things.
        2.   Make a list of questions.
        3.   Write out lists or diagrams that help you figure things out and make sense of your experiences.

F.   Keep on learning (keep your mind active).
    1.   Read at least 3 pages every day.
    2.   That's over 1,000 pages each year.

G.   Seek the wisdom of people who are wise and/or experienced.
    1.   Choose carefully where you get instruction and advice.
    2.   Don't trust just anyone, even if they appear to have "credentials."

H.   Ask yourself questions that are helpful.
    1.   "What is the real issue here?"
    2.   "What are some reasonable solutions to this?"
    3.   "How real is this?"
    4.   "Am I overreacting here?"
    5.   "How would (a wise person) handle this?"
    6.   "What do I really want in this situation?"
    7.   "What would be a reasonable outcome?"

I.   Stop over reacting.
    1.   Don't be reactive → instead, use your brains.
    2.   Get into the habit of thinking your way through situations.
    3.   If you can think your way through a situation, you can usually handle it.
    4.   Be solution focused in your actions.

J.   Develop your self-awareness.
    1.   Begin monitoring your own thoughts and actions on a regular basis → keep tabs on yourself.
    2.   With practice, you gain greater control over your ability to manage stressful situations.
    3.   As self-awareness increases, the benefits of therapy begin to "add up."

Chapter 40 – Stress Management Techniques

I.   Stress – Good or Bad?[41]

   A.   Stress is a very natural part of life.

   B.   With absolutely zero stress, there would be no life at all.

   C.   Positive stress (eustress – pronounced "you-stress") motivates us to accomplish tasks and be productive.

   D.   However, when the stress lasts too long and starts wearing us down it becomes "distress" and is harmful.

   E.   The difference is whether we view the stressful event as manageable or not.

   F.   Remember: Positive things in life are stressful too, and can wear us down if we don't cope effectively.

II.   Types of Stress[42,43]

   A.   Minor Changes – daily hassles; small, unexpected events; minor disagreements; delays.

   B.   Major Changes – any positive or negative change that affects your life in a big way (e.g., job promotion, marriage/divorce, moving, death of someone close).

   C.   Stress Overload – circumstances feel unmanageable; feel overwhelmed; don't know how to cope; don't know what to do; feel helpless; think about "just giving up."

III.   We Need to Cope with Stressful Situations in Realistic and Productive Ways

   A.   Strong and decisive actions are needed in extreme situations.

   B.   However, controlled (calm) actions are better for routine, daily events.

   C.   The goal is not to eliminate stress, but learn how to manage it and use it to our benefit.

   D.   We need to find the optimal stress level that motivates and helps us, but does not overwhelm us or wear us down.

IV.   Are You a Responder or an Over-reactor?

		Responder	Over-Reactor
A.	Driving in rush hour	_____	_____
B.	Arriving at the last minute	_____	_____
C.	Misplacing something	_____	_____
D.	Dealing with incompetence	_____	_____
E.	Waiting in line	_____	_____
F.	Stresses I handle well:	_____	
G.	Stresses that are overwhelming:	_____	

V.   Some Stress Management Strategies[42,43]

    A.   <u>Practice Relaxing</u>

        1.   Take small breaks.

        2.   Practice deep breathing exercises for at least 5 minutes 2X each day.

        3.   Break up your day with activity mixed with brief periods of rest.

        4.   We usually perform at our best when our stress is at a moderate level.

    B.   <u>Practice Self-Acceptance</u>

        1.   If something can't be changed, don't dwell on it.

            a.   Distract yourself.

            b.   Try to focus on something else.

        2.   Accept yourself as a valuable person; stop insisting on perfection.

        3.   If you act responsibly and are confident in yourself, you will usually cope better with stressful events.

    C.   <u>Talk Rationally to Yourself</u> (focus your mind)

        1.   What is the reality of this situation?

        2.   "Is this my problem or their problem?"

        3.   What is the best way to handle this?

        4.   Talk to yourself silently in your mind to stay focused and cope.

    D.   <u>Get Organized</u>

        1.   Make a plan for each day.

        2.   Make and use a list for each day or each week.

        3.   Keep your home and work space generally in order.

        4.   Get a large calendar and write down important appointments or events.

    E.   <u>Exercise</u>

        1.   If you have any significant health concerns, check with your physician before starting an exercise program.

        2.   Get your frustrations out through exercise.

        3.   Start with walking for 30 minutes 3X each week if it is realistic.

        4.   Maybe try aerobics, jogging, dancing, swimming, hiking, cycling, weight lifting, etc.

        5.   Make the activity you choose fit your interests, body type, and fitness level.

    F.   <u>Reduce Time Urgency</u>

        1.   Slow down and allow yourself time for the things you need to do.

        2.   Take a few things slower on purpose.

            a.   Examples: driving, eating.

            b.   Check it out → do you still get just as much done?

        3.   Change your approach from "racing" to "pacing."[23]

        4.   Break tasks into small units and work on one at a time – focus on

only one part of a problem or task at a time.

G. Take a Less Aggressive Approach
   1. Not every situation in life requires a competitive or aggressive approach.
   2. Don't raise your voice when it's not called for.
   3. Give up control when it's not critical; stop blaming and putting others down.
   4. Begin to realize that you can usually get what you need without having to attack other people.

H. Spend Some Quiet Time Each Day[37,38,39]
   1. Practice sitting in silence for 5 to 10 minutes each day.
      a. Do the Deep Breathing Relaxation Exercise.
      b. Practice the Meditation Exercise.
   2. Enjoy a good hobby a little each day.
   3. Remember: Rest time is just as important as work time.

I. Develop Healthy Habits
   1. Eat a balanced diet.
      (lean meat, fruits, and vegetables; minimize fats and carbohydrates)
   2. Avoid unnecessary nonprescription drugs; minimize alcohol use.
   3. Limit your caffeine and sugar intake.
   4. Stop smoking.

J. Make Good Friends and Talk With Them Frequently
   1. Find people who accept you for the person you are.
   2. Share your thoughts and feelings about a wide range of topics.
   3. Have at least some conversation with another person every single day.

Chapter 41 – More Stress Management Techniques

I. **We Need Several Stress Management Strategies**[41,42,43]

    A.   When it comes to stress management, not every strategy works for every person.

    B.   It often helps to try many different strategies.

        1.   If it works → keep doing it.

        2.   If it doesn't work → try something else.

        3.   If something is no longer effective (stopped working) → something else.

    C.   Remember: We need several tools at our disposal.

    D.   "If the only tool you have is a hammer, you tend to see every problem as a nail." -Abraham Maslow

    E.   In PTSD, if your hammer didn't work, you usually just get a bigger hammer!

II. **Some More Specific Stress Management Strategies**[41]

    A.   <u>Become aware of your stress and your reactions to it.</u>

        1.   Look for cues and notice when you start feeling stressed.

        2.   Identify specific people, places, events, situations, etc. that are stressful.

        3.   What specific ways do you react to stress?

        4.   What have been your typical ways of coping?

        5.   When we are aware of stress, we are then in a position to do something about it (i.e., manage it).

    B.   <u>Identify what things you can change.</u>

        1.   Some stresses can be avoided, others cannot.

        2.   Limit your exposure to stressful situations if possible.

        3.   If it is within your power, then change it.

        4.   Alter the situation if you reasonable can.

        5.   If it is beyond your control, then let it go, focus on something else, and move forward.

    C.   <u>Reduce the intensity of your reactions.</u>

        1.   Do I typically exaggerate or overreact?

        2.   Am I trying to please everyone? (which is not possible)

        3.   Just how critical is this situation?   *Low   Medium   High*

        4.   Work to cope with the stress rather than staying overwhelmed.

        5.   Try to gain some perspective on the situation?

            a.   Stop focusing on the negatives and the "what-ifs."

            b.   Refocus on a good solution.

D.   Gain control over your physical reactions.
   1.   Control your breathing (use slow, steady breaths).
   2.   Choose one thing and focus your mind on it.
      a.   Example: Focus on a spot on the wall.
      b.   Stay focused on this one thing.
      c.   Keep doing Deep Breathing until you are back in control.
   3.   Use medications appropriately to manage anger or anxiety (as pre-scribed).
   4.   Go to your safe place.

E.   Build up your physical reserves.
   1.   Do aerobic, fitness, or strength training exercises 3 to 5 times each week. (Start with walking and build up.)
   2.   Eat 3 to 5 small, balanced meals each day; maintain your ideal body weight.
   3.   Avoid nicotine, excessive caffeine, excessive alcohol, and/or stimulants.
   4.   Get enough sleep if at all possible.
   5.   Maintain a fairly consistent schedule.
   6.   Remember: Having some reserves to draw upon during a stressful time can help get you through some tough times or unexpected events.

F.   Maintain your emotional reserves
   1.   Enjoy healthy friendships.
   2.   Expect to have some frustrations, failures, set-backs, sorrows, and successes.
   3.   Be kind and compassionate toward yourself and others.
   4.   Recall how you have dealt with some emotionally difficult times in the past and use those healthy strategies now.

III.   Other Stress-Relieving Strategies

A.   Plan your time well → give yourself enough time to do what you need to do.
B.   Take time out to get perspective a few times each day.
C.   Develop your sense of humor → try to find some humor every day.
D.   Give and receive love.
E.   Have hobbies and enjoy them regularly.
F.   Try new things.
G.   Get your feelings out through talking or writing.
H.   Schedule some things that you enjoy each week.
I.   Get a massage.
J.   Prepare yourself for times that you will need to be patient and wait.
K.   Accept help when you need it.

L.   Create a "safe zone" in your home where you can feel comfortable and relaxed.

M.   Change your perspective → try to see a different viewpoint.

N.   Count your blessings → write in a thankfulness journal each day (or week).

O.   Get rid of clutter around your home → eliminate things you'll never use again.

P.   Give yourself some extra time when driving so you won't feel rushed.

Q.   Wear clothing that is appropriate but comfortable.

R.   Write yourself notes: Most people cannot remember everything.

S.   Say "No" when you need to → don't take on everything.

T.   Develop your patience and persistence → stick with the things that are important and give yourself enough time.

U.   Keep developing your coping skills.

V.   Compensate for your weaknesses.

IV.   Benefits

A.   Some simple preparation for dealing with stress can pay great dividends.

B.   By working a little each day on at least one of the above strategies, we will become more equipped to deal with those things we encounter throughout life.

C.   More coping skills provide us more "tools" to use in managing the daily stresses we encounter.

Chapter 42 – Self-Care: Listening to Your Body

I. **The Need for Physical Self-Care** [1,41]
    A.   Most things need some maintenance to function well on a regular basis.
        1.   If you never provide any maintenance for your car, it won't last very long or run very well.
        2.   The same is true of our physical body.
        3.   However, many individuals with PTSD do very little in the area of self-care.
        4.   It is also common for many people to abuse their bodies with drugs, workaholism, and dangerous activities.
        5.   Neglecting one's own health is common.
    B.   We need to work toward having balance in life.
        1.   Most things work best when all the parts are in balance.
            a.   care for self $\rightarrow$ care for others
            b.   activity $\rightarrow$ rest
            c.   productivity $\rightarrow$ recreation (or rest)
        2.   How much balance do you have in these areas of your life?

II. **Reasons for Lack of Self-Care in PTSD** [1,40]
    A.   Unaware that there is a problem or need – "There's nothing wrong with me."
    B.   Denial – refusing to acknowledge that there is a problem or need.
    C.   Survivor guilt – "I don't deserve to be healthy."
    D.   Low self-esteem – Not valuing yourself as a person; "I'm not worth it."
    E.   Refusing – "I don't want to take care of my health"; "I just won't do it."

III. **Possible Problem Areas in Physical Health Related to PTSD** [1,2,42,43,44]
    A.   Nutrition
        1.   Many people with PTSD don't feel hungry very often due to an overactive sympathetic nervous system. [41]
        2.   Many individuals eat one meal per day (or less).
        3.   Over use of alcohol or an insufficient diet can leave a person malnourished.
        4.   Remember: It is possible to take in a large number of calories and be malnourished at the same time.
    B.   Rest
        1.   The body needs rest to heal and repair itself.
        2.   Nightmares and a lack of sleep can wear us down physically.
        3.   Getting better requires a focus on learning to relax and making "rest" a priority.

C.   <u>Recreation</u> – the ability to play and have fun without worry.
   1.   With PTSD we usually don't feel safe most of the time.
   2.   It can be very difficult to relax enough to play and have a good time.
   3.   We need to find a place that's safe enough to let down our guard and enjoy some activities.

D.   <u>Medical Problems</u> – chronic stress often leads to medical problems.[44]
   1.   Ulcers; stomach problems; headaches, backaches.
   2.   Heart or circulation problems; heart attack; arteriosclerosis.
   3.   Slow healing of physical injury.
   4.   Colds; infections; suppressed immune system.
   5.   Are you willing to start taking better care of your health to help with the PTSD recovery process?

IV.   We Need to Strive for the "Range of Healthy Functioning" in which We Function Best

A.   In many things, a normal "range" is considered an appropriate goal rather than a single point or measurement.
   1.   Example: <u>Blood pressure</u>
   2.   120 / 80 is considered the ideal.
   3.   Readings within a certain range above or below this are NOT considered abnormal or unhealthy.

B.   There is also a general middle range that is considered "normal" when dealing with issues of mental health.
   1.   Example: <u>Mood</u>
   2.   Some days we feel a little better or more happy, and other days we feel a little worse.
   3.   This is normal.
   4.   Feelings in this general middle range can be a useful goal in measuring how we are coping.
   5.   Nobody feels totally happy all of the time.
   6.   Be aware that our mood can often be related to our physical health.

V.   Getting Better

A.   To get better, we need to begin by changing our attitudes toward ourselves.
   1.   Old attitude = "I'm not worth it."
   2.   New attitude = "I am valuable"; "I am worth taking care of."
   3.   New behavior = begin doing things that are necessary to take care of yourself.

B.   New self-care behaviors
       1.   Get medical care for your ailments.
       2.   Eat a balanced diet (make this a priority).
       3.   Take medications exactly as prescribed.
       4.   Get the best sleep you possibly can; take some time to rest every day.
       5.   Work your mind and body each day; rest your mind and body each day.
       6.   Stop doing things that put unnecessary strain, wear, and tear on your body.

Chapter 43 – Self-Care: Nutrition, Rest, and Healthy Habits

I.   **Why We Need Self-Care**[41,44]

    A.   Many trauma survivors feel undeserving of good things in life following the trauma(s).

    B.   This can lead to a lack of basic self-care in most areas of the person's life.

    C.   By doing routine physical and mental self-care, we can increase the chances of benefiting from treatment and recovering a good level of functioning.

    D.   Regular self-care can also reduce the strain of coping with symptoms.

II.   **Nutrition Basics**[41,46]

    A.   <u>Body Repair</u>

        1.   The body needs good nutrition to heal, repair itself, and maintain physical health.

        2.   This requires a balanced diet including vitamins, minerals, protein, and essential fats.

            a.   We get this by eating fruits, vegetables, lean meats, and small amounts of fats and carbohydrates.

            b.   Taking a good multivitamin each day is also a good idea. (and is recommended in a recent medical journal article)[45]

        3.   Balanced nutrition also provides the brain the raw materials needed to produce chemicals involved in thinking and regulating emotions.

            a.   Without this, it is hard for the brain chemistry to stay in balance.

            b.   We simply need the proper raw materials (i.e., nutrition) to make the body function properly.

    B.   <u>Immune System</u> (fighting infection and disease)

        1.   Many doctors believe that the body has the ability to heal itself from most diseases.[46]

        2.   For this to happen, we need to feed our immune system.

        3.   This requires a balanced diet.

        4.   The immune system is like a fighting force.

        5.   Without proper nutrients, it becomes weak and ineffective.

III.   Rest
    A.   <u>Up-time and Down-time</u>[23]
        1.   Nobody can work 100% of the time.
        2.   We need to recognize this and practice balancing periods of productivity with periods of rest (called "down time").
        3.   The rest periods are just as important as the time spent working.
        4.   When we practice taking periods of rest, we are usually more productive during work time.
    B.   <u>Sleep</u>
        1.   Many people throughout the world are sleep-deprived much of the time.
        2.   Most people require between 5 and 10 hours of sleep per night.
            a.   The exact amount of sleep required varies from person to person.
            b.   There is no set amount that applies to everyone.
        3.   If sleep is difficult, consult with your doctor.
            a.   Use medication if necessary.
            b.   Some sleep problems are symptoms of more severe underlying medical disorders.
            c.   A change in certain behaviors is often necessary to improve our sleep.
    C.   <u>Don't overwork yourself</u>
        1.   Don't push yourself to the point of collapse.
        2.   If we deplete our mental and physical reserves, there is little to draw upon when we encounter stress.
        3.   We get more done when rested and ready to accomplish the task.

IV.   Healthy Habits [42]
    A.   The following behaviors are healthy habits that can improve daily coping.
    B.   Basic hygiene.
        1.   Take a bath or shower every day.
        2.   Comb or brush your hair.
        3.   Shave.
        4.   Brush your teeth.
        5.   Wear deodorant.
        6.   Don't overdo the cologne or perfume.
    C.   Stop smoking.
    D.   Eat a balanced diet.
        1.   Eat 3 to 5 small meals per day.
        2.   Get a healthy variety of foods (don't forget fruits and vegetables).

E.   Exercise 3 to 5 days per week at least 30 minutes each time.
    1.   Start with brisk walking.
    2.   Later, try cycling, treadmill, weight lifting, etc.
    3.   Make sure to match the exercise to your physical abilities and fitness level.
F.   Avoid nonprescription drugs if possible.
G.   Minimize alcohol use.
H.   Limit caffeine, sugars, and excessive carbohydrates.
I.   Maintain healthy social contacts.
    1.   Talk with at least one or two people each day.
    2.   Total isolation usually increases anxiety and depression in the long run.
J.   Spend some quiet time each day.
K.   Work a little each day on spiritual growth and connectedness.
L.   Work on your hobbies at least some every day.
M.   Exercise your mind daily.
    1.   Read, write, do puzzles, etc. (anything that requires thinking or problem solving)
    2.   This can possibly reduce chances of developing Alzheimer's Disease in the long run.[83]
N.   Practice the Serenity Prayer – when you can't change it, then let it go!
O.   Get some sunshine every day you can.
P.   Take a multivitamin each day (only 1 per day unless prescribed by your doctor).[45]
Q.   Get a routine physical check-up at least once a year.

Chapter 44 – Perception and Stress Management

I.   **The Importance of Perception**[35]
    A.   Events don't cause stress by themselves.
    B.   Our perception of events is what determines how stressful they are.
        1.   Perceptions affect whether we respond or react to the situation.
        2.   Combined with our beliefs and skills, perceptions affect the way a situation impacts us.
    C.   When we are aware of an event and then interpret it as a threat, we become stressed by it.
    D.   If we think something is upsetting or troublesome, then our minds and bodies react accordingly.
    E.   When we view something as manageable, we remain alert but not alarmed.
    F.   Remember: peace of mind does not come from the absence of problems, but from the ability to cope with them effectively.

II.   **The Johari Window** [47]
    A.   The Johari Window illustrates 4 possible mental conditions in which we operate.
    B.   These conditions directly affect how we view the world and choose our behaviors.
    C.   In PTSD recovery, it is important to pay special attention to the "Hidden" and "Blind" windows.

	Known to Self	Not Known to Self
Known to Others	OPEN	BLIND
Not Known to Others	HIDDEN	UNKNOWN

    D.   The 4 Windows (conditions).[47]
        1.   Open – information that I know about myself, which is also obvious to other people.
            a.   Possible difficulty – embarrassment; shame.
        2.   Blind – information other people know about me, but that I am unaware of.
            a.   Possible difficulty – I might be doing things that cause a problem and I'm not even aware of it.
            b.   In PTSD, many people have the viewpoint that they have no problems while other people frequently see the problems associated with the PTSD symptoms.

          c.   Is there something I'm not aware of that's still causing me problems?

          d.   Am I willing to become aware of those things?

    3.   <u>Hidden</u> – information I know about myself, but other people don't know.

          a.   Possible difficulty – keep unhealthy secrets; self-disclosure can be uncomfortable and even quite painful.

          b.   In PTSD, many people experience intrusive thoughts and flashbacks, or other thoughts they don't want people to know about.

          c.   We bear the burden of those things that are overwhelming, but seem to us "unspeakable" because we feel they are so awful.

          d.   Some things we don't ever want to talk about because we are certain that it will invite judgment and rejection from the other person.

    4.   <u>Unknown</u> – information neither I nor you know about.

          a.   Possible difficulty – the unknown information may be crucial to the success of treatment, but nobody knows what it is.

          b.   We may not know what we should be looking for.

III.   Perception and Distorted thinking [35,43]

    A.   Distorted thinking compromises our ability to accurately perceive stressful situations and cope with them appropriately.

    B.   How do we know that we are perceiving events or situations accurately?

         1.   What standards are we using in coming to our conclusions?

         2.   Each person must come to a conclusion as to what is "good enough" evidence for them to believe something.

    C.   We need to examine our thinking to see if we are coming to inaccurate conclusions (based on erroneous perceptions or distorted thought processes).

    D.   If unsure, then check things out with someone who is intelligent, rational, and reliable.

IV.   Thought Patterns that Make Coping with Stress Much More Difficult [35,43]

    A.   <u>Catastrophizing</u> – by "blowing things out of proportion" we increase our reaction to a situation beyond what is really called for; (called "Making a mountain out of a mole hill").

         1.   The focus on possible catastrophic outcomes is so strong that more likely or reasonable possibilities are dismissed or overlooked.

         2.   This increases physical and mental arousal and creates a feeling of helplessness.

B.   Persistent Negative Expectations
    1.   Start out expecting the absolute worst outcome you can possibly imagine.
    2.   This puts a negative mental filter on everything you see and do.
    3.   With this thinking, it is very difficult to enjoy anything because you are living in "negative-ville" → do you want this to be your "hometown"?
C.   See Everyone as an Enemy
    1.   Have the attitude that everyone is either an enemy or a potential enemy.
    2.   This mindset puts us in an ongoing defensive position, but it is not accurate.
    3.   Most people you come in contact with are usually in "their own little world" trying to make themselves as happy as possible.
    4.   They are not an enemy – they just want to be left alone.
    5.   "How to gain, how to keep, how to recover happiness is in fact for most men at all times the secret motive of all they do, and of all they are willing to endure." - William James
D.   One Little Mistake Means . . .
    1.   Many individuals with PTSD try to achieve perfection in everything they do.
    2.   When even the slightest mistake is made, this is seen as a total failure.
    3.   Many people say "if it can't be perfect, then why do it at all?"
    4.   This view is unrealistic, because in this lifetime we can achieve excellence in many things, but not perfection; → it is more realistic to work toward "a job well done."
    5.   Would you accept 95% of perfection in most things you do?
E.   There is only one way to do things → my way.
    1.   When we insist that our way is the only way to do something, we are claiming to be the ultimate authority on the subject.
    2.   This view does not allow any other strategies or methods that could work just as well.
F.   Tunnel Vision – paying attention to only one aspect of a situation.
    1.   Our perspective gets fixed on only one thing; we don't see the bigger picture.
    2.   As a result, our perspective is distorted and out of balance.

V.   **To Cope More Effectively, We Need to Examine Our Perceptions and Conclusions**

      A.   Are there other ways of viewing this situation?

           1.   What would my doctor say about this situation? How would he/she handle it?

           2.   What feedback would people in my therapy group give in this situation?

           3.   What are the names of 2 people I can talk to? → check out your perceptions.

      B.   What does this look like if I slow down, step back, and see the bigger picture in this situation?

      C.   What reference material could I use to help me get information for figuring this out?

      D.   Make a list of the facts you have and are certain about.

      E.   What is the most logical conclusion based on the facts?

Chapter 45 – Personality and Stress Management

I.   **Personality [48] (a person's typical ways of thinking, feeling, and acting)**
    A.   A person's characteristics are long term patterns of thoughts, feelings, and behavior.
    B.   There are many ways of understanding personality, and very few people agree on any single approach.
    C.   Personality tends to be fairly stable over the long run (many years).
    D.   However, it can be changed under certain (usually extreme) circumstances.

II.   **Personality Determines How We Deal with Stressful Things in Life [8]**
    A.   If a person is willing to change how they think and what they do, they can often cope more effectively with stress, daily hassles, upsetting emotions, and specific psychiatric symptoms.
    B.   It is important to keep in mind that willingness to take positive steps is crucial to good stress management.
    C.   Why change can be difficult [19]
        1.   Some actions or behaviors may have been useful in the past, but are not helpful now.
        2.   To change means I have to take some risk.
        3.   It can be uncomfortable or frightening to change.
            a.   Fear of the unknown.
            b.   Maybe I'm more comfortable in my suffering.
            c.   Some people are unwilling to give up the benefits of behavior that also brings them pain.
        4.   If I don't change, at least I know what to expect most of the time. (It helps me feel safe and in control; I can predict how things will go.)
        5.   Maybe, I don't know how else to think or act.

III.   **Some Behavior Patterns Make Coping with PTSD Much More Difficult**
    A.   Type A Behavior[48]
        1.   Intensely Competitive – "I have to win; always be first; have to be the best."
            a.   Anything less than the best in everything will never do.
            b.   Always seem to be in competition with everyone else.
            c.   The result is that you are competing with everyone else most all of the time, and ultimately, everything winds up being a fight.

2.   <u>Over-achieving</u> – "I always have to do more than what is expected."
    a.   Doing "just good enough" is never good enough.
    b.   There's always more that can be done.
    c.   Things can always be improved.
    d.   Eventually, doing more becomes unrealistic.

3.   <u>Time urgency</u> –"I want it now!"
    a.   Faster – Faster – Faster!!!!!!!!!!!!
    b.   Trying to cram more and more into less and less time.
    c.   In the end, you wear yourself down.
    d.   Maybe, turn to drugs like caffeine, cocaine, or speed to "keep going."

4.   <u>Impatience</u> – "I should not have to wait for anything."
    a.   I don't have time to wait.
    b.   Everyone else is so slow (what's their problem?).
    c.   Why can't they work up to my expectations?
    d.   You become more and more intolerant of others and their lack of intensity (which you put so much value on).

5.   <u>Hostility</u> – antagonism; aggression; venting negative emotions.
    a.   It manifests as refusing to accept the natural limits of a situation.
    b.   Lack of empathy for other people.
    c.   Focus exclusively on the outcome of a situation without consideration for anything else.
    d.   Always insisting on having things your way in spite of limits, what is practical, or the reality of the situation.

6.   <u>Perfectionism</u> – "anything other than perfection is a TOTAL failure."
    a.   My way is the <u>best</u> way and the <u>only</u> way.
    b.   If I'm not <u>all good,</u> then I must be <u>all bad.</u>
    c.   I will only accept <u>what I want</u>.
    d.   I allow no room for compromise.
    e.   Perfectionism ultimately leads us to attempt things that are unrealistic, and then wind up in despair.

B.   While Type A behavior can be useful in certain situations, it is very harmful if used chronically day after day.
    1.   Hostility increases the chances of certain health problems. [44]
        a.   Higher risk of coronary artery disease.
        b.   Higher risk of heart attack.
        c.   Acid reflux, ulcers, other digestive problems.

IV. **New Thoughts (which lead to more productive and healthy coping)**

A. Not everything is personally directed at me, even though it might feel that way.

B. I do not have to compete with everyone I encounter.

    1. Sometimes, just give people some space.

    2. Let other people learn and live their own life.

C. I do not have to be in complete control of everything all of the time.

D. I don't have to always prove that my ideas and opinions are always right. (Even if I am right and the other person is wrong!)

E. I don't have to be tough on myself all of the time.

    1. I will practice forgiving myself on a daily basis.

    2. I choose to start being more gentle with myself.

F. Are there other ways of doing the job that will get the same outcome?

G. Some things I cannot change, so I will focus on those things that I can change.

H. Some things are more important than others, so I will not waste my efforts on things that are insignificant or unproductive.

I. I will exercise patience. Waiting just a little will not hurt me.

J. I will choose where to focus my energies.

    1. Some things require top quality performance.

    2. For other things, good enough really is good enough.

    3. On insignificant things, more time and effort add nothing of value.

K. By focusing on the truly important things I can work less hard each day and actually be more productive.

L. I will choose my battles.

    1. Some things are really worth getting upset about.

    2. Some things are not.

    3. If it is insignificant, I choose to let it go and move on.

M. Perfection is not possible in this life time.

    1. I will put forth my genuine best effort.

    2. I can live with that.

N. As I understand myself better, I choose to go easier on other people.

Chapter 46 – Panic Attacks

I. **Panic Attack [49] (a sudden surge of physical and mental arousal that occurs unexpectedly or in response to a particular upsetting person, place, situation, or object)**
   - A. <u>What does it feel like?</u>
     1. A panic attack comes on quickly (has a sudden onset).
     2. Builds to a peak rapidly.
     3. Feels like there is a serious danger, even if you can't identify it.
     4. Feels like something terrible is about to happen.
     5. You might believe you are going to die.
     6. Have a strong urge to escape the situation.
     7. This intense peak of extremely unpleasant symptoms usually lasts 10 minutes or less.
     8. A less extreme feeling of high anxiety can last for several hours.
   - B. Before being diagnosed, you might think you are losing your mind or "going crazy."

II. **Physical and Mental Symptoms in Panic [42] (circle all that you have experienced)**
   - A. <u>Physical Symptoms</u>
     1. Pounding heart (accelerated heart rate).
     2. Sweating.
     3. Trembling or shaking.
     4. Shortness of breath (feel like you are smothering).
     5. Feel like you are choking.
     6. Chest pain or discomfort.
     7. Nausea or abdominal distress.
     8. Feeling dizzy, unsteady, lightheaded, or faint.
     9. Numbness or tingling sensations (in one or many parts of the body).
     10. Chills or hot flashes.
   - B. <u>Mental Symptoms</u>
     1. Feeling that things are not real .
     2. Feeling detached from your body.
     3. Believe you are going crazy.
     4. Think you are losing your mind.
     5. Think that you might die.
     6. Have an intense desire to escape or get out of the situation.
     7. Fear of having a heart attack.
     8. Fear of doing something terrible .
     9. Think you might be losing control of yourself.

III.   **Panic Is Actually a False Alarm** [42]

    A.   There usually is <u>no real physical danger</u> in a panic attack.

    B.   Often people go to an emergency room thinking they are having a heart attack.

    C.   In a panic attack, we are over reacting to physical sensations, specific distressing thoughts, or overwhelming emotions.

IV.   **Panic Attack vs. Heart Attack**

    A.   Panic attacks are very frightening, but will not kill you.

    B.   It is important to recognize if you really are having a heart attack, or if it's a panic attack.

    C.   <u>Symptoms of a Real Heart Attack</u> [50]

        1.   Chest pain or pressure (usually in the center of the chest).

        2.   A "cold and clammy" feeling.

        3.   Jaw pain.

        4.   Heartburn and/or indigestion.

        5.   Arm pain (more commonly the left arm, but it can be either).

        6.   Pain that travels down the left arm or up the neck.

        7.   Upper back pain.

        8.   Feeling ill or weak all over.

        9.   Nausea.

        10.   Shortness of breath.

        11.   If you really are having a heart attack, then take it seriously → have someone take you immediately to the emergency room or call 911.

V.   **Coping with a Panic Attack** [42,43,75]

    A.   To cope with a panic attack, we must <u>calm the mind</u> and <u>calm the body</u>.

    B.   <u>Calming the Mind.</u>

        1.   Your thoughts will make the situation better or worse.

        2.   The thoughts that come to mind during a panic attack feel like an overwhelming flood of thoughts, feelings, and images passing through your mind all at once.

        3.   We need to <u>focus on only one thought</u> during a panic attack, no matter what it is.

            a.   Examples: focus on breathing, a spot on the wall, or a particular word ("calm").

            b.   Focus your mind to reduce the flood of thoughts.

            c.   <u>Coping thoughts</u> – have a pre-planned thought that you will focus on.

    C.   <u>Calming the Body.</u>

      1.   In a panic attack, the body "gets revved up", but this happens without what seems like a reasonable explanation for it.

      2.   The body "gets revved up" when there is no need for it.

      3.   We need calming exercises or strategies to use when this happens.

           a.   Practice the deep breathing technique every day.

           b.   Learn to respond to the anxiety in this way.

           c.   Drink very cold water.

VI.   Other Treatment Components [75]

    A.   Systematic Desensitization [35] – for situation-specific panic attacks.

      1.   Gradually learn to approach the feared situation without panicking.

      2.   Learn to respond in a calm and controlled way to regain control over your reactions.

    B.   Increase your confidence and self-control.

      1.   As your mental skills improve, you don't have to be afraid that a panic attack might happen at any moment, because you are now prepared to deal with it.

      2.   <u>Anticipatory anxiety</u> – sets you up to possibly have another panic attack.

      3.   We need to overcome the <u>fear of losing control</u> and stop anticipating the worst.

    C.   Decrease caffeine and nicotine [44] (which can mimic panic attack symptoms).

      1.   They are stimulants and decrease blood flow (by constricting blood vessels).

      2.   They can cause the body to be overexcited (physically) when it's not necessary.

      3.   By eliminating caffeine and nicotine, many people can reduce or eliminate panic attacks.

    D.   Use medication appropriately. [20,25,29]

      1.   Take all medications as prescribed.

      2.   Realize that if you take a medication right when the panic attack begins, the attack will be over long before enough medicine gets into the bloodstream to help calm you down.

      3.   To be effective for panic, anti-anxiety medications must be taken on an on-going basis.

      4.   Medication in combination with relaxation (calming) techniques usually produce the best results.

Chapter 47 – Regulating Emotions

I.   **The Ability to Regulate Your Emotions Is a Skill** [8,43,44]
    A.   If you don't use emotion-regulation skills, you will feel like you are on an "emotional roller-coaster" (mood swings).
    B.   This can result in feeling like "a victim of your emotions."
    C.   When extremely severe, a person becomes totally overwhelmed and has a "break down" with little or no ability to cope.
    D.   By using emotion-regulation skills, we can get back in control, function as we need to each day, and enjoy more of the good things in life.

II. **The Nature of Emotions** [1,8]
    A.   <u>Emotions change over time.</u>
        1.   If you are feeling down, it is likely that you will "come back up" and feel better later.
        2.   If you are feeling especially good, expect to have a "let down" and feel not quite as good for awhile.
    B.   Most people have positive and negative feelings at different times and in different situations.
    C.   The intensity of emotions varies from person to person (this is expected and normal).
    D.   For some people, one or two feelings may predominate their mood most of the time.
    E.   This may cause discomfort or impair our functioning.
    F.   What moods are typical of how you feel most of the time?

III. **Ways to Regulate and Manage Emotions** [1,8,43,44]
    A.   <u>Talk</u>
        1.   Express your thoughts and feelings to someone who listens and cares.
        2.   This might be a good friend, a therapist, or in a journal.
        3.   Talking with just anyone (who may not understand or care) may not help.
        4.   By talking, we can process our feelings and reduce tension, inner conflict, and anxiety.
        5.   A person can suppress feelings, which protects them emotionally for short periods of time; but they will eventually come out and cause problems if we don't deal with them.
        6.   Talking can help us get the feelings out and possibly increase our insight and understanding.

B.   Express feelings through actions
    1.   Have outlets for your feelings.
        a.   Enjoy wholesome activities – exercise, music, games, hobbies, etc.
        b.   Use pre-planned activities to express anger and "let off steam" in a safe and controlled way.
    2.   Write in a journal – get the feelings down on paper.
        a.   This helps some people to cope with the distressing emotions.
    3.   Listen to music – different styles of music can set a different "emotional tone" and help shift or change your mood.

C.   Grounding [1,2] – the process of getting back in touch with the "here and now."
    1.   Use the 5 senses (sight, sounds, smell, taste, touch) to bring you back to the reality of what is going on right where you are right now.
    2.   Use things that help you focus on the fact that you are now safe and not helpless in your current situation.
    3.   Examples: listen to a favorite song; smell vanilla, apple pie, a scented candle; taste cinnamon, lemon, peppermint; touch a rough or smooth surface; squeeze a hand gripper or rubber ball.
    4.   Grounding helps us get back in control when negative feelings start to feel overwhelming.

D.   Sleep – when sleep deprived we tend to be irritable, short-tempered, tired, anxious, and may become depressed.
    1.   Getting appropriate amounts of rest restores our ability to think clearly, tolerate some frustration, and not overreact.
    2.   Poor sleep can cause problems with mood regulation by itself.
    3.   It also compounds the problem if other factors are causing problems.
    4.   A person may need to use medication to get back into a more healthy sleep pattern.
    5.   A regular sleep pattern is necessary for good physical and mental health.

E.   Exercise
    1.   Use exercise to get your frustrations out.
    2.   Express anger in a safe and controlled way.
    3.   Exercise usually creates positive changes in body chemistry that can help your mood.
    4.   While exercise is usually a healthy outlet, we need to make sure we don't "over-do it" or injure ourselves.

F.   Nutrition
  1.   The body needs many different nutrients in order to regulate the body and brain chemistry.
  2.   Without proper nutrition, it is difficult for the body to stay in chemical balance, and a person's feelings can become unregulated as a result.
  3.   A well-balanced diet can have huge benefits for helping you stay physically and mentally healthy.

G.   Medication
  1.   When feeling completely overwhelmed, medication may be necessary to get back in control.
  2.   Some people need medication for only short periods of time.
  3.   Other people may need to take medication on an ongoing basis.
  4.   Medication should be used to help you get back in control and improve your functioning.
  5.   Use medication only as prescribed.
  6.   If you have questions, write them down and ask your doctor or other medication provider.

Chapter 48 – Humor and Stress Management

I.   Humor Is Normal

    A.   Humor is a playful discovery, expression, or appreciation of the absurdity or incongruity of life's situations.

    B.   Humor is woven into the fabric of life as one of many types of experiences.

    C.   Humor can be used to help us cope with stress, unbearable tension, or fear.

    D.   Sigmund Freud said this is one of the more mature (healthy) coping mechanisms for dealing with our anxiety.

II.   Trauma and Humor

    A.   Trauma often has devastating effects on a person's sense of humor. [1]

        1.   We can lose our sense of humor or the desire to enjoy humor after trauma.

        2.   Our sense of humor can become morbid.

            a.   Some people joke about death or disturbing issues.

            b.   Other people may not understand why these things are humorous to you.

        3.   We can lose the ability to enjoy humor that was previously funny (before the trauma).

        4.   Many people feel disconnected from friends they used to laugh and joke with before the trauma(s).

    B.   A sign of recovery is getting a sense of humor back.

    C.   Without humor a person's thoughts are likely to become stuck and narrowly focused, leading to distress and negative feelings.

    D.   The lack of a sense of humor is often related to a lower self esteem.

III.   Benefits of Humor

    A.   By being able to laugh at something, you gain a new perspective. [8,42]

        1.   This insight (or new perspective) is one of the cornerstones of how therapy works.

    B.   Humor and laughter can enhance work performance, support learning, facilitate relaxation, and improve coping.

    C.   Humor channels emotions for a positive benefit to the mind and the body.

    D.   Humor can assist us in making positive connections with other people.

        1.   It is often used as "an ice-breaker."

    E.   Laughter can shift our perspective, resulting in less distress.

    F.   Humor helps us replace distressing emotions with more enjoyable feelings.

        1.   It is difficult to laugh and be angry at the same time.

    G.   Humor can increase our energy level.

H. Laughing at yourself can be a way of accepting and respecting yourself during a rough time.

    1. <u>Note</u>: This laughing at oneself can be unhealthy if it insults or degrades.

I. Humor can help us manage our emotions.

J. When we realize that we are free to laugh again, we are in the process of healing!

IV. Activity

A. If used in a therapy group, have each member of the therapy group bring one or more joke(s) and share them in the therapy session.

B. <u>Remember</u>: Getting your sense of humor back is a sign of getting better.

C. <u>Note</u>: Make sure the jokes are appropriate; If in doubt, no jokes with questionable content.

Section VI: Advanced PTSD Issues

Patients with PTSD have said . . .

" . . . there's just a lot you have to deal with if you really want to get better."

"Until therapy, I didn't realize that the trauma had affected every single area of my life."

"In therapy, I realized that PTSD is complicated, and yet it's pretty simple once you understand it."

Chapter 49 – Trust: Part I

I.   **Trust: Reliance on the Character, Ability, Strength, or Truthfulness of Some-one or Something (essentially, depending on someone else to be reliable and to look out for your best interest)**

    A.   Trauma causes loss of trust because we don't feel safe enough to take the chance.

    B.   The typical response is wanting to trust, but then saying "I know better than to do that." [51]

II.   **Loss of Trust Is Often Related to the Type of Trauma Experienced** [3,14]

    A.   <u>Natural Disasters</u> – less severe PTSD; less loss of trust in people; less stigma.

        1.   Maybe it was "an act of God."

        2.   Maybe it was "due to bad luck."

    B.   <u>Man-made </u>(human caused) – usually results in longer and more severe PTSD.

        1.   Stigma is often long-lasting; the person is seen as lacking courage, strength, or moral integrity .

        2.   Society often "blames the victim" or suggests the trauma survivor was at fault for what happened to them.

        3.   Examples of man-made traumas include war, rape, incest, and child abuse.

III.   **Basic Assumptions About the World**

    A.   Before Trauma (personal invulnerability).

        1.   "Nothing bad will happen to me."

        2.   "Those really bad things happen to other people, but not me."

        3.   "The world is a fair and just place."

    B.   After Trauma (radical changes in worldview)

        1.   Most individuals with PTSD have a radically different view of the world after the trauma(s) that is usually more guarded, and pessimistic.

        2.   Trauma Survivors often will say, "I don't trust because I know it will only get you hurt."

IV.   **At Times It Is Safer to <u>Not Trust</u> than It Is to <u>Trust</u>** [14]

    A.   In war (or other types of trauma), it makes sense to divide people into two groups.

        1.   Friends.

        2.   Enemies (threats).

B. In between is not useful or safe.

C. If in doubt, it is safer to consider someone an enemy.

D. For survivors of man-made traumas, it is often difficult to move beyond this "Friend vs. Enemy" approach, which was useful in the past but usually not today.

E. In another form of mistrust, the trauma survivor operates on the assumption that "It is safer to anticipate the worst than to hope for the best."

F. The trauma survivor uses mistrust and defensiveness as a way to stay safe, even when the actual dangers are minimal or nonexistent.

G. Eventually, a person develops an all-or-nothing view as to whether it is safe to trust someone.

V. **Trauma Survivors Often Experience Some Situations as Being Dangerous when in Fact They Are Not Dangerous.**

A. The persistent feelings of un-safety and doom experienced as part of PTSD usually feed into:

1. Hypervigilance.

2. Depression.

3. Anxiety.

B. Other people often label the trauma survivor as cynical, paranoid, negative, or at minimum "over-protective."

C. However, the intense need to feel safe and in control after trauma can prevent a person from trusting most all of the time.

VI. **Trauma Survivors Need to Work Toward Healthy Reconnection with Other People**[1,2,14]

A. Need to work toward a balanced ability to trust.

1. We should not trust everyone because not everyone is trustworthy.

2. However, trusting no-one usually further isolates us.

3. The trauma survivor needs to develop some partial trust in at least a few people.

B. The key: Be wise in your choices about who you trust!

C. It takes time to figure out who to trust.

1. Who do I trust?

2. In what ways?

3. Just how far?

D. Trust must be grounded in reality.

1. Initially, we are mistrustful or at least neutral toward people.

2. Then, we observe the person's behaviors over a period of time.

3. What do their actions tell you?

E.   <u>The goal regarding trust</u>: To not view current experiences as a replay of past traumas.

1.   Is your gut feeling always saying "Don't trust" with every person in every situation?

2.   If so, this is a product of the traumas.

3.   To develop healthy trust, we need to be good investigators → check things out, and then act accordingly.

Chapter 50 – Trust: Part II

I. **Complete Trust vs. Partial Trust** [14]
    A.   Under traumatic conditions, a person usually Trusts 100% or Distrusts 100%.
    B.   Under non-traumatic conditions, we usually exercise only partial trust. This is because in most daily situations "not everything" is at stake.
    C.   We usually ask questions like:
         1.   "How much should I trust?"
         2.   "With what things?"
         3.   "Under what conditions?"

II. **Pitfalls Involved in Distrusting Everyone All of the Time**
    A.   Maintaining total distrust in spite of good evidence to the contrary (an over reaction).
    B.   Being unwilling to learn more about the other person to either confirm or reject your "gut-reaction" to them (not open to new possibilities).
    C.   Being unwilling to give others a chance to earn your trust (shutting people out keeps you isolated and detached).

III. **Trauma-Survivor Intuitive Skills – The 6th Sense** [1,8,14]
    A.   Many trauma survivors possess insights into many things such as human frailty or weaknesses, human cruelty, inadequacies, contradictions, and corruption in human institutions that other people do not see.
    B.   This can actually be a good source of information for making decisions!
    C.   However, it should not be your ONLY source of information.
    D.   This "6th sense" can help you survive extreme situations, but needs to be balanced with other thoughts and information for healthy daily living.

IV. **How to Develop Healthy Trust**
    A.   When we first meet someone, we are usually a little mistrustful or at least neutral.
         1.   This is usually considered good judgment.
         2.   We are "sizing things up."
         3.   This "wait and see attitude" helps us evaluate new people and situations.
    B.   Gather information from several sources (including your intuition, or 6th sense).
    C.   Form an opinion about the person or situation.
    D.   See how that opinion matches up with the person's behavior or the facts of the situation (test it out!).

E.   Revise your opinion as new information comes in.

F.   Trust only to the point that the person proves trustworthy.

V.   Some Conclusions about Trust – Choose Wisely Who You Trust!

A.   If your gut feeling is always saying "don't trust" <u>with every single person you meet</u>, then that impression is most likely based on your traumatic experiences and not on your real experiences today.

B.   There are some people who SHOULD NOT be trusted at all.

C.   There are some people who should be trusted with only very little.

D.   There are some people who should be trusted only in certain ways – with some things and not with other things (selectively).

E.   There are some people who are generally trustworthy with most things.

F.   A blanket distrusting approach to the world <u>was a survivor skill at one time.</u>

G.   However, in non-traumatic situations this may cause problems and will be an obstacle in your relationships and daily life.

H.   Try learning to trust at least a few people who do prove trustworthy with some things.

Chapter 51 – Control

I. **What Is Control?**
   A. Having power over something.
   B. Exerting influence over the outcome of a situation.
   C. Directing how something turns out.
   D. It is natural to feel the need to be in control of most areas of your life.
   E. Feeling in control helps us to ward off anxiety.
   F. However, the desire to be in complete control of everything around you all of the time creates problems for you and the people around you.

II. **The Importance of Our Beliefs about Control**
   A. Locus of Control [52] (LOC) (or, where is the control?)
      1. Personal beliefs about the extent to which you are able to control or influence how things turn out have a large impact on our behaviors.
      2. These are beliefs about the connection between our actions and the outcomes we get.
      3. How do your behaviors relate to the consequences you experience?
   B. Internal or External Locus of Control?
      1. Internal LOC ("I have the power")
         a. I try to exert control over the situation.
         b. I have the power to make a difference and be effective.
         c. When I take action, I get the results I want.
      2. External LOC ("I'm powerless")
         a. Things are outside of my control.
         b. Powerful other people or situations are in control of what happens.
         c. Maybe think that chance or luck determines how things turn out.
      3. Which approach typically describes how you feel about things?
      4. Does that approach account for all situations you encounter?
      5. Research has shown that pessimists tend to view things more accurately, but die sooner, while optimists are a little less accurate in their perceptions, but are happier and live much longer. [44,53]
         a. How does this relate to your view of control?
         b. Which pattern is more typical of how you feel most days?

III. **Three Levels of Control**
   A. Primary Control (directly control the situation)
      1. Being in direct control of a situation by taking direct action.
      2. A "hands on" approach.
      3. Being able to directly determine the outcome.
      4. This is what most trauma survivors strive for most of the time.

    B.   The Circle of Influence
1. In some situations, we do not have direct control, but we still are able to exert some influence.
2. This is a middle ground between direct control vs. secondary control.
3. Sometimes, influence is enough to help get what we want or need without having to be in complete control.

    C.   Secondary Control (change yourself)
1. Changing your behavior to adapt to the environment.
2. Delegating direct control to other people.
3. Changing your attitudes about a situation.
4. The control you exercise is over your own behaviors and responses to the situation.

III. Indicators that the Control Issue Has Become a Problem in Your Life

A. Make sure that you are always in control at all costs.
B. Believe that not being in complete control = being totally vulnerable.
C. It seems reasonable to always be in control of everything around you all of the time.
D. Leave no room for "middle ground" or compromise on non-critical issues.
E. Absolutely not trusting anyone who has a different background or different life experiences from your own.
F. Believe that being hypervigilant is the only way to ensure total control and personal safety.
G. Not accepting reality when direct control is clearly not possible.
H. Believe that secondary control is never an option.

IV. Control and Our Health

A. A higher need for control is associated with several physical problems. [54,55,56]
1. Increased risk of heart disease.
2. More "wear and tear" on the body.
3. Anxiety and frustration in situations where direct control is not possible.
4. Harmful effects on the immune system. [44]
B. People who believe that they have the ability to exert control and then act on it in a productive way usually have better long-term health outcomes.
C. People who take an active part in their own treatment usually do best in the long-term.

V.   **Some Conclusions about Control**
- A.   Appropriate planning is required to exercise personal control at the necessary level.
- B.   Take responsibility for those things under your control, and adapt to those things you cannot control.
- C.   If you can't fix it, then get some help or let it go.
- D.   Worrying and fretting over upsetting things that you cannot change helps nobody.
- E.   Accepting things you cannot change does not mean that you like those things or agree with them.
- F.   It means you are facing the facts of reality, doing what you can, and moving forward in a healthy way.
- G.   Developing more secondary control is absolutely necessary for a healthy adjustment as we age and our abilities decline.

Chapter 52 – Guilt

I.   **Guilt Is a Normal Human Emotion**
- A.   Guilt can be directed in either a toxic or healthy manner. [1]
- B.   If you do something wrong, it is normal to feel some guilt.
- C.   The guilt feeling is a warning signal designed to motivate you to take a corrective action.
- D.   Once you deal with the issue and fix the problem behavior, the guilt should go away.
- E.   If the guilt persists after you have dealt with the issue, it becomes very destructive mentally and emotionally.
- F.   Other unhealthy forms of guilt include:
  - 1.   Using guilt to motivate someone to do what you want.
  - 2.   Guilt used to shame or punish someone.
  - 3.   When guilt is used to control someone.

II.   **Healthy Guilt (feeling bad about wrong, unethical, or immoral behavior)**
- A.   Guilt is an internal moral compass or guide designed to motivate us to behave appropriately and correct past mistakes or bad behavior.
- B.   Healthy guilt is a sign of having a conscience → a good thing for the benefit of society and yourself.
- C.   If you never feel any guilt about anything, this is a warning sign! [57]
  - 1.   People who never feel any guilt are very dangerous people.
  - 2.   What keeps their behavior in line with the law, ethics, and morals?
  - 3.   Guilt should be corrective, and then go away.

III.   **Toxic Guilt (guilt feelings based on self-punishment and/or attempts to justify or fix the original behaviors that were considered wrong)** [1,9]
- A.   Toxic guilt eats you up inside.
  - 1.   Stay tired; difficulty staying focused; always feel inadequate/unworthy.
  - 2.   Often involves the belief "what I did was so bad, I could never be forgiven."
- B.   Toxic guilt manifests itself in several ways that are self-punishing.
  - 1.   Substance abuse.
  - 2.   Workaholism.
  - 3.   Getting into fights so that others can hurt (punish) you.
  - 4.   Grudges; always angry; "chip on your shoulder."
  - 5.   Medical problems (diabetes, stomach problems, heart disease, stroke, etc.).

IV. **Working Through Guilt vs. Guilt Paralysis** [9]
- A. We need to identify trauma-related guilt feelings through therapy, journaling, or self-reflection.
  1. What type of guilt is it?
  2. What caused this guilt?
  3. Is this guilt toxic or healthy?
  4. Is it helping or hindering me?
  5. Is the guilt correcting something or just causing suffering?
  6. Am I willing to forgive others and also accept forgiveness for wrong things I have done?
- B. Healing from toxic guilt involves understanding the trauma from a new perspective.
  1. Realistically, what were my options at the time of the trauma?
  2. What were the conditions under which I had to make decisions?
  3. Realize that I had to do the best I could under the worst of conditions.
  4. Start to "give yourself some slack" or "cut yourself a break" because of the nature of the situation.
  5. Realize that at the time the trauma happened, you did not have the luxury of time or all the information learned since then.
  6. Healing requires considering the nature of the situation when the trauma occurred and forgiving ourselves.
  7. Continued suffering and self-punishment does not fix anything and does nobody any good.

V. **Tasks for the Future**
- A. Acts of Positive Contribution [14]
  1. Become active in at least one activity or organization that makes a positive contribution to society.
  2. Examples: volunteering, church, community groups, organizations that focus on helping others, etc.
  3. Use what you have learned to help others.
- B. Begin putting energy into positive and constructive activities.
  1. Do not allow the guilt to paralyze you.
  2. Start living your life from this point forward.
  3. If another person caused your trauma, then refuse to let them win.
  4. Forgive them and be determined to get better.
     (Getting better is the best revenge! A grudge only hurts you.)
  5. Rebuild your personal beliefs (including religious beliefs).

6. Address the ethical, moral, and spiritual aspects of your guilt, and work toward a healthy resolution (work individually with a psychotherapist on this if necessary).
7. Refuse to carry the burden of the whole world! (which is not your job anyway).
8. Refuse to let the guilt hold you back any longer.

Chapter 53 – Grudges and Resentments: Part I

I. **The Origins of a Grudge**
  A. How a grudge works.
    1. First, somebody wrongs you.
    2. Now you feel angry about what happened.
    3. Next, a decision is made: "I will hold this against them." [58]
    4. At this point, a person often indulges in revenge fantasies. [1,2]
      a. Plan out ways to hurt them.
      b. How will I "get them back?"
      c. How can I "get even?"
    5. Feel completely justified in this because you were wronged by them.
    6. Steps 2-5 become an endless cycle.
  B. The longer you invest in the grudge the more nasty, angry, and bitter you become.
  C. With this pattern, we are not moving toward health.
  D. By holding a grudge, you are feeding your own pain and misery.
  E. You are preventing your own healing and recovery.
  F. While most people feel fully justified in holding the grudge, it is only hurting them.
  G. A grudge is poison that you give to yourself, all the while thinking it is a reasonable thing to do!

II. **The Purpose of a Grudge**
  A. Holding a Grudge is an attempt to convince ourselves that we have more control over what happened than we really do.
    1. A grudge is usually focused on the fact that we were injured or offended by someone else.
    2. We then invest effort and energy into staying upset that this happened, thinking that somehow this would protect us.
    3. Over time holding a grudge changes you into a very rude, nasty, hateful, bitter person.
    4. Often, the insult happened by accident, and the other person doesn't even know they hurt you.
    5. The offending party often knows nothing about the grudge!
    6. The only person hurt by the grudge is you.
    7. The bottom line in holding a grudge is:
        "You hurt me → now I'm going to hurt me and keep hurting me."

B. In trauma, <u>Self-Blame</u> is an attempt to convince ourselves that we had more control over something that happened than we really did. [9]
   1. Continuing to blame ourselves does not change what has happened in the past.
   2. It usually just prevents us from having a better future.
   3. Self-blame is like holding a grudge against yourself about a situation that was actually beyond your control.
   4. At this point, we need to practice self-forgiveness in order to heal.
   5. We need to stop holding ourselves responsible for things that were not our fault or were beyond our control.
   6. Self-forgiveness helps us focus our efforts toward understanding, coping, and healing.

III. **What Happens When We Hold Onto a Grudge** [44]
A. <u>Revenge</u> – to inflict harm in return for an injury or insult; to retaliate.
   1. Focusing on revenge increases a person's stress level overall.
   2. This almost always harms our health by keeping our stress level up and contributing to physical illnesses.
   3. At first, revenge can feel very sweet; However, once we get revenge, we may then feel guilty about what we did.
   4. While revenge sounds appealing, it does not really fix what happened.
B. <u>Misplaced Anger</u> – when we hold a grudge, we let the anger build up inside and then finally explode. [34]
   1. We direct the anger at someone or something.
   2. This someone or something is usually not the person or situation we are really angry with.
   3. This expression of anger is <u>often called "Lashing Out"</u>.
   4. This behavior often makes little or no sense to others or to ourselves.
   5. Holding grudges keeps our anger level high, but without appropriate targets or outlets for the anger.
   6. In time, we can become dangerous and out of control (i.e., a time bomb just waiting to go off!).

IV. **Some Realities of Holding a Grudge**
A. The person who hurt you might not ever ask for forgiveness or be sorry for what they did.
B. People who do take revenge usually say later that it did not make them feel better or fix the situation like they had hoped, even though they thought it would before hand.

C.   Forgiving DOES NOT magically take away all the memories or hurt feelings that were caused by the injury.

      1.   You will still be able to feel some hurt from the injury.

      2.   However, this can be dealt with when we forgive.

      3.   In time, the painful feelings are reduced and dealt with.

D.   When you forgive, you are not responsible for the other person's response.

      1.   They might never be sorry.

      2.   However, you can still resolve the issue within yourself.

      3.   Healing is possible regardless of the other person's choice.

E.   Holding a grudge hurts only you.

      1.   Forgiving is an investment in your own healing.

      2.   Do you want to stay angry and stuck, or have peace of mind?

      3.   Is a grudge really worth all of the torment (to yourself)?

      4.   What does a grudge prove?

      5.   Are grudges part of the way you define yourself?

      6.   Are they a key part of your identity?

      7.   Who or what would you be without your grudges?

      8.   Does holding a grudge help you become the person that you really want to be?

F.   <u>Remember</u>: By holding a grudge, you are making a choice that poisons your own mental health.

      1.   Is this what you really want?

      2.   Are you willing to exercise forgiveness in order to heal?

Chapter 54 – Grudges and Resentments: Part II (Forgiveness and Healing)

I.   **What Is Forgiveness?**
- A.   To forgive is to give up resentment or the claim to get repayment for having been hurt, injured, or offended.
- B.   Grudges are started and maintained not by the offense, but by our choice. [58]
- C.   Forgiveness also happens by choice.
- D.   Forgiveness is an investment in our own healing.
- E.   When we forgive, it frees us to move beyond the hurt.

II.   **Who Needs Forgiveness?**
- A.   The fact is that we have all been hurt or offended in some way.
- B.   No one is free from this aspect of life.
- C.   To be free of past hurts, we all need to practice forgiveness.
- D.   We also need to forgive ourselves.
  - 1.   We are sometimes harder on ourselves than we are on other people.
  - 2.   Are you sometimes:
    - a.   Your worst critic?
    - b.   Your own worst enemy?
    - c.   Harder on yourself than you are on others?
  - 3.   Many people unmercifully beat up on themselves internally over past wrongs.
- E.   We need to forgive ourselves (as well as others) if we are to fully recover.
- F.   What does it take to actually forgive?

III.   **Steps Involved in Forgiveness** [35]
- A.   STEP #1 – Acknowledge the fact that you have been hurt, injured, or offended.
  - 1.   Focus on the <u>facts</u> of the situation.
  - 2.   Denial that an injury occurred does not resolve the hurt or pain.
  - 3.   Name the facts of what happened → be specific.
  - 4.   This is often a very upsetting step in the process.
- B.   STEP #2 – Identify how you feel about the facts of what happened.
  - 1.   Angry; hurt; wounded.
  - 2.   Taken advantage of; betrayed; used; other _____
      _____
  - 3.   The natural thing is to feel hurt and angry, and then want to get back at them.
- C.   STEP #3 – CHOOSE to NOT hold this against the person (or group) any more.

D. STEP #4 – CHOOSE to let go of the anger, resentment, and bitterness.
    1. Practice the following statements.
    2. "I choose to forgive them for _____."
    3. "I choose to let go of the anger, resentment, and bitterness."
    4. "I choose to be healed of this hurt."
E. STEP #5 – Practice Steps 3 and 4 again, and again, and again when anger and other painful feelings pop up.
F. This process might take days, weeks, months, or years.
G. Continue to CHOOSE to forgive every time you experience feelings of hurt, anger, resentment, or bitterness about the event.
H. In time, the hurt feelings are lessened and we become free to move beyond those hurts.

IV. **Myths about Forgiveness:**
A. MYTH: Forgiving means you are saying that what happened was O.K.
    1. This is a popular idea about forgiveness that holds people back.
    2. If you have been hurt, the last thing you want to say is, "That was O.K."
B. FACT: If forgiving was the same as saying "That was O.K.", then you would be saying "You can hurt me anytime you want and that's O.K."
    1. Actually, forgiveness IS NOT excusing, denying, hiding, or ignoring the hurtful event.
    2. Forgiveness does not justify bad behavior.
    3. Instead, it acknowledges what in fact did happen, and chooses to deal with it in a healthy way so that healing can happen.
C. MYTH: We should "Forgive and Forget."
    1. Many people believe that to forgive we must totally forget what happened.
    2. Most people know that you can't just magically erase your memory.
    3. "Forgive and Forget" is an unrealistic expectation.
D. FACT: We cannot erase the memory of the hurtful event from your brain.
    1. "Forgive and Forget" is bad advice.
    2. Trying to forget the hurtful event is like trying to ignore what happened. (How can we forget something that was so painful?)
    3. If we try to forget past events in which we got hurt, we might be choosing to ignore information that could prevent us from getting hurt again in the future.
    4. If we do this, we did not properly learn from the experience.
    5. It is more reasonable to forgive the person and use what you learned in order to keep from being hurt again.
    6. Better advice is: "Forgive, and then use what you learned to prevent further harm in the future."

V. **Conclusions about Forgiveness**

A.   Everyone has been hurt or offended at some time in their life.

B.   The hurts that start grudges are often very painful experiences.

C.   Forgiving others is usually very difficult for most people to do. We usually feel justified in holding a grudge.

D.   The main purpose of forgiving is to <u>invest in your own healing</u>.

      1.   Forgiveness can sometimes restore relationships.

      2.   It also plays an important role in personal growth, healing, and maturity.

E.   If you are never able to forgive, your personal maturity will always be limited.

F.   To forgive is a choice – it does not just happen automatically.

G.   Be careful that you are not suppressing, "stuffing," or using denial just to get past a situation.

H.   Forgiveness is a process and requires making an intentional choice several times until the hurt feelings are reduced.

I.   When we truly forgive, we then become free to move forward without the baggage of those old hurts always dragging us down.

J.   When we choose not to forgive, we are choosing to hold onto those old hurts and continue hurting ourselves.

K.   In the end, the choice is yours. Forgiveness of yourself <u>and</u> others is one of the most important keys to healing.

Chapter 55 – PTSD Mindsets Part I: Extremes of Thinking

I. **Certain Mindsets Are Often Produced when a Person Survives a Traumatic Experience** [1,2,35]

    A. All-or-Nothing Mindset

        1. In combat (or other trauma), less than a full effort can get you hurt or killed.

        2. Also, there are times when being very passive can keep you alive.

        3. "Gray areas" become viewed as dangerous and unhelpful to our survival.

    B. Now-or-Never Mindset

        1. In combat, if you wait you might never get a second chance.

        2. This sense of urgency stays with many people after a trauma.

        3. This approach is then applied to most every situation you encounter.

    C. Perfectionism Mindset

        1. No mistakes allowed → "mistakes get you hurt or killed."

        2. Anything less than perfection is unacceptable.

        3. This is an attempt to maintain an ultimate level of control.

    D. Denial of Personal Difficulty Mindset

        1. In a combat situation, you have to handle anything thrown your way.

        2. It is easy to convince ourselves that we should live that way in civilian life.

        3. When we believe that our best efforts have kept us alive, why should we do any less now?

    E. Worst Case Scenarios Mindset

        1. In traumatic experiences, survival is the bottom line.

        2. If we are prepared for the worst, we can probably handle anything else that comes along.

        3. This is a way of "preparing mentally" in an effort to avoid being caught off guard or traumatized again.

    F. Fatalism Mindset

        1. "I have seen the absolute worst things in the world."

        2. "I'm permanently damaged because of what I've been through."

        3. "What's the use?"

II.   **Understanding the Importance of Mindsets** [35,43]
A.   A person's mindset guides the way they going about doing things.
B.   It is a large part of being mentally healthy.
C.   Unhealthy mindsets can also perpetuate the symptoms of a mental illness.
D.   Mindsets play a large role in how we manage the symptoms of PTSD.
E.   To get better, we must examine our mindsets and replace the harmful thought patterns.
F.   While new mindsets often "feel" strange or untrue, more accurate and productive ways of viewing the world help us cope more effectively.
G.   Recovery requires an openness to seeing things differently and reworking our understanding and conclusions.
H.   Answer the following:
1.   Is it possible that I might have been wrong about a few things through the years?
2.   Could it be that my knowledge and insight have been limited by the PTSD symptoms?
3.   Is it O.K. to change your thinking in order to get better?

III.   **Healthier Mindsets (for coping)** [1,35,42,43]
A.   <u>Learned Optimism</u>
1.   PTSD makes life very difficult.
2.   However, I can develop a better quality of life.
3.   I don't have to stay stuck.
4.   I will use the fighting spirit to not let PTSD win.
B.   <u>Life Balance</u>
1.   Most things work best when all the parts are in balance.
2.   I am in a retraining process to improve my coping skills and overall quality of life.
3.   I choose to not live in the extremes like I did in the past.
C.   <u>Seeing New Colors</u>
1.   "Black-and-white thinking" was useful in the traumatic situation.
2.   However, in civilian life this often works against me.
3.   A more informed view of the world helps me cope better.
4.   I choose to see the "gray areas" and make intelligent choices accordingly based on good judgment.
D.   <u>Flexibility</u>
1.   If you are completely inflexible, eventually you will break.
2.   I have found that some things are worth making a big deal about and some things are not.
3.   Most things in civilian life are not life-and-death.
4.   I will use flexibility in the way I handle most situations.

E.   <u>Forgiveness</u>
      1.   Today, I choose to invest in my own healing by practicing forgiveness.
      2.   I refuse to let those people who hurt me in the past have any power over me or my feelings anymore.
      3.   I refuse to be their victim anymore.
      4.   I will not hold it against them anymore so that I can be healed.

F.   <u>Self-acceptance</u>
      1.   I am a valuable person.
      2.   I choose to not beat up on myself anymore.
      3.   I choose to release feelings of guilt that are not serving a corrective function.
      4.   I accept myself for the person that I am.
      5.   I choose to love myself.
      6.   I am a valuable person.

Chapter 56 – PTSD Mindsets Part II: The PTSD Thought Patterns

I.   **People Who Are Coping with PTSD Often See the World in "All – or – Nothing" Ways**[1,2]
    A.   This is sometimes called "black – or – white" thinking.
    B.   This was useful in combat (or other types of trauma) → it kept you alive.
    C.   Now, in society this makes coping with PTSD much more difficult.
    D.   Things that were useful in the past can make daily life more difficult now.

II.   **Some Ways of Thinking that Make Coping with PTSD More Difficult**
    A.   <u>PTSD Thought Patterns</u>
        1.   I Don't feel safe → I need to always be on guard.
        2.   I Don't want to experience feelings → it seems dangerous.
        3.   I am unworthy; I don't deserve good things.
        4.   It's all my fault.
        5.   I can feel in control (safe) by being angry. (In control = safety)
        6.   Worry helps you watch out for every possible danger.
        7.   I must do everything perfectly. ("If you want it done right, you must do it yourself.")
        8.   One little mistake means that I'm a total failure (all-or-nothing thinking).
        9.   Everyone out there is either stupid or incompetent.
      10.   If people would do things my way, then things would turn out okay.
      11.   My way is the right way and the only way.
      12.   Don't trust anybody because it will only get you hurt.
      13.   If I let people get too close to me, then I might lose them or hurt them, so I push people away.
      14.   I don't need anyone; I can and will do everything for myself.
      15.   I have been wronged, so I have a right to hold grudges.
      16.   There's nothing wrong with me, but everyone else is sure screwed up.
      17.   There is nothing real to believe in.
      18.   I will apologize if I'm wrong about something, but I'm never wrong.
      19.   If one little thing goes wrong, then my whole day is ruined.
      20.   I need to look for everything that's wrong to prove that everything is all messed up.
      21.   People are out to get me. I must watch everyone very carefully (paranoia).
      22.   If you make plans, then something will happen to ruin them.
      23.   If things start going too good, then something bad has to follow.
      24.   If you really knew me, then you would reject me.

    B.   <u>The Problem</u>
1. These thought patterns can be useful and might even help you survive a traumatic situation.
2. However, these thoughts actually work against you in "normal" (non-traumatic) daily life.
3. These thinking patterns usually keep us acting in ways that prevent recovery.

III.   **Some New Ways of Thinking that Help in Coping with PTSD** [35,59]
    A.   There can be many perspectives and opinions about most situations.
    B.   Understanding things in a more accurate way will help me to cope better with PTSD symptoms and my current situation.
    C.   There are usually several possible view points in any given situation.
1. Am I positive that my view point is the most accurate perspective?
2. How do I know for sure that mine is the "right" one?
3. Why am I convinced that I'm right and everyone else is dead wrong?

    D.   Understand that the above PTSD thought patterns are usually not helpful or adaptive in civilian life.
    E.   Are you willing to challenge the "PTSD thoughts" and begin thinking in more adaptive and productive ways?
    F.   <u>New Thoughts</u> (write on a card and carry in your pocket to read 3 times daily)
1. I don't always have to be on high alert to stay safe.
2. Feelings won't kill me → it's okay to feel more than anger and sadness.
3. I don't have to be angry to be in control.
4. It's okay if not everything is absolutely perfect all of the time.
5. Not everyone is out to get me.
6. Most people are not trying to provoke me.
7. There is more than one way to get things done.
8. I can trust a few people who really are trustworthy.
9. I choose to accept help when I need it.
10. Grudges only hurt me → I choose to give them up.
11. A small setback does not have to ruin my whole day.
12. I choose to look for what's right in most situations.
13. I can be alert without having to be paranoid.
14. I choose to be flexible in my planning.
15. I accept that I am a valuable person.

Chapter 57 – PTSD Mindsets Part III: Thought Retraining

I.   **The Importance of Our Thoughts** [35]
   A.   Because traumatic experiences are completely overwhelming, they can set us up to think in depressive, self-defeating, and angry ways.
   B.   To cope more effectively with PTSD, we need to identify the thoughts that perpetuate symptoms, and replace them with productive thinking.
   C.   Without examining our thinking, our very own thoughts will contribute to our symptoms, keeping us stuck, and we won't even know it.

II.   **PTSD Thought Patterns** [1,2,60,61,62]– see if you have any of the following.
   A.   Depressive Thoughts [61,62]
      1.   I'm hopeless (nothing can help or make things better).
      2.   I'm helpless (there's nothing I can do).
      3.   I'm unlovable (nobody would really love me if they knew me or the things I've done).
      4.   I'm so stupid.
      5.   I'm no good (worthless, terrible, good-for-nothing).
      6.   My circumstances are awful and nothing will ever get any better.
      7.   The future is hopeless – why should I even try?
      8.   "Should"-ing on ourselves → beat up on ourselves with "should statements" that are unrealistic.
         a.   "I should be handling everything with no trouble at all."
         b.   "I should be loved by everybody."
         c.   "I should not have these problems."
   B.   Negative Thoughts about Myself [61,62]
      1.   I will never accomplish anything that's good.
      2.   It was all my fault.
      3.   I don't deserve anything good in my life.
      4.   I'm a complete failure.
      5.   I deserve to be punished.
      6.   I am lower than scum.
   C.   Angry Thoughts [33,61]
      1.   All those stupid people out there.
      2.   People are out to get me.
      3.   People do things to me on purpose (to provoke me).
            (taking everything personally, when it's really not personal.)
      4.   I can never back down or I'll be seen as weak.
      5.   Being angry is the only way you can get things to happen.

    D.   <u>Anxious Thoughts</u> [42,61]

        1.   What if _____ happens? I could never handle it.

        2.   Where's the danger?

        3.   Who's watching me? Who's out to get me?

        4.   What's going to go wrong next?

        5.   I should have _____.

        6.   _____ is so awful.

        7.   I'm afraid of what could happen.

III.   **To Get Better, We Need to Practice New Thinking Habits** [35,60,61,62]

    A.   Write each statement below on a note card, and read each one aloud at least 2-3 times each day.

    B.   <u>Positive Self-Statements</u>

        1.   I'm here now.

        2.   They (it) can't hurt me now.

        3.   I'm safe now.

        4.   It's not happening now.

        5.   It was not my fault.

        6.   I'm in control.

        7.   I don't have to be afraid now.

        8.   I will win this thing.

        9.   I will survive.

        10.   I am a valuable person.

        11.   There are people who care about me.

        12.   I am not alone in this.

        13.   It's okay to feel good.

        14.   It's okay to feel good about myself.

        15.   It's okay to have good things in my life.

        16.   It's okay to live in an enjoyable way.

        17.   I do not have to live in constant fear.

        18.   When I encounter a trigger, I will handle it; it will not control me or my behavior.

        19.   I don't have to be afraid of getting better.

        20.   I choose to take control of my own life.

        21.   I choose to not let the past have power over me.

        22.   I choose to confront the realities of my life.

        23.   I refuse to be totally overwhelmed by my past anymore.

        24.   I will not let fear and uncertainty rule my life.

        25.   I forgive myself for where I've messed up.

        26.   I don't want to be angry all of the time.

        27.   I don't have to be angry all of the time.

        28.   I don't always have to prove myself.

29.   Most people are probably not out to get me.
30.   I will manage my anger and control myself.
31.   I will get better.
32.   I'm going to make it.
C.   When we retrain our thinking to be more positive and productive, our ability to cope with symptoms and stress improves.
D.   Now we need to practice.
E.   Practice some more.
F.   Practice every single day.

Chapter 58 – Depression: Part I

I. **What Are the Symptoms of Depression?** [64]
   - A. A mood that feels extremely low, sad, or empty.
   - B. Anhedonia – a loss of interest in things that used to be enjoyable.
   - C. Extremes of appetite that lead to weight gain or loss (too much or very little).
   - D. Extremes of sleep → too much or very little sleep.
   - E. Agitation and/or restlessness.
   - F. Excessive fatigue or lack of energy that doesn't get better with sleep.
   - G. Feelings of worthlessness; inappropriate or extreme guilt.
   - H. Poor thinking or concentration; indecisiveness.
   - I. Frequent thoughts of death or suicide.

II. **The Impact of Depression on Daily Life** [60,61,62,64]
   - A. Have you had 5 or more of the above symptoms for a period of 2 weeks or longer?
   - B. Have the above symptoms interfered with your work, schooling, relationships, or other important parts of your life?
   - C. Mild depression can make us less productive and interfere with relationships.
   - D. Moderate to severe depression can be extremely debilitating.
   - E. Example: Don't get out of bed or take a shower for several days at a time; become unable to complete routine tasks at work or home.
   - F. It feels as if you are "carrying the weight of the world on your shoulders."
   - G. Feel like crawling into a dark pit to escape from everyone and everything.
   - H. Gets hard to fulfill basic responsibilities or tasks each day.

III. **What Can Lead to Depression?**
   - A. Loss and Grief [8,61] – depression can result from the loss of someone or something that was loved, highly valued, or very important to you.
     1. The loved one (or thing that was valued and lost) could include a person, cherished ideal, patriotism, certain spiritual values, or self-respect. [1,9]
        - a. Example: Losses due to war (or other trauma).
        - b. Loss of youth, health, hopes, dreams.
     2. Losing a long-held value or one's dignity can also lead to depression.
        - a. Example: The requirements of war conflicted with values learned as a child.
        - b. Either new values were formed or you walked away confused about what you think and believe.

3.   Depression can result if a person's dignity or self-respect was assaulted by the trauma and/or the negative reactions of other people.

    a.   Example: As a result of war experiences, I came to see myself differently.

    b.   Also, I was mistreated by people after getting back home.

    c.   Ever since then, I have felt terrible about myself.

4.   If assumptions about the goodness and justice in the world were shattered by the trauma, depression may arise.

    a.   Example: Traumatic experiences "removed the rose-colored glasses."

    b.   This creates a new understanding that the world is not a fair or just place.

    c.   Many soldiers lost faith in military authority and experienced lessened patriotism.

    d.   The resulting feelings included anger and grief.

B.   Lack of Reinforcement [65,66,67]

1.   Everyone needs a certain amount of reward, recognition, and positive experience on a regular basis.

2.   If rewards are absent from a person's life, they will naturally become depressed.

3.   Depression can also occur when people are unable to appreciate, reward, or care for themselves.

4.   Trauma survivors often lack reinforcement from themselves and from other people.

5.   Life becomes all work and struggle with no payoff or benefits that we can see.

6.   Many veterans were rejected when they returned home and even treated in abusive ways.

IV.   **Understand the Depression**

A.   What important things have you lost that you never grieved?

B.   What did the trauma(s) take that you can never get back?

C.   What is your view of the world now (after the trauma)?

D.   How do you see yourself now?

E.   Are you able to get positive rewards in life, or is life just a struggle with no benefits or enjoyment?

F.   Do you feel valued?   YES   NO

V.   **Behaviors that Often Help Counteract Depressive Symptoms** [68]

A.   Get some sunlight everyday if possible (you don't have to be directly in the sun).

B.   Get some exercise everyday if possible (e.g., walking 30 minutes 3X per week).

C.   Express anger outwardly in appropriate, non-destructive ways.

D.   Replace negative ways of viewing the world with more positive, productive thoughts.

E.   Add some positive, enjoyable activities to your life on a daily basis.

F.   If you have losses that have contributed to the depression, work through the grieving process.

G.   Find ways to get positive, appropriate rewards for yourself when you do a good job at something.

H.   Reward yourself for doing a good job on _____ recently.

I.   Forgive those people who have rejected or hurt you (be the bigger person).

Chapter 59 – Depression: Part II

I.   **Anger Is Often Present when a Person is Depressed** [8,33]
    A.   When anger is not expressed outwardly, it is often directed inwardly at ourselves.
    B.   This increases depression.
    C.   Many people don't know how to appropriately express anger.
    D.   Many trauma survivors are afraid of their own anger.
        1.   What might I do if I lose control?
    E.   The habit of suppressing anger can be difficult to unlearn or replace.
    F.   There may be no clear target for the anger → angry and don't know why.
    G.   It often feels easier and safer to turn anger inward on ourselves, resulting in beating up on ourselves.
    H.   The bottom line: Anger will be expressed → either outwardly or inwardly on ourselves.

II.   **Feeling Depressed About Being Depressed**
    A.   Some people may interpret the fact that they become depressed as a sign of personal failure or weakness.
    B.   Some people may feel ashamed or guilty about becoming depressed.
    C.   Often society blames people for their own pain or difficulties.
    D.   Depression is very common and does not need to be a reason for feeling ashamed.
    E.   It needs to be recognized and treated.
    F.   Realize that depression is often a self-protective strategy in response to real hurts or emotional injuries that have occurred.

III.   **Self-Esteem (to set a value on; to appreciate the worth of [the self])** [69,70,71]
    A.   With depression, a person may feel bad about themselves as a person (feel worthless, bad, unlovable, unworthy).
    B.   When depressed, a person may question their own value as a human being.
    C.   Thoughts of hopelessness and helplessness often arise and serve to keep us depressed. (There's nothing I can do.)
    D.   We need to confront these thoughts and replace them with realistic, positive thoughts about ourselves.
    E.   Say out loud, "I am a valuable person."

IV.   **Depression and Our Thinking** [60,62]
      A.   When depressed, our thinking takes on a particular pattern.
           1.   We view ourselves negatively.
           2.   "I'm bad; unlovable; a terrible person."
           3.   See our circumstances as awful and beyond our control.
           4.   Think of the future and see only doom and gloom.
           5.   Feel and think there is absolutely no hope.
           6.   Believe there is nothing we can do about our situation and how we feel.
      B.   We need to identify these thoughts and replace them with positive thought patterns that are realistic.

V.   **Addressing the Depression**
      A.   Begin by writing a short description of why you think you are depressed.
      B.   When did this start?
      C.   How long has it lasted?
      D.   What makes it worse? (be specific)
      E.   List the exact thoughts that go through your mind when depressed.

           _____   _____   _____

           _____   _____   _____

           _____   _____   _____

      F.   What important things in your life have you lost?
           1.   Have you accepted the loss?
           2.   Are you still in denial about the loss?
      G.   Make a list of the things you are angry about from the past or present.
           1.   Do you "bottle it up?"
           2.   How do you express this anger?
      H.   How do you feel about yourself as a person?
      I.   Write down anything else that you think might possibly relate to the depression.

VI.   **Behaviors that Often Help Counteract Depressive Symptoms** [68]
      A.   Add some positive, enjoyable activities to your life on a daily basis.
      B.   If using medication, take exactly as prescribed.
      C.   Talk with someone you can trust about what is going on in your life.
      D.   Find meaningful, productive activities for yourself and stay fairly busy (projects).

E.   Force yourself to do the basics:
   1.   Get up.
   2.   Take a bath or shower.
   3.   Shave.
   4.   Wash your face.
   5.   Brush your teeth.
   6.   Get moving (start to doing something productive, no matter how small).
   7.   Stay active (the majority of your time).
   8.   Talk with a positive, uplifting friend.
   9.   Open the blinds and get some sunlight.

Chapter 60 – Depression: Part III

I.   **Certain Types of Beliefs Contribute To and Perpetuate Depression** [60,61,62]
  A.   The things we believe have a powerful influence on how we feel and how we act.
  B.   Many beliefs were learned during childhood.
    1.   These beliefs have effects on our lives many years later.
    2.   We are often not fully aware of these beliefs.
  C.   We can challenge many of our old beliefs and choose new beliefs that help us to "move away from the depression."

II. **Specific Beliefs Related to Depression** [61,62]
  A.   I'm Hopeless – the belief that my situation and the future will never get any better.
    1.   When feeling hopeless, we expect a bad outcome in most situations we encounter.
    2.   We feel that "it will never get any better."
    3.   We tell ourselves "there is nothing to look forward to."
    4.   We feel like the world is totally awful with nothing good in it.
    5.   When feeling hopeless, we conclude "what's the use?"
  B.   I'm Helpless – the belief that I am unable to do anything positive to improve my situation or how I feel.
    1.   "I am ineffective, inadequate, and unable."
    2.   "Nothing I do ever works out."
    3.   If I try, I'm sure to fail."
    4.   We become convinced that we have no power to change our situation.
    5.   Self-doubt can become paralyzing.
    6.   Words frequently used to describe feelings of helplessness:
      a.   Inadequate
      b.   Powerless
      c.   Trapped
      d.   Inferior
      e.   Ineffective
      f.   Incompetent
      g.   Weak
      h.   Vulnerable
      i.   Failure
      j.   Defective
      k.   Don't measure up
      l.   Not good enough

                m.   Loser

                n.   Needy

                o.   Out of control

C.   <u>I'm Unlovable/Worthless</u> – the belief that I have no personal value.

    1.   When depressed, we believe negative things about ourselves that we ordinarily would not.

    2.   When feeling this way, we "beat up on ourselves inwardly" and confirm our negative feelings with derogatory self-statements.

    3.   We tell ourselves certain things inside our minds:

        a.   I'm no good.

        b.   I'm a loser.

        c.   I'm a failure.

        d.   I'm just damaged goods.

        e.   I'm not worth the effort.

        f.   I have nothing to offer.

        g.   I'll never amount to anything.

        h.   I'm stupid.

        i.   Nobody could ever really care about me.

        j.   I am the lowest scum of the earth.

    4.   When depressed, we believe that other people feel as badly toward us as we feel toward ourselves.

III.   Other Depressive Thought Patterns

A.   <u>Negative Thought Patterns</u>

    1.   When depressed, we see most everything in a negative and depressing way.

    2.   Positives are turned into negatives and negatives are magnified.

    3.   Our ability to enjoy positive things is reduced or eliminated.

    4.   Our perspective changes leaving no room for anything positive or enjoyable.

B.   <u>Pessimistic Outlook</u>

    1.   When depressed, we diminish anything potentially positive.

    2.   After long enough, we become cheerless, gloomy, joyless, unhappy, critical, blaming, derogatory, judgmental, and dejected.

IV.   Replacing the Old Beliefs [35]

A.   <u>Challenging the Hopeless Beliefs</u>

    1.   What evidence supports the idea that I'm hopeless? (i.e., what are you basing this on?)

    2.   What is the result of believing that I'm hopeless?

    3.   If I changed my belief, what might the result be?

    4.   What do I have to lose?

    5.   What would I tell a friend who expressed this belief?

B.   <u>Challenging the Helpless Beliefs</u>

1.   I Can't = I am <u>unable</u> and it is beyond my control.
2.   I Won't = I <u>choose</u> not to for some reason.
3.   In depression, feeling helpless is related to difficulties getting motivated and believing that any action we take will not be effective.
4.   What are some examples of where you were effective in the past?
5.   Are you willing to take the first little step to make a positive change now?

C.   <u>Challenging the Unlovable/Worthless Beliefs</u>

1.   Say to yourself right now, "I am a valuable person."
2.   I don't have to be loved by everyone.
3.   If some people don't like me, that's OK.
4.   I can be happy without everyone's approval.
5.   I have a mix of positive and negative traits – just like everyone else and that's OK. I choose to use the positive and will work to improve the negative.
6.   There really are people who care about me.
7.   It's OK to have good feelings about myself.

V.   Using Questions to Help Change Our Conclusions and Beliefs

A.   What is the evidence for believing these negative things?
B.   How do I know that these negative thoughts are really accurate or true?
C.   Is it possible to test these beliefs?
D.   What is the worst thing that could happen if I took a more positive view?
E.   Will I be any worse off believing something different?
F.   What would a good friend say if I expressed my negative beliefs to them?
G.   Where do I want to go from here?

Chapter 61 – Anxiety and Our Thinking

I.   **What Is Anxiety?**
   A.   <u>Symptoms of Anxiety</u> [42,43,72]
      1.   Trembling, feeling shaky or restless, muscle tension.
      2.   Shortness of breath, feeling like you are smothering.
      3.   Rapid heartbeat.
      4.   Sweating, cold hands and/or feet.
      5.   Lightheadedness or dizziness; feeling as if your head might explode.
      6.   Tingling sensations.
      7.   Diarrhea, frequent urination, or both.
      8.   Feeling as if things aren't real; feeling like you are outside your body.
      9.   Problems falling asleep; can't shut off the flood of thoughts.
      10.   Difficulty paying attention or concentrating.
      11.   Feeling nervous, edgy, or tense.
   B.   <u>What Does It Feel Like?</u>
      1.   Uncomfortable; jittery inside; body feels tense.
      2.   Uneasy; feel nervous; weak legs or weak all over.
      3.   Feel unsure of myself.

II.   **How Common Is Anxiety?**
   A.   Anxiety is the most common psychiatric complaint. [13]
   B.   Most people feel a little nervous or tense from time to time or in certain situations.
   C.   However, when anxiety lasts too long or makes you unable to do the things you need to do, it becomes a concern worthy of attention and possible treatment. [29]

III.   **Normal vs. Abnormal Anxiety** [61]
   A.   <u>Normal Anxiety</u>:
      1.   When we consider that we are in danger, we tend to feel anxious. This is normal → no pathology here.
      2.   Anticipation that we will lose something valuable to us brings anxiety.
      3.   Anxiety is a warning signal → it tells us that some kind of protective or preventive action is needed.
      4.   Anxiety alerts us so we can take action in order to cope with a threat (to protect yourself).
      5.   Anxiety is normal when is arises in response to a real and present danger, and then it goes away when that danger passes.

B.   Abnormal Anxiety:
   1.   The anxiety is disproportionate to the degree of danger. (anxiety is too high; an emotional over reaction).
   2.   Anxiety occurs when no real danger is present.
   3.   It is a problem when anxiety lasts too long → find that you are still anxious after the danger is gone or the situation has resolved.
   4.   If anxiety is continually present with no apparent or immediate danger, then a person is reacting in a way that does not match up with the reality of the situation.
   5.   The anxiety impairs our coping ability → limits you from doing what needs to be done.
   6.   It is a problem when our mind and body stay revved up, but no good benefit is gained from it.

IV.   **How Anxiety Affects Our Thinking** [42,43,61]
   A.   Anxiety makes it hard to think clearly.
   B.   Decision making is more difficult.
   C.   Fear and doubt dominate our thoughts.
   D.   We focus on our own inadequacies and have doubts about our ability to cope.
   E.   We convince ourselves that we won't be able to manage the situation.
   F.   Anticipatory Anxiety (how it works)
      1.   We create worst-case scenarios in our mind.
      2.   Focus on extremely unlikely outcomes (based on unrealistic thinking).
      3.   Expect things to turn out badly.
      4.   Then, these scenarios almost never come true.
      5.   As a result, we stay anxious or "keyed up" most of the time.
      6.   With this pattern, we are "working really hard" for almost no benefit.

V.   **Coping Thoughts**
   A.   What we say to ourselves inside our minds has a profound impact on how we handle anxiety (and also difficult life situations).
   B.   Our thoughts will either make things better or worse.
   C.

Don't Say	Instead, Tell Yourself
1. I'll never make it.	1. I will get there.
2. I can't.	2. I can do it.
3. It's too much.	3. I can deal with this.
4. I'm afraid.	4. I will overcome this.
5. What if _____ happens?	5. I will find a way to handle it.
6. What will I do?	6. I have options.

VI.   Coping Behaviors (to gain control over our anxiety)

    A.   Confront those things you are afraid of.
         1.   Go at this slowly.
         2.   Use good judgment.
         3.   If feeling overwhelmed, back off a little and try more later.
         4.   Consult a good therapist to help with this if necessary.

    B.   If planning ahead, ask a friend to help you with uncomfortable situations until those things become easier or more manageable.

    C.   <u>Keep a record</u>
         1.   Just how many of those negative predictions actually came true?
         2.   Write down exactly what happened in those situations that you feared.

    D.   Start with small steps toward bigger goals and work your way up .
         1.   Take baby steps at first.

    E.   Practice coping thoughts every day whether you feel anxious or not.

    F.   <u>More Coping Thoughts</u>
         1.   I will make it.
         2.   I can handle it.
         3.   I'm not helpless here.
         4.   There are things I can do in this situation.
         5.   I can figure this out.
         6.   I have skills and will use them here.
         7.   I am a valuable person.
         8.   I refuse to live in fear and uncertainty.
         9.   I refuse to be a victim of fear and anxiety.
         10.   Most problems have reasonable solutions → I will find them!

Chapter 62 – Understanding Your Anxiety

I.   We First Need to Understand Anxiety [61]

A.   Fear and anxiety are related but not the same thing.

B.   <u>Fear</u> is an unpleasant, strong experience caused by the anticipation of danger or the expectation of being hurt.

C.   Synonyms for fear are dread, fright, alarm, panic, terror, trepidation.

D.   <u>Anxiety</u> – an abnormal and overwhelming sense of apprehension marked by physical signs (e.g., sweating, tension, increased pulse), doubt concerning the reality and nature of the threat, and self-doubt about your ability to cope with it.

E.   Notice the Difference.

    1.   <u>Fear</u> is the anticipation of being hurt or damaged in some way (a particular kind of thinking).

    2.   <u>Anxiety</u> is the unpleasant emotional and physical reaction associated with fear (a particular feeling or emotion).

F.   Once we understand how anxiety works, we can confront our fears and those things that perpetuate the symptoms.

II.   Types of Anxiety [73]

A.   There are at least 6 different types or sources of anxiety.

B.   To get better, it is important to know which type(s) of anxiety you are working on.

C.   A person can have one or more of the following:

    1.   <u>Anxiety about our own potential destructiveness</u> (ID anxiety)

        a.   What might I do if I lost control of myself?

        b.   What might happen if my destructive impulses were unleashed?

        c.   Many people put enormous effort into keeping their impulses under control.

    2.   <u>Anxiety about a real and present danger</u> (EGO anxiety)

        a.   This can be based on past experiences in which you were in danger.

        b.   Now, you feel anxious when the same or similar danger is present.

        c.   Some people become anxious simply anticipating the danger (when it is not really present).

3.   <u>Anxiety from your conscience</u> (SUPEREGO anxiety)
a.   Fear of punishment, shame, or guilt.
b.   Feel like you can never measure up; feel "not good enough" or "less than."
c.   No matter what you do, it's never good enough; your efforts are not fulfilling.

4.   <u>Anxiety about the fear of annihilation</u>
a.   Afraid of becoming overwhelmed or engulfed by a powerful outside force.
b.   This often results from experiences in childhood.

5.   <u>Separation Anxiety</u>
a.   Fear of being utterly alone with no connection to anyone.
b.   Results in feeling empty, inconsequential, unimportant, or worthless.

6.   <u>Anxiety Due to a Medical Condition</u> [29]
a.   Some medical conditions create physical states of the body that produce anxiety.
b.   Ex. Adrenal insufficiency, Cushing's Syndrome, hyperthyroidism, mitral valve prolapse, Parkinson's disease, certain tumors, and other medical conditions.

III.   Using Our Thoughts to Reduce Anxiety

A.   <u>We need to Confront and Challenge the Thoughts that keep us Anxious</u> [35]
1.   Make a list of exactly what you feel anxious about.
2.   Choose one item and describe in detail the <u>worst case</u> scenario.
3.   Now imagine that the worst thing really does happen.
4.   What would you do if that happened?
5.   Could you handle it?
a.   YES
b.   Even though it is undesirable, it probably wouldn't kill you, it wouldn't be the end of the world, and you wouldn't go crazy.
6.   Often, looking at "the bottom line" reduces our anxiety and worry by helping us face up to our fears and then move forward.
7.   Next, describe in detail the <u>best</u> possible outcome for that situation.
8.   Could you handle that?
a.   YES
9.   <u>Conclusion</u>: If you can handle the worst <u>and</u> best case scenarios, then any outcome in between can also be managed.
10. Now tell yourself: "I see that I will probably be able to manage this!"

11.   Take a deep breath and tell yourself: "I will be able to handle this!"

12.   If you are still anxious, you are probably stuck focusing only on the worst case scenario.

B.   We Need to Think more in terms of "What are the Chances?" [74]

    1.   What are the chances that (the feared situation) will happen?

        Low   Medium   High

    2.   How do I know?

    3.   What is my experience in this type of situation?

        a.   Has it happened before? What usually happens in this situation?

        b.   Does it ALWAYS happen? What information do I have?

    4.   Many times, we stay anxious by focusing on things that are extremely unlikely.

    5.   Now, let's decrease our anxiety by focusing on the most likely outcome.

    6.   If the chances of this negative thing happening are low, then I refuse to worry about it!

    7.   What are the chances that I will be able to cope with this situation?

        Low   Medium   High

    8.   I can now be more relaxed because I see that it is manageable.

    9.   I am ALERT but NOT ALARMED → I can now handle the situation without reacting.

C.   Change Your Attitudes and Thoughts

    1.   Most situations do not turn out the worst possible way most of the time.

    2.   Say, "I expect that I will be able to cope with most things that come my way."

    3.   Most problems have good solutions → I will figure them out!

    4.   I refuse to be a victim of my fears → I will overcome past fears.

    5.   I will use my brains, test things out, and cope effectively.

IV. Confronting Fears

A.   Avoiding vs. Confronting [42,43]

    1.   Avoiding those things that make us anxious reduces our anxiety in the short term, but strengthens it in the long term.

    2.   To ultimately overcome anxiety, we must confront our fears without being overwhelmed.

    3.   When our fears are confronted and conquered, they no longer have power over us.

    4.   When we confront feared situations, this usually increases anxiety in the short term, but reduces it in the long term.

    5.   Necessary Steps

a.   Make a plan for what to confront and how to confront it.
b.   Choose a time and go at it slowly.
c.   When feeling too anxious, remain at that point until the anxiety reduces.
d.   Go a little further now that you are more calm.
e.   Repeat "c" and "d" above until you no longer have anxiety.
f.   With practice, you will learn to confront the feared situation without feeling anxious or overwhelmed (you are now in control).

B.   Be aware that many people need to consult a good therapist to assist with confronting fears.

Chapter 63 – Victim Thinking

I.   Most People Who Have Been Traumatized Feel Like a Victim [1,2,5]

    A.   This is expected because <u>you were</u> victimized by the trauma.

    B.   When a person is victimized, several thoughts, feelings, and behaviors are common.

        1.   Feel trapped, shamed, vulnerable, incompetent, unworthy, deprived.

        2.   Can't talk about it.

        3.   Feel that it's not safe to trust anyone.

        4.   Want to fight or do harmful behaviors.

        5.   Focus on safety above all else.

        6.   Want to hide, isolate, and alienate others.

        7.   Feel abandoned.

        8.   Have difficulty feeling anything positive, and managing feelings in general.

        9.   Have unrealistic standards of perfection.

        10.   Become overly critical and sensitive.

        11.   Show poor self-control.

        12.   Often, find it hard to stick with anything.

        13.   Have a negative attitude about most things.

        14.   Become pessimistic and punitive toward others.

    C.   While it is expected that a person will have these types of experience after a trauma, keeping this mindset prevents recovery.

II.   Victim Thinking Can Become a Vicious Cycle [1,8,9]

    A.   First → feel victimized (see section I above).

    B.   Second → repeatedly seek out situations that result in re-victimization.

        1.   Feel hurt all over again.

        2.   Feel like a magnet for trouble.

    C.   Third → become convinced that you will always be a victim.

        1.   Maybe I'm just a terrible person.

        2.   Maybe I deserve it.

    D.   Now, the person feels like a victim all over again and the cycle repeats.

III.   Untreated PTSD Results in a Severe, Negative Downward Spiral [1,9]

A. Cope as best you can while being confused most of the time, often feeling overwhelmed.

B. Live in denial – " I don't have a problem, but everyone else sure does."

C. Efforts to cope (e.g., drugs, alcohol, fights, etc.) provide bits of short-term relief, but overall make things worse in the long term.

D. Privately think "maybe I'm just crazy."

E. Most actions are motivated by the lasting effects of the trauma and not by positive choices for how we want to live today.

F. Struggle to be in control, wondering when you might lose control or become overwhelmed next.

G. Have minimal to nonexistent relationships → wind up feeling rejected and alone.

H. Without treatment, most people never figure it out or get much better.

I. When PTSD goes untreated, the long term prognosis is often poor.

J. What direction was your life headed before therapy?

IV. Steps Toward Recovery [1,2]

A. To get better, we <u>must become determined</u> that we will get back in control of our lives.

B. <u>Victim Stage</u>
   1. Stay trapped, powerless, and always fearful.
   2. Feel sorry for yourself (keeps you trapped).
   3. Focus on how you were wronged and your inability to do anything about it.
   4. Remain paralyzed by fear and indecision.

C. <u>The Surviving Stage</u>
   1. Survive the best you can.
   2. Use coping skills in an unhealthy way.
      a. Unhealthy skills (alcohol, drugs, anger, intimidation, fighting).
      b. Short term solutions for a long term problem (denial, stuffing feelings, etc.).
      c. Overuse healthy strategies (workaholism, over-controlling, "analyze it to death").
   3. Go thru life confused and uninformed about your condition, not knowing what to do about it.
   4. Be convinced you're on the right track because "your method got you this far."
   5. Eventually, hit bottom, your life starts "falling apart", and you're not sure what to do or where to turn.

D. <u>The Recovery Process</u>

1.   Become educated about what happened to you.
   a.   We must figure it out to start getting better.
   b.   Staying confused will keep you stuck.
2.   Begin taking care of yourself so that you can recover.
3.   Reduce and eliminate unhealthy behaviors.
4.   Replace unhealthy attempts at coping with healthy, productive coping skills.
5.   Begin taking some small risks to connect with other people in positive ways.
6.   Set and observe healthy boundaries.

E.   <u>Living Again</u> (thriving)
1.   Start plugging back into life in a healthy way; start "living again."
2.   Manage your anxiety and fear so that most of the time it is no longer overwhelming.
3.   Learn and practice skills to get your anger under control.
4.   Acknowledge your positive traits and ability to survive.
5.   Learn to love and play again.
6.   Identify and use the wisdom gained from surviving the trauma and the recovery process.
7.   Manage your triggers and their effects.
8.   Understand the meaning of your trauma and share this with others at appropriate times.
9.   Reach out to help others.

F.   Progress occurs as we move fully into the thriving stage (i.e., living again).

V.   New Conclusions

A.   I was a victim in the past, but I refuse to be a victim anymore.
B.   I will not let the trauma(s) dominate my life anymore.
C.   I choose to live in a healthy way from now on.
D.   I am replacing "reaction mode" with intentional choices for handling things.
E.   I am understanding more and more all the time.
F.   I am no longer powerless to deal with the trauma(s) → I choose to respond and not react!
G.   I choose to recover and thrive in spite of the trauma(s).

Chapter 64 – Worry

I. **What is Worry?** [75,76]
 A. Frequent distressing thoughts about a wide range of potential threats or dangers.
 B. When we feel helpless, we often attempt to "do something" about the situation.
 C. Worry is an attempt to reduce negative physical and mental feelings when there is no specific action to be taken at that moment.
 D. A small amount of negative feeling is reduced, and we are therefore "rewarded" for worrying.
 E. We come to believe that worrying has prevented some negative outcome, and we think that it has "helped us."
 F. However, we have actually increased our own stress and anxiety in the long term.

II. **Thought Patterns Involved in Worry** [42,43,44,45]
 A. <u>Selective Attention</u>
  1. Focusing on possible dangers or threats.
  2. Discounting positive outcomes that are more likely.
  3. Not looking at the "big picture" or larger situation.
  4. This results in tunnel vision and a focus on problems instead of solutions.
 B. <u>"What If's"</u>
  1. Creating worst-case scenarios with elaborate details in your mind based on "what if" catastrophic thinking.
  2. Ignoring the possible positive outcomes for a particular situation and considering only the negative ones.
  3. Example: What if my spouse has an automobile accident driving home and is killed. I could never handle that.
  4. With this pattern, we stay focused on the worst case scenario and how awful it would be.
 C. <u>Perfectionism</u>
  1. Expecting perfect performance from yourself in everything you do.
  2. Perfectionism is seen as the only way to prevent catastrophic events or consequences.
  3. Anything less than perfection is seen as a total failure and is considered completely unacceptable.
  4. This sets you up to be disappointed and depressed because nobody does everything perfectly.
  5. Less than perfect behavior in other people is seen as incompetence and evidence that they can't be trusted at all.

D. <u>Difficulty Tolerating Uncertainty</u>
   1. When uncertain about how things will turn out, we put effort into figuring things out and trying to have some control over the situation.
   2. However, worry consists of distressing thoughts, but without positive action to help the situation.
   3. When worrying, this process can continue indefinitely.

E. <u>Low Confidence in Our Own Problem-solving Ability</u>
   1. When worrying, we try to work out the "best solution" to our fears.
   2. We are convinced there is always a better solution, so we strain ourselves with worry in order to feel a sense of control.
   3. Our doubts motivate us to "work harder" mentally to find a feeling of safety and security.
   4. This results in mental work that does not produce solutions or increased confidence.
   5. We usually stay anxious, and then worry more.

III. Confronting and Challenging the Worry [42,43]
(This requires <u>deliberate action</u> based on your <u>choice</u> to stop worrying)

A. <u>Reduce physical tension</u> [41]
   1. We need to reduce our physical tension in practical and productive ways.
   2. Practice deep breathing for 5 minutes 2 to 3 times each day.
   3. Exercise regularly at a level your body is able to handle.

B. <u>Challenge your "worry thoughts"</u>
   1. Imagine that the worst thing really does happen.
   2. Will you be able to handle it?   → YES
   3. Now choose to focus on the most likely outcome for the situation.

C. <u>Set aside time just to worry</u>
   1. Stand or sit by a trash can (this symbolizes what worry does to us).
   2. Set an alarm for 15 minutes.
   3. Worry as hard as you can about every concern for 15 minutes.
   4. After 15 minutes, you are done worrying for the day.
   5. Make this a ritual – get all of your worrying done so the rest of the day can be more productive.
   6. In time, the "worry session" becomes a time for productive planning.

D. <u>Use planning</u>
   1. A lack of simple planning often increases our stress and worry.
   2. Use planning (with flexibility) to become more effective in your daily tasks.
   3. The need to worry begins to decrease when you plan ahead and are prepared.

E. <u>Get information</u>
    1.   What are the chances that _____ will happen?
    2.   How do I know?
    3.   What is my experience in this type of situation?
    4.   What usually happens?
    5.   Decrease worry by thinking your way through the situation and focusing on the most likely outcome.

F. <u>Confront feared situations</u>
    1.   Anxiety and worry usually prevent us from taking positive actions.
    2.   When our fears are confronted, they no longer have power over us.
    3.   Slowly confront the situations you worry about and find practical solutions.

G. <u>Use your spiritual beliefs</u> [2,77]
    1.   Many people trust God in situations where they have no control.
    2.   This reinforces our beliefs and helps us cope with situations that are beyond our control.
    3.   This is a key part of spiritual growth and mature faith for many people.

H. <u>Imagine</u>
    1.   What would it be like to not be a worrier?
    2.   Would that be an OK way to live?
    3.   Is that something that I want?
    4.   Am I willing to work toward getting there?

Chapter 65 – Identity

I.   **Identity (the distinguishing character or personality of an individual)**
  A.   Who are you?   What makes up who you are?
  B.   What direction is your life headed?
  C.   How do you define yourself?
  D.   What is your role in life?
  E.   Erik Erikson, the psychologist who coined the term "identity crisis," stated that the identity crisis is the most important conflict people experience when going through the eight developmental stages of life. [78]

II.   **Importance of Identity**
  A.   Many experts in the field of psychology agree that the development and growth of the "self" (i.e., a healthy identity) is a necessary part of mental health. [8,48]
  B.   During adolescence, the task of growing up is to figure out our identity.
    1.   We must figure out who we are, or who we want to be.
    2.   In order for teenagers to achieve a sense of identity, they must engage in exploration. (Trying out new ways of thinking and acting.)
    3.   This involves trying new ways of looking, new ideas, new groups or friends, new music styles, various clothing styles, etc. (in most every area of life).
    4.   After exploring several options, a person usually commits to a solid identity.
  C.   There are two potential outcomes to the identity search process.
    1.   Identity Achievement – once a solid, well-developed identity is formed, it guides how we live, how we see ourselves, and how we relate to others.
      a.   A firm sense of self (know who you are and why).
      b.   Healthy self-esteem (feel comfortable with who you are; feel valuable as a person).
      c.   Socially skilled (able to relate well with other people).
    2.   Identity Diffusion – people without a solid identity often struggle to understand themselves and where they "fit in."
      a.   Not sure who you are, or not comfortable with your identity.
      b.   Low self-esteem; feel rejected or unimportant.
      c.   Trouble making friends and relating to other people.
      d.   Difficulty being successful in life or going in a positive direction.

III.   Traumatic Experiences and Identity [1,8,9]

    A.   Traumatic experiences can disrupt a person's sense of identity.

    B.   They can become confused about their inner sense of who they are, how they think, what they believe, and how they should act.

    C.   Many trauma survivors report that they feel "permanently damaged" by the trauma(s).

    D.   Also, many report feeling that their personality (identity) was radically changed by the trauma(s).

    E.   This disruption causes some people to take on a "victim identity."

    F.   Others struggle to create a new healthy identity, and simply go through life trying to survive, stay safe, and "feel in control."

    G.   The inner turmoil of untreated PTSD leads many people to try building their self-esteem "any way possible", including through what are actually destructive behaviors.

    H.   A specific problem that arises from a damaged identity is that the person feels empty and worthless inside.

    I.   When deprived of external supports that had allowed the person to hold him or herself together, the person feels like they are beginning to disintegrate.

    J.   This "crumbling self" may result in depression, anxiety, rage, emptiness, and an overall sense of confusion. The person may even become suicidal.

IV.   Repairing a Healthy Identity [8]

    A.   Some things helpful to healing:

        1.   Realize you are not the only person dealing with PTSD.

        2.   Hear how other people's lives have been affected by PTSD.

        3.   Learn what PTSD really is.

        4.   Gain an understanding of the symptoms and their impact.

        5.   Realize that as chaotic as your life might have been, you are not "crazy."

        6.   With this new understanding, start deciding what you really believe and what you don't.

    B.   Healing Requires Empathy. [8,9,14]

        1.   Empathy may be defined as one person taking the time and effort to listen to and understand another person.

        2.   Walk in their shoes.

        3.   See the world through their eyes (as much as possible).

        4.   When a person feels understood and accepted, it feels safe enough to make inner changes that are needed for healing.

C.   If you find yourself in an identity crisis, you can look at the following areas that are important to having a healthy identity.

    1.   <u>Time perspective</u>
        a.   Can you distinguish immediate gratification from long-term goals?
        b.   Have you learned to balance between impulsive action and working steadily towards your long-term goals?

    2.   <u>Character and Self Consistency</u>
        a.   Do you feel consistent in your self-image and the image you present to others?
        b.   Are you confident enough in who you are to give up "wearing the mask?"

    3.   <u>Roles and Intentions</u>
        a.   Have you tried different roles in search of the one(s) that feels right to you?
        b.   Are you comfortable with the direction you are now headed in life?
        c.   Are you able to be either a leader or follower, whichever is called for in a given situation?
        d.   Are you true to your own beliefs, even in stressful situations?

    4.   <u>Anticipating Achievement</u>
        a.   Do you believe that you will be successful in the things you choose to do?
        b.   Do the things you do matter? Are they worthwhile?

    5.   <u>Sexual Identity</u>
        a.   Are you comfortable in being male or female?

    6.   <u>Attitudes and Core Values</u>
        a.   Do you have good reasons for believing the things you believe?
        b.   Are you confident in your core values and the direction they provide?

    7.   <u>Beliefs, Convictions, and Guiding Principles</u>
        a.   Do you have a set of basic social, religious, and philosophical beliefs and values that you base your life upon?
        b.   Do you have good reasons for those beliefs, or are you simply taking on the beliefs of others?

D.   As a person gets better through therapy, they rebuild a healthy identity that includes confidence, healthy attitudes, core values, self-esteem, and purpose.

E.   Eventually, each person must decide the kind of person they want to be, and work toward becoming just that.

Chapter 66 – Grieving and Loss: Part I

I.   **Grief [79] (a deep and poignant distress caused by the loss of people or things that are valuable to us)**
A.   This is usually experienced in the form of intense feelings of sadness and sorrow.
B.   While grief is emotionally painful, it needs to be processed.
C.   When losses are not grieved, anger about the loss can be turn inward onto ourselves, resulting in depression.
D.   <u>Mourning</u> – the process by which we identify, express, and deal with our grief.
1.   Mourning is necessary for us to adjust to the world after a loss.
2.   The terms "Grieving" and "Mourning" are usually used inter-changeably.

II.   **Some Basics About the Grief Process [79,80]**
A.   Everyone experiences grief a little bit differently.
B.   The pain of your loss can be deeper than you might expect.
C.   Grief can last longer than you anticipate (often many months up to a few years).
D.   The experience can take an unpredictable course and be disruptive to your daily functioning.
E.   The grieving process cannot be rushed (even though other people may try to "hurry you along").
F.   Time alone does not heal → we have to work through the process to get healing.
G.   Multiple losses usually extend the amount of time required for grieving.

III.   **Stages of Grief [79,80]**
A.   The process of grieving does not always follow a predictable pattern.
B.   Each person might pass through the stages in a different order.
C.   You might repeat some of the stages several times as you work through the loss.
D.   <u>Stages</u>
1.   <u>Denial</u> – initial shock at the loss; "This is not really happening!"
2.   <u>Anger</u> – a natural reaction at having no control over losing what's important to you.
   a.   Anger at the fact of the loss (we did not want this to happen).
   b.   Possibly anger at the person for "leaving you"; maybe anger at other people.
   c.   Sometimes anger at God; maybe angry, but not sure at whom or what.

3.   <u>Bargaining</u> – wishing to get the person or thing back.
    a.   Imagining "what if _____"; "if only I had _____."
    b.   This is often an attempt to convince ourselves that we can get back the person or thing when we really can't.
    c.   Not wanting to let the person or thing really be gone.

4.   <u>Depression</u> – a reaction to the loss and the fact that it is permanent.
    a.   We acknowledge that we can't bring the person back and feel helpless.
    b.   This is a normal way to feel in this situation, even though it may be very intense and painful at times.
    c.   Various societies and cultures have differing amounts of time that are considered "normal" or "typical" for the grieving process as a whole.

5.   <u>Acceptance</u> – facing the facts of what has happened.
    a.   This <u>does not</u> mean that you like what happened or that you are happy about it.
    b.   Depression and feelings of rage about the loss become greatly reduced in time.
    c.   Understand that any compensation for the loss can only be partial at best.
    d.   Accept help from others and begin integrating these new facts about how your life has changed into your self and daily activities.
    e.   Become less self-punitive; become more patient and kind toward yourself.

IV.   Myths that Complicate the Grieving Process [79,80]
    A.   <u>Myth</u>: Grief is a weakness.
        1.   <u>Fact</u>: Grief is a normal human experience when we lose people or things that we value.
        2.   By grieving, we feel the pain of the loss, express it, and move forward with fewer negative long-term effects.
    B.   <u>Myth</u>: If I grieve or cry, then I will lose control and cry forever.
        1.   <u>Fact</u>: Losing control is very unlikely.
        2.   More likely, you will feel sad and cry for a while, and then recover.
        3.   You may feel overwhelmed during grieving. However, when this happens the person has already felt overwhelmed and they are now acknowledging it and beginning to deal with it.
    C.   <u>Myth</u>: If I grieve, then I will lose the gains made in other areas of my life.
        1.   <u>Fact</u>: Instead of losing ground, the grieving process helps us deal with our losses and move toward future productivity.

2.   Unresolved losses usually detract from our ability to function and enjoy the good things in life.

3.   While grief work takes some time, it is an investment in our ability to cope and live well in the future.

D.   <u>Myth</u>: If I recover from the grief and pain, then that means I don't care about the person.

    1.   <u>Fact</u>: Resolving the pain of the loss does not mean betrayal of the lost person, and it doesn't mean that you don't care.

    2.   Would that person want you to "stop living" and just exist in emotional pain for the rest of your life? (probably not)

    3.   Instead of intense and prolonged pain, healthy grieving and retaining the good memories offer dignity and a healthy form of pride.

E.   <u>Myth</u>: If I stop grieving, then I will forget the person (or thing).

    1.   <u>Fact</u>: When the intense emotional pain has reduced, we then remember the person more completely, with less pain to burden us.

    2.   We can value them by keeping all the good memories and going on living.

F.   <u>Myth</u>: Grief means that you lack spiritual faith.

    1.   <u>Fact</u>: Grief does not mean that you have no spiritual beliefs, lack faith, or that you don't believe in God.

    2.   It does mean that you are human and having normal feelings in this kind of situation.

    3.   While we might question some things during these difficult times, our beliefs remain and sometimes are strengthened.

V.   Overall Tasks Involved in Grieving

A.   Identify the loss.

B.   Accept the reality of the loss.

C.   Work through the pain and grief of the loss.

D.   Adjust to a world without the lost person or thing (which you valued).

E.   Move forward in life keeping positive memories, but without the intense pain of the loss.

VI.   The First Step in Grieving

A.   Write down the persons or things that you valued but have now lost.

_____

_____

_____

Chapter 67 – Grieving and Loss – Part II

I.   **Necessary Steps in the Grieving Process** [79,80]

    A.   <u>Identify the person(s) or thing(s) that you valued but have now lost.</u>

        1.   Make a list – e.g., loved ones, friends, prized possessions, jobs, etc. (Anything that was valuable to you that you lost)

        2.   Be as specific as possible.

        3.   Emotional losses:

_____

_____

        4.   Financial losses:

_____

_____

        5.   Medical/Physical losses:

_____

_____

        6.   Spiritual/Moral Losses:

_____

_____

        7.   Ability Losses:

_____

_____

        8.   Hopes/dreams Lost:

_____

_____

    B.   <u>Describe how the loss affected you emotionally.</u>

        1.   How did the loss make you feel? Angry, hurt, sad, hollow, empty, disturbed, abandoned, deprived, distraught, etc.

_____

_____

_____

        2.   Let yourself experience the emotional hurt and pain of the loss.

        3.   The best way to get rid of a painful feeling is to let yourself feel it. (This can be frightening, but the pain reduces in time.)

    C.   <u>Identify the positive and negative characteristics of the person or thing that was lost.</u>

        1.   Make a list of the positive characteristics of the person or thing that was lost.

        2.   Make a list of the negative characteristics.

        3.   Describe in detail why each of the positive characteristics was important to you.

D.   Begin releasing yourself to the reality that they will not be coming back.
1.   Acknowledge the fact that the valued person or thing is gone.
2.   Accept that they are gone.
3.   Acceptance does not mean that we like the fact they are gone. It does mean we are acknowledging and dealing with this fact.
4.   If there is any unfinished business with this person (or thing), we need to resolve it at this point.

E.   Adjust to living in the world without this person or thing.
1.   We remember and retain those valued aspects of the cherished person or thing, while letting go of the intense pain that they are gone.
2.   Reinvest in living and develop healthy connections with others.

II.   **Obstacles to Grieving** [1,79,80]

A.   Fear of losing control; fear of being vulnerable.
B.   Not wanting to be seen as weak or mentally unstable.
C.   Fear of feeling or confronting the pain of the loss.
D.   Grieving for "too long" is seen by other people as self-pity or dwelling on the past.
E.   Stoicism is looked upon positively in many cultures.
F.   Reminders of the person you lost make you "feel ambushed" even by routine experiences.
G.   Special days (birthdays, anniversaries, holidays, etc.) can be especially difficult.
H.   Suppressed feelings can build up and explode later.
I.   When grief is not resolved, it can lead to bitterness, destructive behaviors, or compulsions.
J.   To grieve in a healthy way, we must overcome these obstacles and engage in grieving.
K.   However, unresolved grief can lead to resentments, depression, regret, self-pity, loneliness, loss of purpose and direction in life, and a focus on the unfairness of what you experienced.

III.   **Signs of Complicated or Unresolved Grief (problematic)** [79,80]

A.   Excessive and persistent denial.
B.   Preoccupation with anger and rage at the loss.
C.   Feelings of ambivalence or confusion toward the person or thing that was lost is not acknowledged.
D.   Anger is displaced → It gets directed toward someone or something not related to the loss.
E.   Unresolved guilt or shame.

F. Traumatic events surrounding the loss may have occurred too suddenly or were too overwhelming to confront → unable to mentally process what happened.

G. Other people discouraged grieving; they did not recognize or appreciate the losses you experienced.

IV. Moving Forward in a Healthy Way

A. <u>Moving Forward Does Not Mean</u>
1. We forget the person.
2. We never feel the pain of the loss ever again.
3. We believe that life is fair.

B. <u>It Does Mean</u>
1. The pain of loss is reduced over time.
2. We treasure our best memories of the person.
3. We realistically accept the different aspects of our loss.
4. In time, we can form new relationships and try new things.
5. We accept the reality of our loss, and forgive other people.
6. Understand that both joy and loss are parts of life.

C. <u>New Learning Through Grief</u>
1. Our perspective on life changes and matures.
2. New priorities are formed.
3. Reestablish healthy convictions and beliefs.

V. When is Grieving Finished? [79,80,81]

A. When we are able to think about the person or thing who was lost without the overwhelming and disabling emotional pain, although some sadness may remain.

B. When a person can reinvest their thoughts, feelings, and efforts into living in the present instead of mainly in the past.

C. While mourning can sometimes be a long process, the frequency and severity of the pain associated with the loss is <u>greatly reduced.</u>

D. Some people claim that mourning never ends. Instead, the pain is felt less often, and we are able to feel more hopeful and adapt to new things in life.

Chapter 68 – PTSD and Aging

I. **PTSD Age of Onset** [1,2,9]
    A. Many people who were traumatized at a young age and did not immediately get full-blown PTSD often develop PTSD symptoms when nearing retirement.
    B. Physical decline and failing health can trigger or increase symptoms.
    C. The decline in our abilities during the later years of life often reminds us of the vulnerability we felt during the trauma(s).
    D. This can bring up symptoms that had been repressed, or make existing symptoms worse.

II. **Age at the Time of Trauma** [13]
    A. The age at which a person is traumatized often affects the person's ability to cope.
    B. How old were you at the time of the trauma(s)? _____
    C. Many people with PTSD feel "stuck at that age" in many ways throughout life.
    D. The age of a person at the time of the trauma usually dictates the level of life skills they use in trying to cope with their PTSD symptoms.
    E. Children who are traumatized are less mature than adults and have fewer coping skills.
    F. Elderly individuals who are traumatized also struggle due to declining abilities as a result of the aging process. [82]

III. **Normal Age-Related Changes** [82]
    A. <u>Physical Changes</u>
        1. Graying hair; Loss of hair and teeth.
        2. Continued growth of the ears and nose.
        3. Loss of subcutaneous fat.
        4. Skin becomes thin; bruise easily.
        5. Wrinkling of the skin.
        6. Fading eyesight and poor hearing.
        7. While 80% of the elderly have one or more chronic health problems, around 95% are still able to live in the community. [82]
    B. <u>Mental Changes</u>
        1. As we age, some mental abilities decline while others remain constant or improve.
        2. Short-term memory gets a little worse.
        3. Long-term memory remains generally intact.

        4.   Physical reaction time slows some, and thinking speed might slow for some people.

        5.   Problem solving for real life problems often improves (due to life experience).

C.   Other Changes (positive and negative)

        1.   The elderly are either highly respected or scorned in many cultures.

        2.   Elderly people are often seen as a valuable source of wisdom or as a burden to society.

        3.   Income is often drastically reduced in the later years → this can lead to financial stress.

        4.   Problems often associated with aging include grief, guilt, loneliness, depression, anxiety, rage (at things beyond our control), disability, fear, and social disconnection.

IV.   Challenges to the Aging Trauma Survivor

A.   Several life events have the potential to bring about or increase many PTSD symptoms.

B.   Challenging life events include the following:

        1.   Retirement.

        2.   Children leaving home.

        3.   Death or separation from family or friends.

        4.   Physical illness.

        5.   Being hospitalized.

        6.   Job stress.

        7.   Situations beyond your control.

        8.   Changes in existing relationships.

        9.   Declining physical abilities.

        10.   New losses in your life.

        11.   Additional traumas at this point in life.

        12.   Being confronted with extreme situations or images such as war, violence, cruelty, etc. either in person or on TV.

C.   The trauma survivor needs to finds healthy ways of coping with declining abilities that accompany old age.

V.   Using Age (and maturity) to Our Advantage [1,2,82]

A.   Many trauma survivors learn to cope with adversity through experience.

B.   Some develop a high level of self-discipline and self-control to manage symptoms.

C.   Many trauma survivors who have matured through life experience and therapy value life more and have a clearer sense of direction in life.

D.   Some individuals use their own success in therapy to share with younger individuals who are just now beginning to cope with PTSD symptoms.

E.   Other positive effects of aging include a broader perspective, increased coping skills, more self-discipline, and independence.

F.   Maturity often brings coping skills that were unavailable to us at younger ages.

Chapter 69 – Adapting to Retirement

I. **What if PTSD Forces Me to Retire?** [13,72]

    A.   For some people with PTSD, symptoms can cause either partial or total debilitation.

    B.   <u>What is a Disability</u>?

        1.   The inability to pursue an occupation because of physical or mental impairment.

        2.   A restriction or disadvantage due to a physical or mental condition.

    C.   Some disabilities can be completely debilitating → become totally unable to work.

    D.   Others are only partially debilitating.

    E.   A healthy adjustment requires compensating for specific limitations and accepting help when you need it.

II. **Disability and Stigma**

    A.   Individuals with disabilities are often stereotyped in negative ways. Examples

        1.   Crazy; strange.

        2.   Weird; unstable.

        3.   Lazy; con artists.

        4.   Dangerous; social outcasts.

        5.   Other labels you've heard: _____

    B.   Ways of handling the question "So, . . . , what do you do?"

        1.   "I'm retired."

        2.   "I'm medically retired."

        3.   "I was injured and had to retire."

        4.   "I worked as a _____, but had to retire."

        5.   "I do volunteer work at _____."

        6.   "I was retired by the military."

        7.   Other _____

III. **How to Know When to Retire (and possibly file for a disability)**

    A.   Professionals' Opinions and Recommendations.

    B.   Current functioning is below minimum acceptable standards.

    C.   You become unable to do work you had been doing for many years.

        1.   Get to where you don't know how to accomplish familiar tasks.

        2.   Get overwhelmed by several aspects of the job and don't perform as usual.

D.   High level of lethality → thinking of killing people very often.

E.   Other people observe that you are unable to meet the demands of work.

F.   Problems regulating your emotions.

    1.   Chaotic emotions lead to poor functioning at work.

    2.   Unstable emotions → leads to continual conflict with others.

G.   You are seriously considering killing yourself.

H.   You frequently do risky things for no good reason.

I.   You are close to giving up on everything in your life.

J.   Your symptoms are so severe you are close to a melt down at any moment.

K.   Symptoms are so overwhelming that you can no longer function.

IV.   **Strategies for Healthy Adjustment to Retirement** [1,82]

A.   Develop a positive identity

    1.   Give up the identity that says "I am a disabled person" (damaged goods).

    2.   Instead "I am a valuable person, who happens to have certain limitations."

    3.   Instead of "I'm now ruined" → "I now have new limitations to deal with and also new opportunities."

B.   Fill your time in positive ways

    1.   Make a schedule and generally stick to it (with some flexibility, of course).

    2.   Have projects for yourself to do.

    3.   Idle time feeds depression, anxiety, and feelings of worthlessness.

    4.   If boredom sneaks up on you, reconnect with a friend or get started on a project.

C.   Stay active physically and mentally

    1.   Exercise 3 to 5 times per week at a level that does not cause injury.

    2.   Stay mentally active.

        a.   Learn something new.

        b.   Read, work crossword puzzles, get interested in new things check out videos from the library, watch the discovery channel, watch historical documentaries, learn a new skill, etc.

    3.   Inactivity, boredom, and lack of purpose lead to deterioration mentally and physically.

D.   Be productive

    1.   Find new ways to be productive or make a positive difference.

    2.   Do something positive for someone else; contribute to their well-being.

    3.   Do volunteer work.

4. Help someone when it is within your power to do so.
5. Give of your time, effort, wisdom, knowledge, etc. without expecting repayment (don't give all of your money away and still expect to pay your bills).

E. <u>Guard your attitudes</u> [81]

1. It can be easy to focus on what you "can't" do rather than what you "can" do.
2. This makes you a nasty, bitter, resentful, and unhappy person.
3. Instead, focus on:
    a. Things I <u>can</u> do.
    b. Positive things in my life.
    c. Ways I can still contribute to family or society.
    d. Ways to improve things.
    e. Things that make me laugh.
    f. Things I am thankful for.
    g. Ways to use experience and/or wisdom productively.

Section VII: Healthy Outcomes

Patients with PTSD have said . . .

"Today I can live with it and around it."

**"The symptoms don't have as big a hold on me as they used to.
I'm actually in control of my life again, and it feels good."**

**"Fear ruled my life for too many years. Today, it's not controlling me like it used to.
I'm actually the one doing the driving now."**

**"In therapy, I've learned that you can get better, and make a new direction for your life.
I am beginning to see what that feels like."**

Chapter 70 – What is "Better?"

I.   **Expectations About the Outcome of Treatment** [1,2,8]
    A.   Many people coping with long-term symptoms of a diagnosable mental disorder expect that after treatment they will never have a single symptom or problem ever again.
    B.   For long-term conditions, this is often unrealistic.
    C.   Many behaviors have become long-term patterns of attempting to cope with symptoms.
    D.   It usually takes a great deal of effort and practice over long periods of time to develop more effective behaviors and new life patterns that are more productive.

II.   **What "Better" Is Not**
    A.   Never having any symptoms ever again.
    B.   Eliminating all bad memories.
    C.   Never having negative or "bad" feelings.
    D.   Not having any problems at all.
    E.   Not having to put forth effort and "magically" feeling better.

III.   **What Is Required to "Get Better"** [1,8,35]
    A.   Acknowledge there is a problem and be determined to get better.
    B.   Gaining an accurate understanding of your symptoms and overall condition (knowing exactly what you are dealing with).
        1.   What is the name of the condition? _____
        2.   What are the symptoms? _____
        3.   How does it affect a person's thoughts, feelings, and behaviors?
                _____
        4.   What are the long-term effects of this condition?
                _____
        5.   How many books have you read about this condition?_____
    C.   A commitment to work at applying new coping skills each day.
    D.   Active participation in treatment on a regular basis.
        1.   Ask for help instead of getting into trouble.
        2.   Be willing to actually work on your own issues.
    E.   Working to change your thought patterns and behaviors.
    F.   Casting a positive vision for your future and working toward it.
    G.   We must confront and work through the real issues to ultimately get better even though this is difficult and painful.
    H.   Become determined that you will be responsible and take healthy care of yourself.
    I.   Relearn how to get along with most people (most of the time).

J.   Confront your fears → refuse to be a victim of fear and anxiety.
  1.   Get help with this if necessary.
  2.   Be determined to overcome challenges in your life.
K.   Come to terms with the reality that each of us must stand up for ourselves and take responsibility for our own happiness.
L.   Accept that you have strengths and use them; compensate for your weakness.
M.   Become more intelligent and clever in how you manage your symptoms, deal with stress, and live your life.

IV.   **What "Better" Looks Like in Action** [9,35,43]
A.   Use coping skills to manage symptoms.
  1.   Replace behaviors that are no longer useful with more productive coping strategies.
  2.   Learn and practice new skills (deep breathing, time outs, mental focus, anger management, stress management).
B.   Know your limits and appropriate boundaries.
  1.   Recognize limits before you exceed them.
  2.   Live within your limits.
C.   Know what situations to avoid and which ones to handle.
D.   Implement structure in your daily life and observe healthy boundaries.
E.   Change your behavior to get more desirable results.
  1.   Stop drinking and drugging.
  2.   Talk to people you trust when you need to.
  3.   Eliminate self-destructive or damaging behaviors.
F.   Use safety nets – preplan a course of action so you don't have to try to figure it out when feeling overwhelmed.
  1.   Use medications as prescribed to reduce chances of symptom "flare-up."
  2.   Go to your "safe places" when feeling unstable.
  3.   Have the names and phone numbers of at least 3 people you can call when going through a rough time.
  4.   Make use of resources available to you.
G.   Fill your time in positive ways.
  1.   Make a schedule and generally stick to it (with flexibility, of course).
  2.   Have projects for yourself to do.
  3.   Fill your idle time → it feeds depression, anxiety, and feelings of hopelessness and worthlessness.
H.   <u>Eliminate common errors in coping</u>
  1.   Error #1: Lack of Planning.
      <u>Instead</u>: Plan ahead, reduce impulsive and reactive behaviors, be prepared.

2.   Error #2: Reacting without thinking (impulsive behavior).
      <u>Instead</u>: Choose a response to the situation instead of reacting based on how you feel.

3.   Error #3: Inconsistency (ineffective attempts at coping).
      <u>Instead</u>: Use the self-discipline it takes to be stable and consistent in your efforts.

V.   **Remember:** Peace of mind does not come from the absence of problems, but from the ability to cope with them → be realistic in your expectations.

Chapter 71 – What is "Normal?"

I.   **Importance of Daily Functioning** [3]
    A.   A critical part of mental health is being able to do necessary tasks each day.
    B.   When symptoms become moderate to severe, they can interfere with our ability to complete basic tasks each day.
    C.   When daily functioning is impaired, a person's life becomes disrupted.

II.   **How Can Symptoms Affect Daily Functioning?** [1,2]
    A.   Don't practice routine self-care.
    B.   Let basic tasks go undone.
        1.   Cooking.
        2.   Cleaning, laundry.
        3.   Paying bills, lawn care.
    C.   Get behind in fulfilling responsibilities.
        1.   At work.
        2.   At home.
        3.   In relationships.
    D.   Not able to function at work, or productivity is greatly reduced.
    E.   Become socially isolated.
        1.   Avoid people.
        2.   Rude when forced to deal with people.
    F.   Experience frequent problems in getting along with other people.
        1.   Easily irritated.
        2.   Angry at other people's incompetence.
        3.   Argue or fight when things don't go your way.

III.   **What Does Normal Functioning Look Like?** [82]
    A.   The Basic ADL's (activities of daily living)
        1.   <u>Self-Care</u>
            a.   Hygiene/grooming – taking a bath or shower each day.
            b.   Using the toilet.
            c.   Getting dressed.
            d.   Preparing meals, feeding yourself.
            e.   Taking medication as prescribed.
        2.   <u>Basic Tasks</u>
            a.   Walking; moving around as needed.
            b.   Cleaning, housekeeping, laundry, small tasks at home.
            c.   Shopping, Paying bills.
            d.   Driving, transportation.
            e.   Doing minor repairs.
            f.   Using the telephone (and/or computer).

3.   <u>Occupational Functioning</u>
   a.   Am I able to do the tasks required for my job?
   b.   Ability to function in school is included here.
   c.   If not employed, retired, etc., am I able to do some productive activity most every day?
4.   <u>Social Functioning</u>
   a.   Getting along with most people most of the time.
   b.   Using social skills.
   c.   Following most of the rules of society (most of the time).
   d.   Contribute to your school, church, community, etc.

IV.   Personal Experience

A.   What adjustments in functioning have you made as a result of symptoms?

_____
_____
_____

B.   What activities have been modified or given up because of limitations?

_____
_____
_____

C.   What things can you do to get some independence back?

_____
_____
_____

V.   Ways to Improve Daily Functioning

A.   Take personal responsibility for your actions as much as possible.
B.   Do as many things for yourself as you are able (self-care, basic tasks, etc.).
    1.   When we stop doing things for ourselves, our abilities often decline rapidly.
C.   Be creative → modify tasks as needed to maintain independence.
D.   Ask for and accept help when you need it.
E.   Practice skills to help you accomplish tasks and cope more effectively.
F.   Stay physically and mentally active into the later years of life.
G.   Do physical exercise 3 to 5 times each week to maintain your strength.
H.   Read a little every day to keep your mind active → it can reduce the risk of Alzheimers.[83]
I.   Use physical aides to compensate for areas of difficulty.
J.   <u>Remember:</u> It's not about proving how strong, tough, or independent you are → normal functioning helps a person live more effectively.

Chapter 72 – Living Again

I. **What's the Goal?** [1,2]
    A. <u>To get my life back</u>
        1. This is a common desire among individuals with PTSD.
        2. Realize that you can't go back and be the person you were before the trauma(s).
        3. However, you can build a new life that is good (and in some ways better).
    B. <u>What do we recover through therapy?</u>
        1. A feeling of sanity.
        2. The ability to cope with stresses (and with life in general).
        3. Personal stability.
        4. The ability to lead a healthy life.

II. **What Success in Therapy Looks Like**
    A. Now you have a good understanding of:
        1. Symptoms.
        2. Where they came from.
        3. How your life was affected.
        4. Have a healthy acceptance of the diagnosis and symptoms.
        5. Have a healthy self-image.
    B. Have positive coping skills now.
        1. Use healthy skills on a daily basis.
        2. Recognize stress and cope with it.
        3. Don't get angry as easily; manage the anger you do have appropriately.
        4. Exercise appropriate self-confidence.
        5. Don't rely on alcohol or illegal drugs for coping or emotional relief.
    C. Have new, more healthy behaviors.
        1. Less confrontational in most situations.
        2. Less argumentative.
        3. Fewer outbursts; less legal trouble.
        4. Listen to others more.
        5. Able to socialize in some situations.
        6. Can set and abide by healthy boundaries.
    D. Symptoms <u>no longer control you</u> or your life.
        1. Less anxiety most days.
        2. Don't have to be on high alert in relatively safe situations.
        3. Nightmares are less frequent and less intense.
        4. Don't get revved up so easily.

E.   No longer fear the memories or get overwhelmed by them.
    1.   Can talk about the traumas now.
    2.   Not overwhelmed by the memories.
    3.   No longer a prisoner inside your own mind.

III.   Where We Go From Here?
A.   Move forward with life.
B.   Able to prioritize.
C.   Develop your own beliefs without undue influence from the traumas.
D.   Able to pursue goals now.
E.   Live a life full of meaning and purpose.

IV.   Indicators that Emotional Maturity has Developed Through Therapy [8,13]
(circle all that you now have)
A.   Taking personal responsibility for your own actions.
B.   Being rational (most of the time).
C.   The ability to delay gratification.
D.   Living up to your word.
    1.   Doing what you say you will do.
    2.   Keeping commitments.
E.   Minimizing impulsive behavior.
F.   Use of planning → looking ahead.
G.   Exercising PATIENCE – the ability to wait.
H.   Observing healthy boundaries.
I.   Adaptability → changing according to what different situations require.
J.   Don't get "shocked" or "rattled" easily.
K.   Sensible.
L.   Accountable to others.
M.   Integrity – truthful to self and others; live according to your principles.
N.   Sincere – not fake, superficial, or manipulative.
O.   Resourceful.
P.   Able to relate to others and generally get along.
Q.   Not self-centered.
R.   Open to new ideas – not narrow minded.
S.   Able to deal with tough situations without taking offense or personalizing.
T.   Refuse to let people "push your buttons."
U.   Be persistent; stick with things; don't be a quitter.
V.   Strive to be intelligent and wise – use your brains.
W.   Do things the smart way, not always the hard way.
X.   Be responsive, not reactive.

V. **Maturity and Coping with Symptoms**
    A. Maturity brings the benefit of increased coping skills for dealing with symptoms.
    B. Immaturity limits the thoughts, skills, and behaviors available to us for handling symptoms and/or difficult life situations.
    C. How have my past experiences affected my current level of emotional maturity?
    D. What is my goal regarding maturity?
        1. Am I happy where I am now?
        2. Do I see benefits of increased maturity?
    E. What new levels of maturity have I developed in therapy?
    F. What would I like to do regarding my own emotional maturity from this point forward?

Endnotes

1. Matsakis A. *Post traumatic stress disorder: a complete treatment guide.* Oakland, CA: New Harbinger Publications. 1994.
   I consider this a "must read" for any therapist doing trauma work.

2. Schiraldi G R. *The post traumatic stress disorder sourcebook: a guide to healing, recovery, and growth.* Los Angeles: Lowell House. 2000.
   A good resource for therapist and patients alike.

3. American Psychiatric Association. *Diagnostic and statistical manual of mental disorders, 4th ed text revision*: 463-468. 2000.

4. Foa EB, Keane TM, and Friedman MJ. *Effective treatments for PTSD.* New York: The Guilford Press. 2000.

5. Herman JL. *Trauma and recovery.* New York: Basic Books. 1992.

6. van der Kolk BA, McFarlane AC, and Weisaeth L. (Eds.). *Traumatic stress: the overwhelming experience on mind, body, and society.* New York: Guilford Press. 1996.
   This is the definitive, authoritative text for professionals wishing to understand the effects of trauma.

7. Dean C. *Nam vet.* Winepress Publishing. 1999, 10th printing.

8. McWilliams N. *Psychoanalytic diagnosis.* New York: The Guilford Press. 1994.
   A very "rich" resource that will expand the therapist's depth and breadth of practice.

9. Matsakis A. *I can't get over it: a handbook for trauma survivors, 2nd ed.* New York: New Harbinger Publications. 1996.
   Some higher functioning patients may be able to read this text and benefit greatly.

10. Bachom S. *Denial is not a river in Egypt.* Center City, Minnesota: Hazelden. 1998.

11. *Living sober.* New York: Alcoholics Anonymous World Services, Inc. 2001, 34th printing.

12. *Twelve steps and twelve traditions.* New York: Alcoholics Anonymous World Services, Inc. 2002, 63rd printing.

13. Inaba DS and Cohen WE. *Uppers, downers, all arounders: physical and mental effects of psychoactive drugs.* Ashland, Oregon: CNS Publications. 2004.
This is the most comprehensive text on substance use I have read in a long time. A great resource for clinicians.

14. Matsakis A. *Trust after trauma: a guide to relationships for survivors and those who love them.* New York: New Harbinger Publications. 1998.

15. Rosenbloom D and Williams MB. *Life after trauma: a workbook for healing.* New York: The Guilford Press. 1999.

16. Williams MB. *The PTSD workbook.* New York: New Harbinger Publications. 2002.

17. Davis M, Eshelman E R, and McKay M. *The relaxation & stress reduction workbook, 5th Ed.* New York: New Harbinger Publications. 2000.
Every therapist should draw upon this workbook as a mainstay of good practice.

18. Bourne EJ. *The anxiety & phobia workbook, 3rd ed.* New York: New Harbinger Publications. 2000.
Comment: Same as #17.

19. Watzlawick P, Weakland JH, and Fisch R. *Change: principles of problem formation and problem resolution.* New York: W.W. Norton & Company. 1974.

20. Shay J. About medications for combat PTSD. Available at http://www.dr-bob.org/tips/ptsd.html. Accessed 10/13/07.

21. Potter-Efron R, and Potter-Efron P. *Letting go of anger.* New York: New Harbinger Publications. 1995.
This book is brief, yet power-packed with information.

22. Butler RN, Lewis MI, and Sunderland T. *Aging and mental health, 5th ed.* Boston: Allyn and Bacon. 1998.

23. Pitzele SK. *We are not alone: learning to live with chronic illness.* New York: Workman Publishing. 1986.

24. Shiraldi, Sourcebook, 13.

25. Inaba, Uppers, Downers, All Arounders, 343.

26. Ibid., 463-464.

27. Sowell ER, Thompson PM, Holmes CJ, et al. 1999. In vivo evidence for post-adolescence brain maturation in frontal and striatal regions. Nat Neurosci 2(10):859-861.

28. Paus T, Zijdenbos A, Worsley K, et al. 1999. Structural maturation of neural pathways in children and adolescents: in vivo study. Science 283(5409):1908-1911.

29. Preston JD, Talaga MC, and O'Neal JH. *Handbook of clinical psychopharmacology for therapists, 3rd edition.* New York: New Harbinger. 2002.
    Dr. Preston also provides a 2-page summary sheet about psychotropic medications – a great quick reference for non-prescribers.

30. Hollon SD, DeRubeis RJ, Shelton RC, et al. 2005. Prevention of relapse following cognitive therapy vs medications in moderate to severe depression. Arch Gen Psychiatry 62:417-422.

31. Hollon SD, DeRubeis RJ, Evans MD, et al. 1992. Cognitive therapy and pharmacotherapy for depression: singly and in combination. Arch Gen Psychiatry 49:774-781.

32. Jacobson NS and Hollon SD. 1996. Cognitive-behavior therapy versus pharmacotherapy: now that the jury's returned its verdict, it's time to present the rest of the evidence. J Consult Clin Psychol. 64(1)74-80.

33. McKay M and Rogers P. *The anger control workbook.* New York: New Harbinger Publications. 2000.

34. Potter-Efron R and Potter-Efron P. *Letting go of anger.* New York: New Harbinger Publications. 1995.

35. Leahy RL. *Cognitive therapy techniques: a practitioner's guide.* New York: Guilford. 2003.

36. Ellis A and Lange A. *How to keep people from pushing your buttons.* New York: Citadel Press. 1995.

37. Dalai Lama and Cutler H. *The art of happiness: a handbook for living.* New York: Riverhead. 1998.

38. Kabat-Zinn J. *Wherever you go there you are: mindfulness meditation in everyday life.* New York: Hyperion. 1994.

39. Kabat-Zinn J. *Coming to our senses: healing ourselves and the world through mindfulness.* New York: Hyperion. 2005.

40. Matsakis A. *Survivor guilt: a self-help guide.* New York: New Harbinger Publications. 1999.

41. Schafer W. *Stress management for wellness.* New York: Holt, Rinehart, & Winston. 1987.

42. Bourne EJ. *The anxiety & phobia workbook, 3rd ed.* New York: New Harbinger Publications. 2000.

43. Davis M, Eshelman ER, and McKay M. *The relaxation & stress reduction workbook, 5th Ed.* New York: New Harbinger Publications. 2000.

44. Sapolsky RM. *Why zebras don't get ulcers: an updated guide to stress, stress related diseases, and coping.* 3rd Ed.: Holt paperbacks. 2004.
   "Why Zebras . . ." should be a must-read for any clinician treating clients with anxiety disorders or working in behavioral medicine.

45. Fairfield KM and Fletcher RH. 2002. Vitamins for chronic disease prevention: scientific review and clinical applications. (Clinician's corner.) JAMA 287:3116.

46. Eades MD. *The doctor's complete guide to vitamins and minerals.* New York: Dell. 2000.

47. Luft J and Ingham H. The Johari window, a graphic model of interpersonal awareness. *Proceedings of the western training laboratory in group development.* Los Angeles: UCLA. 1955.

48. Merrens MR and Brannigan GG. *Experiences in personality: research, assessment, and change.* New York: Wiley. 1998.

49. APA, DSM-IV-TR, 430-441.

50 Mayo Clinic Staff. Heart attack symptoms: know what signals a medical emergency. Available at http://www.mayoclinic.com/health/heart-attack-symptoms/HB00054. Accessed 10/13/07.

51. Matsakis, Trust after trauma, 57.

52. Rotter JB. 1975. Some problems and misconceptions related to the construct of internal versus external control of reinforcement. J Consult Clin Psychol, 43(1):55-66..

53. Maruta T et.al. 2000. Optimists vs pessimists: survival rate among medical patients over a 30-year period. *Mayo Clinic Proceedings:* March; 75(3)318.

54. Siegrist J, Peter R, Junge A, Cremer P, and Seidel D. 1990. Low status control, high effort at work and ischemic heart disease: prospective evidence from blue-collar men. Soc Sci Med 31:1127-1134.

55. Siegrist J. 1996. Adverse health effects of high-effort/low-reward conditions. J Occup Health Psychol 1:27-41.

56. Appels A. Loss of control, vital exhaustion and coronary heart disease. *Stress, personal control and health.* Edited by A. Steptoe and A. Appels. New York, NY: John Wiley & Sons. (pp. 215-235). 1989.

57. Hare RD. *Without conscience: the disturbing world of the psychopaths among us.* New York: Guildford Press. 1993.

58. Glasser W. *Choice theory: a new psychology of personal freedom.* New York: Harper Collins. 1998.

59. Foa EB and Kozak MJ. 1986. Emotional processing of fear: exposure to corrective information. Psychol Bull 99:20-35.

60. Beck JS. *Cognitive therapy: basics and beyond.* New York: The Guilford Press. 1995.

61. Beck AT. *Cognitive therapy and the emotional disorders.* New York: Penguin Books. 1979.

62. Beck AT, Rush AJ, Shaw BF, and Emery G. *Cognitive therapy of depression.* New York: Guilford Press. 1979.

63. Litz BT. 1992. Emotional numbing in combat-related post-traumatic stress disorder: A critical review and reformulation. Clin Psychol Rev, 12:417-432.

64. APA, DSM-IV-TR, 349-356.

65. Ferster C B. 1973. A functional analysis of depression. Am Psychol 28:857–870.

66. Lewinsohn P M. A behavioral approach to depression. In RM Friedman and MM Katz (Eds.), *The psychology of depression: Contemporary theory and research.* New York: Wiley. 1974.

67. Lewinsohn PM and Atwood GE. 1969. Depression: A clinical-research approach. *Psychotherapy: Theory, Research and Practice*, 6:166–171.

68. Hopko DR, Lejuez CW, Ruggiero KJ, and Eifert GH. 2003. Contemporary behavioral activation treatments for depression: Procedures, principles, and progress. Clin Psychol Rev 23:699-717.

69. Schiraldi, G.R. *The self-esteem workbook.* New York: New Harbinger Publications. 2001.

70. Rutledge, T. *The self-forgiveness handbook: a practical and empowering guide.* Oakland CA: New Harbinger Publications. 1997.

71. DeRoo C and DeRoo C. *What's right with me.* Oakland, CA: New Harbinger. 2006.

72. APA, DSM-IV-TR, 429-484.

73. McWilliams N. *Psychoanalytic case formulation.* New York: Guilford Press. 1999. Also, a must-read for clinicians wanting to strengthen their therapeutic repertoire.

74. Kline RB. *Principles and practice of structural equation modeling.* New York: Guilford Press. 1998.

75. Falsetti S A. 1997. Treatment of PTSD with comorbid panic attacks. *National Center for PTSD Clinical Quarterly*, 7, 46-48.

76. Mathews A. 1990. Why worry? The cognitive function of anxiety. Behav Res Ther 28:455-468.

77. Lewis CS. *The problem of pain.* New York: Macmillan. 1944. This is truly a classic, addressing both physical and psychic pain.

78. *The Erik Erikson Reader.* Edited by Coles. New York: Norton. 2000.

79. Kubler-Ross E and Kessler D. *On grief and grieving: finding the meaning of grief through the five stages of loss.* New York: Scribner. 2007.

80. James JW and Friedman R. *The grief recovery handbook: the action program for moving beyond death, divorce, and other losses.* New York: Collins. 1998.

81. Lewis CS. *A Grief Observed.* Easton Press. 2002.
    If you have not yet dealt with grief in your own life, read this book and your understanding will grow exponentially.

82. Butler RN, Lewis MI, and Sunderland T. *Aging and mental health, 5th ed.* Boston: Allyn and Bacon. 1998.

83. Wilson RS, Mendes de Leon CF, Barnes LL, et al. 2002. Participation in cognitively stimulating activities and risk of incident Alzheimer disease. JAMA 287:742-748.

Bibliography

American Psychiatric Association. *Diagnostic and statistical manual of mental disorders, 4th ed* text revision. 2000.

Appels A. Loss of control, vital exhaustion and coronary heart disease. *Stress, personal control and health.* Edited by A Steptoe and A Appels.. New York, NY: John Wiley & Sons. (pp. 215-235). 1989.

Bachom S. *Denial is not a river in Egypt.* Center City, Minnesota: Hazelden. 1998.

Beck AT. *Cognitive therapy and the emotional disorders.* New York: Penguin Books. 1979.

Beck JS. *Cognitive therapy: basics and beyond.* New York: The Guilford Press. 1995.

Beck AT, Rush AJ, Shaw BF, and Emery G. *Cognitive therapy of depression.* New York: Guilford Press. 1979.

Bourne EJ. *The anxiety & phobia workbook, 3rd ed.* New York: New Harbinger Publications. 2000.

Buckingham M and Coffman C. (Gallup Organization). *First break all the rules.* New York: Simon & Schuster. 1999.

Butler RN, Lewis MI, and Sunderland T. *Aging and mental health, 5th ed.* Boston: Allyn and Bacon. 1998.

Carlson R. *Don't sweat the small stuff.* New York: Hyperion. 1997.

Cialdini RB. *Influence: the psychology of persuasion.* New York: Quill William Morrow. 1993.

Dalai Lama and Cutler H. *The art of happiness: a handbook for living.* New York: Riverhead. 1998.

Davis M, Eshelman ER, and McKay M. *The relaxation & stress reduction workbook, 5th Ed.* New York: New Harbinger Publications. 2000.

Dean C. *Nam vet.* Winepress Publishing. 1999, 10th printing.

De Bono E. *Lateral thinking: creativity step by step.* New York: Harper & Row, Publishers. 1970.

De Bono E. *Six thinking hats.* New York: Little, Brown and Company. 1999.

DeRoo C and DeRoo C. *What's right with me.* Oakland, CA: New Harbinger. 2006.

Eades MD. *The doctor's complete guide to vitamins and minerals.* New York: Dell. 2000.

Einstein A. *Relativity: the special and the general theory.* New York: Crown Publishers, Inc. 1961.

Ellis A and Lange A. *How to keep people from pushing your buttons.* New York: Citadel Press. 1995.

Ellman SJ. *Freud's technique papers: a contemporary perspective.* Northvale, New Jersey: Jason Aronson Inc. 1991.

Erik Erikson Reader, selected and edited by Coles. New York: Norton 2000.

Fairfield KM and Fletcher RH. 2002. Vitamins for chronic disease prevention: scientific review and clinical applications. (Clinician's corner). JAMA 287:3116.

Falsetti SA. 1997. Treatment of PTSD with comorbid panic attacks. *National Center for PTSD Clinical Quarterly*, 7:46-48.

Ferster CB. 1973. A functional analysis of depression. Am Psychol 28:857–870.

Feske U and Chambless DL. 1995. Cognitive-behavioral versus exposure only treatment for social phobia: A meta-analysis. Behavior Therapy 20:695-720.

Foa EB, Keane TM, and Friedman MJ. *Effective treatments for PTSD.* New York: The Guilford Press. 2000.

Foa EB and Kozak MJ. 1986. Emotional processing of fear: exposure to corrective information. Psychol Bull 99:20-35.

Frattaroli E. *Healing the soul in the age of the brain: becoming conscious in an unconscious world.* New York: Viking Penguin. 2001.

Fromm E. *The art of loving.* New York: Harper & Row. 1956.

Glasser W. *Reality therapy.* New York: Harper & Row Publishers. 1965.

Glasser W. *Choice theory: a new psychology of personal freedom.* New York: Harper Collins. 1998.

Griffith SB. *Sun Tzu the art of war.* New York: Oxford University Press. 1963.

Grossman D, Lt. Col. *On killing: the psychological cost of learning to kill in war and society.* New York: Bay Back Books / Little, Brown and Company. 1995.

Hare RD. *Without conscience: the disturbing world of the psychopaths among us.* New York: The Guildford Press. 1993.

Herman JL. *Trauma and recovery.* New York: Basic Books. 1992.

Hollon SD, DeRubeis RJ, Evans MD, et al. 1992. Cognitive therapy and pharmacotherapy for depression: singly and in combination. Arch Gen Psychiatry 49:774-781.

Hollon SD, DeRubeis RJ, Shelton RC, et al. 2005. Prevention of relapse following cognitive therapy vs medications in moderate to severe depression. Arch Gen Psychiatry 62:417-422.

Hopko DR, Lejuez CW, Ruggiero KJ, and Eifert GH. 2003. Contemporary behavioral activation treatments for depression: Procedures, principles, and progress. Clin Psychol Rev 23:699-717.

Inaba DS and Cohen WE. *Uppers, downers, all arounders: physical and mental effects of psychoactive drugs.* Ashland, Oregon: CNS Publications, Inc. 2004.

Jacobson NS and Hollon SD. 1996. Cognitive-behavior therapy versus pharmacotherapy: Now that the jury's returned its verdict, it's time to present the rest of the evidence. J Consult Clin Psychol. 64(1)74-80.

James JW and Friedman R. *The grief recovery handbook: the action program for moving beyond death, divorce, and other losses.* New York: Collins. 1998.

Kabat-Zinn J. *Wherever you go there you are: mindfulness meditation in everyday life.* New York: Hyperion. 1994.

Kabat-Zinn J. *Coming to our senses: healing ourselves and the world through mindfulness.* New York: Hyperion. 2005.

Kline RB. *Principles and practice of structural equation modeling.* New York: The Guilford Press. 1998.

Kubler-Ross E and Kessler D. *On grief and grieving: finding the meaning of grief through the five stages of loss.* New York: Scribner. 2007.

Leahy RL. *Cognitive therapy techniques: a practitioner's guide.* New York: Guilford. 2003.

Lewinsohn PM and Atwood GE. 1969. Depression: A clinical-research approach. *Psychotherapy: Theory, Research and Practice,* 6:166–171.

Lewinsohn PM. A behavioral approach to depression. *The psychology of depression: contemporary theory and research.* Edited by RM Friedman and MM Katz . New York: Wiley. 1974.

Lewis CS. *The problem of pain.* New York: Macmillan. 1944.

Lewis CS. *A grief observed.* New York: Easton Press. 2002.

Litz BT. 1992. Emotional numbing in combat-related post-traumatic stress disorder: a critical review and reformulation. Clin Psychol Rev, 12:417-432.

Living sober. New York: Alcoholics Anonymous World Services, Inc. 2001, 34th printing.

Luft J and Ingham H. The Johari window, a graphic model of interpersonal awareness. *Proceedings of the western training laboratory in group development.* Los Angeles: UCLA. 1955.

Maruta T et.al. 2000. Optimists vs pessimists: survival rate among medical patients over a 30-year period. *Mayo Clinic Proceedings:* March; 75(3)318.

Mathews A. 1990. Why worry? The cognitive function of anxiety. Behav Res Ther 28:455-468.

Matsakis A. *Post traumatic stress disorder: a complete treatment guide.* Oakland, CA: New Harbinger Publications. 1994.

Matsakis A. *I can't get over it: a handbook for trauma survivors, 2nd ed.* New York: New Harbinger Publications, Inc. 1996.

Matsakis A. *Trust after trauma: a guide to relationships for survivors and those who love them.* New York: New Harbinger Publications, Inc. 1998.

Matsakis A. *Survivor guilt: a self-help guide.* New York: New Harbinger Publications, Inc. 1999.

Mayo Clinic Staff. Heart attack symptoms: know what signals a medical emergency. Available at http://www.mayoclinic.com/health/heart-attack-symptoms/HB00054. Accessed 10/13/07.

McAllister WR and McAllister DE. Two factor-fear theory: implications for understanding anxiety-based clinical phenomena. *Theories of behavior therapy: exploring behavior change.* Edited by W O'Donahue and L Krasner. Washington, DC: American Psychological Association. 1995.

McCann IL and Pearlman LA. *Psychological trauma and the adult survivor: theory, therapy, and transformation.* New York: Brunner / Mazel. 1990.

McKay M and Rogers P. *The anger control workbook.* New York: New Harbinger Publications. 2000.

McWilliams N. *Psychoanalytic diagnosis.* New York: The Guilford Press. 1994.

McWilliams N. *Psychoanalytic case formulation.* New York: The Guilford Press. 1999.

Merrens MR and Brannigan GG. *Experiences in personality: research, assessment, and change.* New York: Wiley. 1998.

Mowrer OH. *Learning theory and behavior.* New York: Wiley. 1960.

Musashi M. A book of five rings. Translated by V Harris. New York: The Overlook Press. 1974.

Nadel L and Jacobs, WJ. The role of the Hippocampus in PTSD, panic, and phobia. *HIPPOCAMPUS: functions and clinical relevance.* Edited by N. Kato. Amsterdam: Elsevier Science B.V. 1996.

O'Donohue W, Fisher JE and Hayes SC. *Cognitive behavior therapy: applying empirically supported techniques in your practice.* New York: Wiley. 2003.

Orsillo SM. 1997. Social avoidance and PTSD: the role of comorbid social phobia. *National Center for PTSD Clinical Quarterly* 7:54-57.

Paus T, Zijdenbos A, Worsley K, et al. 1999. Structural maturation of neural pathways in children and adolescents: in vivo study. Science 283(5409):1908-1911.

Pitzele SK. *We are not alone: learning to live with chronic illness.* New York: Workman Publishing. 1986.

Potter-Efron R and Potter-Efron P. *Letting go of anger.* New York: New Harbinger Publications. 1995.

Preston JD, Talaga MC, and O'Neal JH. *Handbook of clinical psychopharmacology for therapists, 3rd Edition.* New York: New Harbinger. 2002.

Rescorla RA. 1988. Pavlovian conditioning: it's not what you think it is. Am Psychol 43:151-160.

Rosenbloom D and Williams MB. *Life after trauma: a workbook for healing.* New York: The Guilford Press. 1999.

Rotter JB. 1975. Some problems and misconceptions related to the construct of internal versus external control of reinforcement. J Consult Clin Psychol, 43(1):55-66..

Rutledge T. *The self-forgiveness handbook: a practical and empowering guide.* Oakland CA: New Harbinger Publications. 1997.

Sapolsky RM. *Why zebras don't get ulcers: an updated guide to stress, stress related diseases, and coping.* 3rd ed.: New York: Holt paperbacks. 2004.

Schafer W. *Stress management for wellness.* New York: Holt, Rinehart, & Winston. 1987.

Schiraldi GR. *The post traumatic stress disorder sourcebook: a guide to healing, recovery, and growth.* Los Angeles: Lowell House. 2000.

Schiraldi GR. *The self-esteem workbook.* New York: New Harbinger Publications. 2001.

Shay J. *Achilles in Vietnam.* New York: Touchstone. 1994.

Shay, J. About medications for combat PTSD. Available at http://www.dr-bob.org/tips/ptsd.html. Accessed 10/13/07.

Siegrist J, Peter R, Junge A, Cremer P, and Seidel D. 1990. Low status control, high effort at work and ischemic heart disease: prospective evidence from blue-collar men. Soc Sci Med 31:1127-1134.

Siegrist J. 1996. Adverse health effects of high-effort/low-reward conditions. J Occup Health Psychol 1:27-41.

Sowell ER, Thompson PM, Holmes CJ, et al. 1999. In vivo evidence for post-adolescence brain maturation in frontal and striatal regions. Nat Neurosci 2(10):859-861.

Twelve steps and twelve traditions. New York: Alcoholics Anonymous World Services, Inc. 2002, 63rd printing.

United States Department of Veterans Affairs. National Center for Posttraumatic Stress Disorder. Available at http://www.ncptsd.va.gov. Accessed 10/13/07.

van der Kolk BA, McFarlane AC, and Weisaeth L. (Eds.) *Traumatic stress: the overwhelming experience on mind, body, and society.* New York: Guilford Press. 1996.

Vasterling JJ and Brewin CR. (Eds.) *Neuropsychology of PTSD: biological, cognitive, and clinical perspectives.* New York: The Guilford Press. 2005.

Watzlawick P, Weakland JH, and Fisch R. *Change: principles of problem formation and problem resolution.* New York: W.W. Norton & Company. 1974.

Williams MB. *The PTSD workbook.* New York: New Harbinger Publications, Inc. 2002.

Wilson RS, Mendes de Leon CF, Barnes LL, et al. 2002. Participation in cognitively stimulating activities and risk of incident Alzheimer disease. JAMA 287:742-748.

Yalom ID. *The theory and practice of group psychotherapy: 4th ed.* New York: BasicBooks. 1995.

Appendix A – Understanding the Technical Terms

I.   Some Terminology

    A.   To gain a working knowledge of PTSD, the symptoms, and recovery, we need to be familiar with some key terms.

    B.   This can help increase our understanding of exactly what we are dealing with.

    C.   It also helps facilitate discussion with your therapist and can help you make better use of the time spent in therapy.

II.   Key Terms

    A.   <u>Trauma</u> [1,2,3] – an extreme stressor involving direct personal experience or observation of an event that involves actual or threatened death or serious injury, or threat to one's physical integrity.

        The person's response to this event must involve intense fear, helplessness, or horror.

    B.   <u>Mental Disorder</u> [3] – any clinically significant behavioral or psychological syndrome characterized by the presence of distressing symptoms, impairment of functioning, or significantly increased risk of suffering death, pain, disability, or loss of freedom.

        1.   Mental disorders are assumed to be the manifestation of a behavioral, psychological, or biological dysfunction in the individual.

        2.   The concept does not include deviant behavior, disturbances that are essentially conflicts between the individual and society, or expected and culturally sanctioned responses to particular events.

    C.   <u>Secondary Wounding Experience</u> [14] – experiences that occurred after the primary trauma(s) in which other people responded to the trauma survivor by disbelieving or discounting the person's experiences, blamed the victim, stigmatized or negatively judged the person because of the trauma.

        1.   These experiences are not "full blown traumas" by themselves.

        2.   They do make the negative effects of the original traumas much worse.

    D.   <u>Re-experiencing Symptoms</u> [1,2,3] – experiences in which it feels as if you are reliving the traumatic experiences.

        1.   <u>Nightmares</u> – frightening or terrifying dreams that are either about the trauma(s) or resemble some aspect or theme of the trauma(s).

            a.   <u>Note</u>: dreams and/or bad dreams are not traumatic nightmares.

            b.   To be a PTSD-related nightmare, the dream must in some way be about the trauma.

        2.   <u>Intrusive Thoughts</u> – disturbing thoughts or images of the trauma that force their way into your mind when you are not wanting to think about it.

        3.   <u>Flashbacks</u> – a brief period of time in which a person feels as if they are

back in the middle of the traumatic situation all over again.

E.   Triggers [1,2] – people, places, or situations that bring to mind the overwhelming feelings associated with the trauma(s).

F.   Traumatic Anniversary Date (Trauma Date)[1,8] – the specific date (or same time of year) that the original trauma(s) occurred.

G.   Stress [41]– any specific situation or event that threatens the health of the body or has a negative (undesirable) effect on its functioning; Anything that challenges or interferes with a person's ability to think, make decisions, or function in life.

H.   Impairment [3]– a limitation or worsening of a person's ability to function due to their symptoms.

I.   Coping Skills [1,2,43,44] – Thoughts, behaviors, and skills that help us deal with stress, daily hassles, symptoms, and painful emotions (feelings).

J.   Acute vs. Chronic [1,3]

1.   Acute – characterized by sharpness or high severity; lasting a short time; in PTSD, the term refers to symptoms lasting less than 3 months.

2.   Chronic – long duration or frequent occurrence; always present; in PTSD, the term is used when symptoms last 3 months or longer.

K.   Avoidance [1] – Actively avoiding contact with people, places, or situations that remind a person of the memories or feelings involved in the trauma(s).

L.   Social Detachment [9] – feeling as if you "don't fit in" with others; feeling rejected or threatened by others much of the time; as a result, being alone for extended periods of time.

M.   Emotional Numbing [63] – shutting down emotions in reaction to the traumatic event; it is a main feature of PTSD and is found in survivors of all forms of psychological trauma.

N.   Hyperarousal [3] – group of PTSD symptoms in which the nervous system and body overall stays "revved up" and stimulated at a high level, with difficulties in calming down or relaxing.

O.   Depersonalization [1] – a symptom in which a person has feelings of unreality and strangeness about one's own behavior; feeling detached from your own body or from yourself.

P.   Catastrophizing [18] – interpreting a situation or specific events as being catastrophic, when in fact the scenario does not warrant such a conclusion.

III.   Using the Terminology

A.   Communication with your therapist can be more productive when you know the correct terminology.

B.   Talking with your medication provider can be more helpful when using these terms correctly.

C.   You now have a framework for better understanding and accurately naming your symptoms.

D.   There is benefit to having correct names for the things you have been experiencing.

Appendix B – Coping Skills Review

I.   **Some Steps to Getting Better** [1,2]

A.   Need an accurate diagnosis
B.   Start treatment
C.   Accept the reality of the diagnosis
D.   Find understanding and acceptance within a therapy group
E.   Learn about the symptoms
F.   Learn how your life has been affected
G.   Develop an understanding of exactly what you are dealing with
H.   Learn and practice coping skills
    1.   To manage symptoms
    2.   To deal with stress
    3.   To handle anger
    4.   To be able to have relationships
    5.   To deal with difficult life situations
    6.   To live a healthy, balanced life
I.   Only when you are ready, talk about the traumas one-on-one with a therapist you trust to reprocess the memories and get some resolution.

II.   **A Review of Coping Skills**

A.   For a good long-term outcome, we need to know what our coping skills are.
B.   Can you name the coping skills you use?
C.   Do you know which skills to use in a particular situation?
D.   Mark each of the skills listed below that are helpful to you (not all will apply)
    1.   Deep breathing
    2.   Take a "time out"
    3.   Stop → Think → Choose → Act
    4.   Pause to get perspective; step back and see the big picture
    5.   Stop reacting to everything; think out what your response should be
    6.   Focus on staying calm and in control
    7.   Think: "What are my <u>options</u>?", and then choose the best one
    8.   Look for a good solution
    9.   Focus on the task at hand
    10.   Practice relaxing in a safe place every day
    11.   Look ahead; consider consequences before acting
    12.   Say "No" when you need to
    13.   Read a little every day
    14.   Just walk away
    15.   Exercise 3 – 5 × per week

16.   Write in a journal
17.   Make reasonable plans and schedule your time
18.   Talk about your concerns with a friend
19.   Listen carefully
20.   Try to understand others (and not judge or condemn them)
21.   Read and recite a coping card; carry a coping card in your pocket and refer to it regularly
22.   Get out of your home at least once each day
23.   Use self-talk to get through a situation
24.   Think before you speak
25.   Stick to a healthy diet
26.   Change what you can and let the rest go
27.   Do something enjoyable every day
28.   Write notes to help your memory; use a small notebook or calendar
29.   Laugh some every day
30.   Enjoy a pet
31.   Grow a garden (or plants indoors)
32.   Enjoy some art
33.   Whistle or sing
34.   Listen to enjoyable music
35.   Smile just for fun
36.   Each day, write down 3 things you are thankful for
37.   Go to an enjoyable place or event
38.   Learn something new each day
39.   Maintain a reasonable schedule/routine (which helps you function better)
40.   Take medication exactly as prescribed
41.   Look for the positive alternative in a situation
42.   Clearly identify your real goals (i.e., know exactly what you are working toward)
43.   Read books that help you grow, become more mature, or develop a skill
44.   Don't react to things; instead, choose your response (which sometimes is to do nothing)
45.   Take time to rest
46.   Ask questions that help you get information or broaden your perspective
47.   Remember to switch between broad-level thinking and detail-level thinking on a regular basis
48.   Think slowly and try to make things as simple as possible
49.   Detach your ego from your thinking and be able to stand back and look at your thinking

50.   Keep in mind the <u>focus of your thinking</u>
        ("At this moment, what am I trying to do?")
51.   Get information and use logic <u>before</u> letting the emotions come to
        bear on a situation
52.   Do perception checking
        a.   Am I seeing this clearly?
        b.   Do I have all the information I need?
        c.   Is there another perspective that is reasonable?
        d.   What am I missing here?
53.   Add to this list _____

        _____

        _____

Appendix C – Emergency Preparedness

I.   The Need for Emergency Preparedness [2]

    A.   Trauma survivors who develop PTSD lose the general sense of feeling safe most of the time.

    B.   This leads to being on guard (hypervigilance) almost all of the time.

    C.   Being prepared for potentially threatening situations ahead of time can help reduce the anxiety that is often felt on a daily basis.

    D.   An emergency preparedness kit can be helpful.

    E.   This does not mean going to extremes, but generally being prepared for potential emergency situations and being able to take care of yourself and your family.

II.   Emergency Kit Items [2]

    A.   The following are suggested items for an emergency preparedness kit.

    B.   However, each person must decide which items will be most useful to them and plan accordingly.

    C.   Try to use only 1 bag and keep it in a safe, readily accessible place.

        1.   A backpack or similar bag that is easy to carry is usually a good choice.

        2.   Get a bag that is waterproof or water-resistant.

    D.   Possible emergency kit items:

        1.   Sleeping bag, blanket

        2.   Change of clothing, underwear, socks, shoes or boots, hat, gloves, poncho

        3.   Money: credit cards, cash ($20-$100), coins, prepaid phone card

        4.   Important papers, addresses, phone numbers

        5.   Food: ready-to-eat meals, tuna, peanut butter, candy bars, etc.

        6.   Candles, flares, flashlight (extra batteries), lighter, waterproof matches

        7.   Multi-tool, pocket knife, can opener, rope/twine, duct tape

        8.   Toilet articles: soap, toothbrush, floss, toilet paper, towelettes, etc.

        9.   Paper, pencil, pen, Ziplock bags

        10.   Sunscreen, insect repellent, lip balm

        11.   First aid: tweezers, aspirin, ibuprofen, gauze, adhesive tape, medications

        12.   Canteen with water; extra water

        13.   Sewing kit

        14.   Towel, washcloth

        15.   Portable radio

        16.   First aid manual, survival manual

        17.   Entertainment: reading material, games, etc.

    E.   Replace perishable items every 6 months.

    F.   Other items might be included depending upon your individual needs.

    G.   By being prepared, we can reduce our anxiety and increase our confidence that we will be able to handle emergency situations that might arise.

Appendix D - Recommended Group Rules and Guidelines

The material in this book has been used as psychoeducational material in a group therapy setting. The following group rules and guidelines were implemented in these groups. Please feel free to use, adapt, or modify the following in accordance with your own needs.

Group Rules:
1. What's said in the group stays in the group   (confidentiality)
2. No "war stories"   (don't talk about the traumas during group time)
3. Keep the language as clean as possible   (no cursing)
4. No putdowns   (be respectful of others)
5. No weapons allowed in the group
6. Don't come to the group if you are drunk, high, or stoned
7. Don't monopolize the group   (allow time for others to participate)
8. Don't give advice, or tell people what to do
9. If you disagree, do it in an agreeable way
10. No political debates or arguments

Focus of the Group:
1. Understand PTSD and how it has affected your life
2. Develop skills for coping
3. Learn how to live a healthy, productive life in spite of PTSD symptoms
4. Increase understanding of PTSD symptoms and mental disorders
5. Increase stress management skills
6. Increase anger management skills
7. Increase healthy self-respect and self-esteem
8. Understand and practice daily living skills
9. Become better able to relate with others
10. Improve our quality of life

Guidelines for Effective Group Participation:
1. Take it slow → don't disclose too much personal information too quickly
2. Be a good listener → try to hear what is said and what is meant
3. Try to understand one another
4. Recognize and respect differences among group members
5. Accept others for who they are   (don't judge or condemn)
6. Be honest, but also use tact
7. Contribute ideas and possible solutions to problems discussed in the group, but don't give advice
8. Consider the ideas and contributions of others with an open mind
9. Ask questions and get clarification.

10.   Be supportive and solution focused
11.   Work toward a common purpose → the group is intended to help every group member
12.   Genuinely care that everyone in the group gets better
13.   Participate in the group process in order to benefit

CPSIA information can be obtained at www.ICGtesting.com
Printed in the USA
BVOW04s1855040814

361634BV00006B/97/P